The Governance of Public and Non-Profit Organisations

Boards play a crucial role in ensuring that public and non-profit organisations are publicly accountable and perform well. Following various failures and scandals they face increasing scrutiny, pressure and expectations. Serious questions have been raised about the ability of boards to govern effectively.

Such concerns have stimulated a renewed interest in organisational governance, and a growing literature on the subject. Much of the current literature, however, has been criticised for underestimating the constraints and conflicting demands that boards face and recommending unrealistic solutions. There have been relatively few detailed empirical studies of what boards do in practice. *The Governance of Public and Non-Profit Organisations* fills that gap by bringing together analyses based upon some of the best recent empirical studies of public and non-profit governance in the UK.

Using a new theoretical framework that highlights the paradoxical nature of governance, this book throws light on the questions at the heart of recent debates about public and non-profit boards:

- Are boards publicly accountable or is there a democratic deficit?
- Are boards able to exercise real power or does management run the show?
- What do boards do? Are they effective stewards of an organisation's resources? Can they play a meaningful role in setting organisational strategy?
- What impact are regulatory and other changes designed to improve board effectiveness having?

The book is essential reading for academics and students with an interest in the governance and management of public and non-profit organisations. It will also be of value to policy-makers and practitioners who wish to gain a deeper understanding of how boards work and what can be done to improve their performance.

Chris Cornforth is Senior Lecturer in Management and Head of the Public Interest and Non-profit Management Research Unit (PiN) at the Open University Business School. His research focuses on the governance and management of non-profit organisations. Recent publications include: *Good Governance*, with C. Edwards (London: CIMA, 1998) and *Recent Trends in Charity Governance and Trusteeship* (London: National Council of Voluntary Organisations, 2001).

Routledge Studies in the Management of Voluntary and Non-Profit Organizations
Series editor: Stephen P. Osborne

The Governance of Public and Non-Profit Organisations

What do boards do?

Edited by Chris Cornforth

Routledge
Taylor & Francis Group

LONDON AND NEW YORK

First published 2003
by Routledge
2 Park Square, Milton Park, Abingdon, Oxon, OX14 4RN

Simultaneously published in the USA and Canada
by Routledge
270 Madison Ave, New York NY 10016

Routledge is an imprint of the Taylor & Francis Group

Transferred to Digital Printing 2006

Typeset in Baskerville by Wearset Ltd, Boldon, Tyne and Wear

British Library Cataloguing in Publication Data
A catalogue record for this book is available from the British Library

Library of Congress Cataloging in Publication Data
A catalog record for this book has been requested

ISBN 0-415-25818-9 (hbk)
ISBN 0-415-35992-9 (pbk)

Contents

Illustrations

Contributors

Lynn Ashburner is currently working as a consultant in health services management for a World Bank project in Bulgaria. She was previously a Principal Research Fellow and Lecturer in Health Services Management at Keele and Nottingham Universities.

Nasa Begum is Principal Research Fellow at the Centre for Institutional Studies, University of East London.

Mike Bieber is an investigator for the local government ombudsman. He has extensive experience as a board member and carried out research on the governance of arts organisations while a PhD student at the Department of Museum Studies, University of Leicester.

Chris Cornforth is Senior Lecturer in Management and Head of the Public Interest and Non-profit Management Research Unit (PiN) at the Open University Business School.

Charles Edwards is Senior Lecturer in the Centre for Comparative Management at the Open University Business School.

Jane W. Grant is a freelance consultant and researcher. She was recently awarded a PhD at the Centre for Women's Studies at the University of Kent and was formerly Director of the National Alliance of Women's Organisations.

Alan Greer is Reader in Politics at the University of the West of England, Bristol.

Jenny Harrow is Professor of Management and Head of the Centre for Public Services Management at South Bank University Business School.

Paul Hoggett is Professor of Politics at the University of the West of England, Bristol.

Michael Locke is a Reader in the Centre for Institutional Studies, University of East London.

Stella Maile is a Senior Lecturer in Sociology at the University of the West of England, Bristol.

Veronica Mole is a Research Fellow in the Centre for Public Services Management, South Bank University Business School.

Shirley Otto is a freelance specialist in management development with voluntary organisations; she completed her PhD on governance at Birkbeck College.

Paul Palmer is Professor of Charity Finance at South Bank University. He is (with Adrian Randall) the author of *Financial Management in the Voluntary Sector*.

Fred Robinson is Research Lecturer in the Department of Sociology and Social Policy, University of Durham and Visiting Professor at the University of Northumberland.

Paul Robson is a Principal Research Fellow in the Centre for Institutional Studies at the University of East London.

Colin Rochester is Director of the Centre for Nonprofit and Voluntary Sector Management at the University of Surrey Roehampton.

Keith Shaw is Principal Lecturer in Government at the University of Northumberland.

Claire Simpson is Research Fellow in the Student Support Research Group, Student Services at the Open University in Milton Keynes.

Acknowledgements

I am very grateful to all the authors in this volume for the quality and timeliness of their contributions, and their patience in responding to the many comments and queries on earlier drafts. I would also like to thank my colleagues Charles Edwards and Rob Paton, who gave timely comments and advice on various aspects of the book. Special thanks are due to Margaret Marchant for splendid secretarial support and encouragement to get the book finished!

Grateful acknowledgement is made to the following sources for permission to use material in this book:

Cornforth, C. and Edwards, C. (1998) *Good Governance: Developing Effective Board–Management Relations in Public and Voluntary Organisations*, London: Chartered Institute of Management Accountants (CIMA) Publishing, © CIMA 1998.

Cornforth, C. and Edwards, C. (1999) 'Board Roles in the Strategic Management of Non-profit Organisations: Theory and Practice', *Corporate Governance: An International Review*, 7, 4, 346–362, © Blackwell Publishers Ltd 1999.

Cornforth, C. and Simpson, S. 'Change and Continuity in the Governance of Non-Profit Organisations in the U.K.', *Nonprofit Management and Leadership*, 12, 4, 2002, © Jossey-Bass Publishers.

Introduction

The changing context of governance – emerging issues and paradoxes

Chris Cornforth

Background and aims of the book

The delivery of public services in the UK has changed dramatically over the last two decades. Increasingly, government has been withdrawing from the direct delivery of public services and programmes. Crucial to this process has been two related reforms: the first has been the creation by government of an increasing number of devolved or quasi-autonomous government agencies (quangos) to deliver public services. The second has been the introduction of market mechanisms into the provision of public services through splitting the 'purchasers' of services from the 'providers' and introducing elements of competition through the contracting out of services to a mix of private companies, voluntary organisations and quangos.

As the importance of quangos and voluntary organisations in delivering public services has grown, they have come under increased public scrutiny. In particular, paralleling developments in the private sector, the governance[1] of these organisations has been questioned. Serious concerns have been raised both about the democratic legitimacy of governing boards and their effectiveness, for example, the ability of what are often lay board members to effectively supervise senior managers, ensure probity and protect the interests of relevant stakeholders and the public.

These concerns have also led to renewed professional and academic interest in organisational governance and a growing literature. Much of this literature is prescriptive in nature and aimed at addressing the perceived shortcomings of governing bodies. However, it has been criticised for oversimplifying the problems, underestimating the conflicting demands and pressures that board members face, and presenting solutions that are difficult to implement in practice (Middleton, 1987; Herman, 1989). These shortcomings point to the need for a greater understanding of the way boards work that is grounded in empirical studies of board behaviour.

In a review of the research literature on boards, Middleton (1987) concluded that empirical and scholarly studies were relatively scarce, and that

there were considerable gaps in knowledge. Since then the research literature has grown steadily and there is now a small but identifiable field of
research on non-profit boards (Ostrower and Stone, 2001), although
largely dominated by work in the USA. The main aim of the book is to
contribute to this field by bringing together some recent empirical studies
and reviews of public and non-profit governance in the UK, that explore a
number of questions and themes that have been at the heart of recent
debates about non-profit governance:

- How are changes in membership affecting boards? Are boards publicly accountable, or is there a democratic deficit? What are the
  implications of involving users on boards?
- What do boards do? Are they able to be effective stewards of an organisation's resources? Can they play a meaningful role in setting organisational strategy?
- What is the relationship between boards and management? Are
  boards able to exercise real power, or is it really management that
  runs the show?
- How are changes in the environment affecting boards and how are
  boards changing?

The aim of this chapter is to set the scene for this analysis by placing it in
an historical and theoretical context. First, it will examine how recent contextual changes have impacted upon the governance of public and non-
profit organisations in the UK, and identify the main problems and issues
that have arisen as a result. Second, it will discuss the main theories that
have been put forward to explain organisational governance. It argues
that each of these theories only gives a partial and limited account of governance and suggests that a new multi-paradigm perspective is required,
which highlights the paradoxical and situational nature of governance.
Finally, it outlines the structure of the book and introduces the subsequent chapters.

The changing context of organisational governance

Until quite recently the way organisations are governed has not attracted a
great deal of public and academic attention. There appears to have been
an implicit assumption that what matters in organisations is the way they
are managed. This picture has been changing rapidly since the mid-1980s.
Stimulated first by public concern over the behaviour and accountability
of some senior business executives, there has been a growing interest in
how to improve the quality of organisational governance, which has
spread to the public and voluntary sectors. Below we map out some of the
most significant changes and developments affecting the governance of
public and non-profit organisations.

The public sector

Much of the public concern about the governance of public service organisations stems from the widespread structural reforms of the public sector
carried out by different Conservative governments during the 1980s and
early 1990s. This led to many public services being removed from the
direct control of elected local authorities and government departments to
be run by 'quangos' operating under contract with central government.
Key reforms included the establishment of independent trusts to deliver
services in the NHS, the establishment of Training and Enterprise Councils and Local Enterprise Councils, and the removal of further education
(FE) colleges and the former polytechnics from local authority control. In
an attempt to improve efficiency the government also sought to introduce
greater competition and a range of management practices from the
private sector. Common changes included: separating the purchase of
services from their provision, replacing elected board members by
appointees (often with business experience), and making greater use of
performance indicators and multiple audits. At a local level these changes
marked a shift from a relatively simple structure of local government,
where services were largely provided by multi-functional local authorities
working with central government, to a complex and often fragmented
system of local governance (Stoker, 1999; Robinson *et al.*, 2000).

The rapid growth in the number of quangos, the variety of their governance arrangements and the perceived increase in central government
control led to concerns about the membership and accountability of these
public bodies. Plummer (1994: 1), for example, suggested that the governance structures of these bodies 'were created without clear and consistent principles and methods', leading to what he called a 'governance
gap' and 'deep public unease about the legitimacy of many of the
quangos'. Skelcher and Davis (1995), in their study of the membership
of what they call 'locally appointed bodies', warned against the
dangers of creating a new closed professional elite or 'magistracy' controlling these bodies. Skelcher (1998) provided the most comprehensive
analysis of these changes in governance, and criticised the decline in
democratic accountability. There was also public disquiet over the lack of
transparency and allegations of political bias over many public appointments. At the same time the rise of managerialism in the public sector
(Pollitt, 1993) challenged the rather simplistic assumption that it is
lay councillors or board members who make policy and officers who carry
it out.

In response to these criticisms, there have been a variety of initiatives to
try to address these problems. Perhaps the most significant impetus for
change has come from the standing Committee on Standards in Public
Life, initially chaired by Lord Nolan. Although originally established to
improve standards among MPs after repeated allegations of 'sleaze', its

focus also extended to those in charge of unelected public bodies. The first report of the committee established seven 'principles of public life' to guide the conduct and behaviour of politicians and those in charge of public bodies, namely: *selflessness, integrity, objectivity, accountability, openness, honesty* and *leadership* (Nolan, 1995). It also recommended the establishment of an independent commissioner to establish a code of conduct for ministerial appointments to public bodies and to ensure those appointments were made on merit after open and fair competition.

The second report from the committee focused on what were called Local Public Spending Bodies, including further and higher education bodies, grant-maintained schools, TECs and LECs, and registered housing associations (Nolan, 1996). While the report made detailed recommendations for each of the sectors that it looked at, it also established some general principles and recommendations. It concluded that best practice conforms to the seven principles of public life set out in the first Nolan report. It proposed that where taxpayers' money is involved, the government or local authority must retain responsibility for ensuring the interests of both taxpayers and users are safeguarded, and local mechanisms should exist to ensure local influence and accountability. It also recommended that various principles of good practice be adopted with suitable modifications across the sectors on: appointments, training, openness, codes of conduct, conflicts of interest and whistle-blowing.

The advent of the New Labour government in 1997 saw a continuation of this process of gradual reform rather than radical change, which has continued into the government's second term of office. There have been various initiatives to improve the openness of board appointment procedures and the diversity of boards. However, the implementation of these reforms has been uneven, and concerns about a democratic deficit remain (see Chapters 1, 2 and 11). The government also espoused a commitment to keeping the number of quangos under control. While overall the numbers have fallen somewhat, the government has created important new quangos, particularly in areas such as health and regeneration, as part of its modernisation programme and emphasis on partnership working.

The voluntary sector

During the 1980s the size and importance of the voluntary and non-profit sector increased dramatically. In large part this was due to the changes in government policy discussed above, and particularly the contracting out of public services. For example, housing associations rather than local authorities were increasingly used as the main vehicle to provide social housing and many social services were contracted out to private or voluntary organisations. These increasing demands on voluntary organisations and recognition of their growing importance led to concerns to improve standards of management and governance in the sector. A few well-publicised problems and failures heightened this concern. By the late 1980s the possibility of abuse was recognised, and the efficiency scrutiny of the supervision of charities, conducted by Sir Philip Woodfield in 1988, called for action to remedy the situation (Holden, 1996: 31).

In England and Wales the government responded to these concerns by introducing the new Charities Act in 1992 and 1993, which tightened the regulatory regime for charities. In addition the main regulatory body, the Charity Commission, was revitalised and began to take a more active supervisory role. As part of this work it devoted effort to trying to improve standards of trusteeship by directing greater attention to the role and responsibilities of trustees. In 1991 the Charity Commission and the National Council for Voluntary Organisations (NCVO) established a Working Party on Trustee Training, which produced the report *On Trust* (NCVO, 1992), which made recommendations to improve the quality of governance among charities and other voluntary organisations. A survey for the report came up with the rather startling evidence that only one in three of those trustees surveyed knew that they were trustees. The main thrust of these recommendations was to provide more advice and training for trustees. As a result, a Trustees Services Unit was established at the NCVO in 1993, with the brief to maintain a strategic role in developing advice, support and training services for trustees. It was also tasked to produce a comprehensive handbook for trustees (Kirkland, 1994), which has regularly been updated (Nunan, 1999). Subsequently the NCVO also established a board development programme to provide more sustained assistance to boards. The Charity Commission itself continued to extend its advice, guidance and educational work on charity governance (Charity Commission, 2000a: 15–19). The development of its website means that this information is easily available to anyone with access to the Internet. In parallel with these developments, there has been a growth in training for board members and trustees at a local level. However, provision and take-up remain patchy.

The Commission on the Future of the Voluntary Sector looked at governance as one of many important issues confronting the sector (NCVO, 1996). It recommended that voluntary organisations should clearly define the respective roles of chair, board members, chief executive and staff; should ensure that boards have an appropriate balance of members; do not become too large; and have adequate recruitment and induction procedures. The report commended the codes of practice developed by the Nolan Committee (1996), which recommended standards for bodies that were involved in spending public money, and suggests they could be used more widely in the voluntary sector. A code of conduct for charity boards was subsequently produced by the NCVO. The idea was also taken up by the Joseph Rowntree Foundation who commissioned a report which gives guidance to voluntary organisations wishing to draw up codes of practice (Ashby, 1997).

Emerging issues

Historically, the traditions of governance in private, public and voluntary organisations are rather different. However, with the government reforms of the public sector, and the growing introduction of management practices derived from business into the public and voluntary sectors, the boundaries between the sectors have become blurred. Increasingly, it is relevant to ask what the similarities and differences are between governance in different sectors, and what lessons is it possible to learn which may have relevance across sectors.

Much of the attention and interest in governance in all sectors has focused on what may be called the stewardship role of boards – the ability to hold management to account and to see that the resources of the organisation are used properly. The main response to these concerns has been to try to improve self-regulation through the development of voluntary codes of practice and by providing more information, advice and training for board members. This raises three important questions. First, are boards able to effectively monitor management and hold them to account? Second, has the attention on the stewardship role of boards meant that other important roles are in danger of being neglected, in particular the ability of boards to add value to policy decisions and organisational strategy? Third, is it enough to try to improve the functioning of boards or is tighter external regulation required?

Another common issue concerns the accountability of boards themselves. In the public sector the removal of many public bodies from local authority control and the move to more corporate style boards have raised alarms about the ability of boards to represent or be accountable to the local communities they serve, their users, or other legitimate stakeholders. In the voluntary sector this issue has echoes in calls for greater user involvement and accountability.

Theoretical perspectives and paradoxes

So far the chapter has examined the various political and contextual changes that have helped to shape the governance of public and non-profit organisations. The focus now shifts to theory and the different theoretical perspectives that have been used to try to understand boards and the roles they play. The governance of non-profit organisations is relatively under-theorised in comparison with the governance of business corporations. In addition, the two literatures have developed largely separately from each other (Middleton, 1987; Herman and Van Til, 1989; Hung, 1998). Noticeable exceptions include resource dependency theory and the study of elites (Middleton, 1987). In contrast, a variety of competing theories have been proposed to try to understand the role of boards in the private sector, e.g. agency theory, stewardship theory, resource dependency theory, a democratic perspective, stakeholder theory, and managerial hegemony theory. Below, each of these theoretical perspectives is briefly examined and how they can be usefully extended to throw light on non-profit boards. It is then argued that, taken individually, these theories give a one-dimensional view of governance, and that a better understanding can be gained by taking a multi-paradigm perspective, which focuses on the paradoxes of governance.

Agency theory – a compliance model

Principal–agent theory, or agency theory for short, has been the dominant theory of the corporation and corporate governance arrangements (see Keasey *et al.*, 1997: 3–5 for an overview). It assumes that the owners of an enterprise (the principal) and those that manage it (the agent) will have different interests. Hence the owners or shareholders of any enterprise face a problem that managers are likely to act in their own interests rather than the shareholders'. While free markets are seen as the best restraint on managerial discretion, agency theory sees corporate governance arrangements as another means to ensure that management acts in the best interests of shareholders. From this perspective the main function of the board is to control managers. This suggests that the majority of a company's directors should be independent of management, and that their primary role is one of ensuring managerial compliance, i.e. to monitor and, if necessary, control the behaviour of management to ensure it acts in the shareholders' best interests.

One difficulty in applying an agency perspective to public and non-profit organisations is that there is much more potential ambiguity over who the principals or owners are. In the case of voluntary organisations, is it, for example, the original founders of the organisation, its beneficiaries or members?; in the case of public organisations, is it the general public, service users, taxpayers or the government itself? However, many aspects of this perspective still have relevance. For example, the principles and regulations concerning charitable trusts, which affect many voluntary organisations, embody similar ideas on the role of governance. Under trust law the trustees of a charity are appointed to look after the money and resources donated to the organisation and to see that it is used to serve the charity's intended beneficiaries, as set out in the trust deed. Hence, a key role of the trustees of a charity is to see that the staff and management of the organisation carry out the charity's objectives. It is enshrined in trust law that the trustees themselves should not benefit financially from the trust, and so employees of a trust cannot normally be trustees. As there is a complete separation of the board members from staff or management, it could be argued that trust law is even more in line with an agency or compliance model of governance than company law. Harris (1994) identifies this as the 'traditional' model for charity boards where the board represents or reflects those who act as 'guardians' of the charity's mission. Similarly, in public organisations it can be argued that the public or state's objectives are at risk from managers pursuing their own interests, and so a key role of the board is again to monitor management and ensure their compliance in furthering the organisation's objectives.

Stewardship theory – a partnership model

Stewardship theory (Donaldson and Davis, 1991; Muth and Donaldson, 1998) is grounded in a human relations perspective (Hung, 1998) and starts from opposite assumptions to agency theory. It assumes that managers want to do a good job and will act as effective stewards of an organisation's resources. As a result, senior management and shareholders (or their representatives on the board) of the organisation are better seen as partners. Hence, the main function of the board is not to ensure managerial compliance or conformance, but to improve organisational performance. The role of the board is primarily strategic, to work with management to improve strategy and add value to top decisions. In this context it is not surprising that management ideas and practices should be applied to governance. From this perspective board members should be selected on the basis of their expertise and contacts so that they are in a position to add value to the organisation's decisions.

This perspective is evident in various models of governance across different sectors. For example, Pound (1995) argues that current models of corporate governance are too concerned with ensuring managerial compliance and suggests an alternative that he calls the 'governed corporation model' for public companies. In this model the board and major shareholders are seen as partners of management, and the prime function of the board is to add value to the organisation by improving its top decision-making and relations with shareholders. Carver (1990), in his policy governance model for non-profit organisations, advocates that the real business of governance is to make policy, articulate the mission and sustain the vision of the organisation.

Resource dependency theory – a co-optation model

Resource dependency theory (Pfeffer and Salancik, 1978) views organisations as interdependent with their environment. Organisations depend crucially for their survival on other organisations and actors for resources. As a result they need to find ways of managing this dependence and ensuring they get the resources and information they need. From this perspective the board is seen as one means of reducing uncertainty by creating influential links between organisations through, for example, interlocking directorates. The main function of the board, whatever sector the organisation is in, is to maintain good relations with key external stakeholders in order to ensure the flow of resources into and from the organisation, and to help the organisation respond to external change.

From this perspective the board is part of both the organisation and its environment. The role of the board is one of boundary-spanning. Board members are selected for the important external links and knowledge they can bring to the organisation, and to try to co-opt external influences. For example, it is quite common for local voluntary organisations to include on their board people with links to important statutory agencies they work with, or receive funding from.

A democratic perspective – a democratic model

Democratic government is a central institution in Western societies. Key ideas and practices include: open elections on the basis of one person one vote; pluralism, i.e. that representatives will represent different interests; accountability to the electorate; the separation of elected representatives, who make policy, from the executive, who implement policy decisions. Democratic ideas and practices have influenced thinking about the governance of organisations, particularly public and voluntary organisations. For example, many voluntary organisations have been established as membership associations, where it is enshrined in the organisation's constitution that the governing body should be elected by and represent the membership in some way. Conversely, as noted above, the governance of many quangos is often criticised for not living up to ideas of democratic accountability that underpin central and local government.

A democratic perspective on governance suggests that the job of the board is to represent the interests of one or more constituencies or groups the organisation serves. The role of the board is to resolve or choose between the interests of different groups and set the overall policy of the organisation, which can then be implemented by staff. Central to this view is that any member of the electorate or membership can put himself or herself forward for election as a board member. Expertise is not a central requirement, as it is in the partnership model.

Stakeholder theory – a stakeholder model

Stakeholder theory is based on the premise that organisations should be responsible to a range of groups in society other than just the organisations' 'owners' (Hung, 1998: 106). By incorporating different stakeholders on boards, it is expected that organisations will be more likely to respond to broader social interests than the narrow interests of one group. This leads to a political role for boards negotiating and resolving the potentially conflicting interests of different stakeholder groups in order to determine the objectives of the organisation and set policy.

Stakeholder theory has developed mainly in debates over corporate governance in the private sector as an alternative to traditional share-holder models, where there has been robust debate about its desirability and likely consequences (e.g. Hutton, 1997; Tricker, 2000: 295). The principles of stakeholder involvement are less controversial in the public and non-profit sectors, and the practice more common, although not always discussed in terms of stakeholder theory. Some of the clearest examples in the UK are in the field of education where government reforms have specified the involvement of various stakeholders on governing bodies. For example, state-funded schools are required to have governing bodies made up of people appointed or elected from various groups, including: parents, the Local Education Authority, teacher governors and, in the case of voluntary aided schools, foundation governors representing the church or charity supporting the school. When FE colleges were taken out of local government control, the government specified that at least half the governors should be business, broadly construed. Due to concerns about lack of balance and accountability the composition was broadened by the government in 1999 to include representatives of staff, students, the local authority and community.

Managerial hegemony theory – a 'rubber stamp' model

Managerial hegemony theory relates back to the thesis of Berle and Means (1932) that although shareholders may legally own and control large corporations, they no longer effectively control them, control having been ceded to a new professional managerial class. A variety of empirical studies have lent support to this thesis. Mace (1971), in his study of US directors, concluded that boards did not get involved in strategy except in crises, and that control rested with the president (chief executive) rather than the board. Herman (1981) came to similar conclusions but argued that managerial power was always in the context of various constraints and the latent power of stakeholders such as external board members. In a more recent study Lorsch and MacIver (1989) concluded that although the functioning of boards has improved since Mace's study, their performance still leaves much room for improvement. Like Mace, they distinguish between boards in normal times and during crises, and conclude that in normal times power usually remains with the chief executive. From this perspective the board ends up as little more than a 'rubber stamp' for management's decisions. Its function is essentially symbolic to give legitimacy to managerial actions.

Although this theory was developed in the study of large business corporations, many of the processes it describes seem just as relevant to public and non-profit organisations: for example, the separation of those who 'own' the organisation from those that control it, and the increasing growth and professionalisation of management. Indeed, it could be argued that the largely voluntary nature of board members' involvement in public and non-profit organisations and the subsequent constraints on their time are likely to mean that board power is even more limited than in the private sector.

The main features of these different perspectives are summarised in Table 0.1. Taken individually, these theories are rather one-dimensional, and have been criticised for only illuminating one particular aspect of the board's work. This has led to calls for a new conceptual framework that can help integrate the insights of these different perspectives (Hung, 1998: 108–109; Tricker, 2000: 295). A paradox perspective offers a promising approach to providing this new conceptual framework.

A paradox perspective

Morgan (1986: 339), in his ground-breaking study of organisations, argues that many of our theories and ways of thinking about organisations do not match the complexity and sophistication of the organisational realities we face. In order to address this problem he argues that it is necessary to take a multi-paradigm or perspective approach in order to 'understand and grasp the multiple meanings of situations and to confront and manage contradiction and paradox, rather than pretend they do not exist'. At the same time there has been a growing recognition that many management problems and issues require a move from linear thinking and simple either/or choices to seeing them as paradoxes (e.g. Hampden-Turner, 1990; Handy, 1995). Managing paradox means embracing and exploring tensions and differences rather than choosing between them. As Lewis (2000) charts in her review of the literature, the concept of paradox has been playing an increasing role in organisation studies.

A similar critique can be made of attempts to understand organisational governance. As Hung (1998: 108) observes in his review of literature, each of the theories of governance discussed above 'focus on a small part and no one is able to perceive the whole picture of corporate governance'. In a similar vein, Tricker (2000: 295) notes, 'At the moment various theoretical insights cast light on different aspects of play, leaving others in the shadow.' He calls for a new conceptual framework that can 'light up the entire stage and all the players'.

One way of addressing this problem is to take a multi-paradigm perspective and focus more explicitly on the paradoxes, ambiguities and tensions involved in governance. As Lewis (2000: 772) discusses, a multi-paradigm approach can be useful as a sensitising device to highlight what are likely to be important paradoxes, by contrasting opposing theoretical approaches. So, for example, contrasting agency theory with stewardship theory suggests that boards may experience pressures to both control and partner senior management. Next, we examine some of the main tensions and paradoxes that the contrasting theories of governance suggest that boards are likely to face. The list is not meant to be exhaustive. A number

Table 0.1 A comparison of theoretical perspectives on organisational governance

Theory	Interests	Board members	Board role	Model
Agency theory	Owners and managers have different interests	Owners' representatives	Compliance/conformance: safeguard owners' interests oversee management check compliance	Compliance model
Stewardship theory	Owners and managers share interests	Experts	Improve performance: add value to top decisions/strategy partner/support management	Partnership model
Democratic perspective	Members/the public contain different interests	Lay representatives	Political: represent constituents/ members reconcile conflicts make policy control executive	Democratic model
Stakeholder theory	Stakeholders have different interests	Stakeholder representatives: elected or appointed by stakeholder groups	Balancing stakeholder needs: balance stakeholder needs make policy/strategy control management	Stakeholder model
Resource dependency theory	Stakeholders and organisation have different interests	Chosen for influence with key stakeholders	Boundary spanning: secure resources maintain stakeholder relations being external perspective	Co-option model
Managerial hegemony theory	Owners and managers have different interests	Owners' representatives	Largely symbolic: ratify decisions give legitimacy managers have real power	'Rubber-stamp' model

of authors have also begun to study governance from a paradox perspective. Demb and Neubauer (1992), in their study of corporate board, identified and examined three paradoxes which stem from the legal and structural aspect of the boards setting. Wood (1996) suggests a similar approach to studying non-profit boards.

Main tensions facing boards

Who governs? – the tension between representative and professional boards

The various theoretical perspectives have different implications for who should serve on boards. The opposition is clearest between the stewardship and democratic perspectives. Stewardship theory stresses that board members should have expertise and experience that can add value to the performance of the organisation. The implication is that board members should be selected for their professional expertise and skills. In contrast, the democratic perspective (and to some extent stakeholder theory) stress that board members are lay representatives there to serve the constituency or stakeholders they represent.

This can raise an obvious tension for public policy-makers – should the boards of public bodies be elected or chosen because of their expertise? The move to non-elected, expert boards in many parts of the public sector has been heavily criticised for its undemocratic nature and the danger of creating a new self-selected elite (Skelcher and Davis, 1995). There is also a dilemma for voluntary sector boards – should members be chosen, or encouraged to stand for election, because of their expertise or because they represent or reflect some stakeholder group? It also raises dilemmas for board members. Are they expected to represent particular stakeholders or to give expert guidance? The professional role also demands a close involvement with the organisation. This may conflict with board members' unpaid status in most non-profit organisations.

Board roles – the tension between the conformance and performance

The different theories of governance put different emphasis on what is the main role of the board. This is most apparent in the opposition between the agency and stewardship perspectives. Agency theory emphasises what Garratt (1996) has called the 'conformance' role of the board to ensure the organisation acts in the interests of its 'owners' and to be a careful steward of their resources. In contrast, stewardship theory emphasises the role of the board in driving forward organisational 'performance' through adding value to the organisation's strategy and top decisions.

These contrasting roles require a very different orientation and behaviour on the part of board members. The conformance role demands careful monitoring and scrutiny of the organisation's past performance and is risk-averse. The performance role demands forward vision, an understanding of the organisation and its environment and perhaps a greater willingness to take risks. Again, boards face a tension concerning how much attention they should pay to these contrasting roles and how to balance the different demands on them.

Relationships with management – the tension between controlling and partnering

The relationship between boards and management is viewed differently within the contrasting theoretical perspectives. The agency, stakeholder and democratic perspectives stress the importance of the board monitoring and controlling the work of managers (the executive). In contrast, stewardship theory stresses the role of the board as a partner to management, improving top management decision-making.

The need to both control senior management and be their support and partner in decision-making can be a source of role conflict and tension for board members. To what extent should board members push the interests of particular stakeholders if this is against the wishes of management? This tension is vividly illustrated by the following comment on a European Union report on parent participation in education by the convenor of the Scottish Parent Teacher Council:

> Quite often the parents on school boards cease to take the parental point of view and start to identify more with management ... in some cases you can see parents on boards closing ranks around the head teacher rather than lobbying on behalf of parents.
>
> (*The Scotsman*, 27 December 1995: 6)

These paradoxes and related tensions are examined and explored throughout the book.

The structure of the book

The book is divided into four main parts. Part I focuses on the question, who should sit on governing bodies? As noted above, the different perspectives on governance give very different answers to this question – should board members be elected to represent or reflect the constituencies the organisation serves, or chosen for the expertise and experience they can bring to directing the organisation? This tension has been one of the major issues in reforms of governance structures in the public sector, as moves towards more appointed boards have been criticised because of a perceived lack of democratic accountability. Two chapters address this question directly. In Chapter 1 Fred Robinson and Keith Shaw examine who runs the many elected and unelected bodies that run one British region, the North East of England. They reveal a complex, and confusing, picture where it is often quite difficult to even find out who runs what and they argue for democratic reform. In Chapter 2 Alan Greer, Paul Hoggett and Stella Maile examine how the perceived tension between democratic accountability and effectiveness has been played out in the development of quangos in the UK. They also argue for democratic reform, but suggest no one model will be suitable across this diverse sector. Another common criticism of organisations providing public services is that the people who use these services do not have sufficient say in how they are run. One response has been to involve users directly on the boards of organisations. This issue is taken up in Chapter 3 by Mike Locke, Nasa Begum and Paul Robson, who draw on action research in a number of voluntary organisations to identify some of the lessons for organisations wanting to increase user involvement, particularly in their governance.

Part II examines the question, what is it that boards do? The prescriptive literature on boards highlights the many responsibilities of board members. However, it has been criticised for giving an unrealistic and idealistic picture of what boards do and ignoring the many constraints they operate under (Herman, 1981). The different theoretical perspectives discussed above give different and conflicting answers. At one end of the spectrum the managerial hegemony perspective suggests boards cannot actually do a lot. Real power remains with management who have the expertise, time and resources to control the organisation, so that boards serve mainly a symbolic function. The other perspectives give more positive but somewhat different answers. Agency theory suggests the board's main role is to oversee management and make sure it acts in the best interests of the organisation's 'owners'. In contrast, stewardship theory stresses the role of the board in working with management to set the organisation's strategy and add value to top decisions.

In Chapter 4 Chris Cornforth and Charles Edwards look at some of the factors that influence the strategic contribution of boards. The results of their research show a more complex answer than that given by any of the perspectives individually. The strategic contribution of boards can vary widely and is influenced by various contextual factors, board inputs and processes. They highlight some of the actions boards can take to improve their contribution to strategy making. In Chapter 5 Jenny Harrow and Paul Palmer look at the contribution charity boards make to financial decision-making. Their review of the empirical literature shows a varied picture often at odds with legal and other prescriptions. Although the vast majority of voluntary organisations are very small (Cornforth, 2001: 5–7), there has been little research on the distinctive challenges the boards of these organisations face. Colin Rochester addresses this issue in Chapter 6. He questions the generic nature of much of the literature on non-profit boards, and draws on case study research to suggest how small voluntary organisations can overcome the 'liability of smallness'.

Part III looks at board roles and relationships, including the balance of power between boards and the managers they work with. The success of the relationship between chairs and chief executives has been regarded as a key factor in the success of boards (Demb and Neubauer, 1992; Roberts and Styles, 1998; Robinson and Exworthy, 1999). The competing perspectives on governance suggest that the boundaries between these roles will inevitably be somewhat ambiguous. For example, the chair may need to both monitor the chief executive and act as adviser and supporter. In Chapter 7 Shirley Otto examines and compares the chair–chief executive relationship in organisations in the private, public and voluntary sectors and asks if and how they differ. While the relationship is characterised by a degree of ambiguity and conflict in all three sectors, an important difference to emerge was the more limited and reactive role played by chairs in the voluntary sector.

Chief executives, because of their position and control of board information, can have an important influence on shaping what boards do. This may be particularly true in the voluntary sector where board members are typically volunteers and are often only able to have a very part-time involvement. Indeed, some research on non-profit boards suggests that they are more likely to be successful where chief executives take responsibility for board development (Herman, 1981). Hence the expectations chief executives have of their boards are important. This is the focus of Chapter 8 by Veronica Mole. Based on interviews with the chief executives of sixty small and medium-sized voluntary organisations, she examines what shapes their attitudes and relationships to boards. Another important aspect of the relationship between boards and chief executives is the balance of power and influence. In Chapter 9 Mike Bieber explores this question in research on the boards of independent museums. In particular, he examines how issues of professionalism and the status of professional work in museums constrain the nature of board involvement and power.

As we saw earlier, the governance of public and non-profit organisations has been subject to a range of external initiatives and reforms in recent years. Part IV picks up this theme and looks at continuity and change, among boards. Chapter 10 by Chris Cornforth and Claire Simpson examines how charity board have changed since the mid-1990s, and looks to see whether there are differences between organisations of different size. In Chapter 11 Lynn Ashburner reviews how governance structures have changed in the National Health Service since the early 1990s. She concludes that a continuing weakness is a lack of local democratic accountability, and argues for new models of governance that can address this weakness. Jane Grant examines how governance is changing in the organised women's movement in Chapter 12 and she demonstrates the value of taking an historical perspective. She reveals an organisational field that is proving very adaptive in the face of external changes, and that shows a degree of convergence in governance structures between organisations in the 'traditional' and 'modern' feminist movements.

Another criticism that can be levelled at much of the theorising about boards (both descriptive and prescriptive) is its generic nature. Little account is taken of how contextual factors, such as organisational size or changes in public policy, influence boards and their behaviour. The importance of contextual factors is a theme that emerges in many of the chapters of the book and is picked up in the concluding chapter. Chapter 13 uses the framework concerning the paradoxical and situational nature of governance, established in this chapter, to draw out and summarise some of the main findings from the various studies and reviews in the book. It examines some of the main contextual influences on boards, and how these shape the various paradoxes of governance. In doing so it briefly examines some of the main implications for policy-makers and practitioners.

Note

1 The term governance has become an important concept in a variety of disciplines including management, public administration, public policy and politics. However, as Kooiman (1999) notes in his useful review, the term is used in many different ways. He suggests one useful way of distinguishing between the different usages is in terms of different levels of analysis. In this book the main focus is on the organisational level, and the term governance is primarily used to refer to the arrangements for organisational and corporate governance, i.e. the systems by which organisations are directed, controlled and accountable. Central to this is the organisation's board or governing body, which carries formal responsibility for the organisation. In particular, the book examines board behaviour, roles and relationships with management and other internal and external stakeholders. The term is also used at higher levels of analysis to refer to new patterns of government and governing, in particular the shift away from a unitary state to a more fragmented system of government where a range of non-governmental bodies participate in the delivery of public services and the development of public policy (Rhodes, 1994). In the public sector these new patterns of political governance provide the context in which the boards of public organisations and quangos operate. The relationship between these two levels is the particular focus of Chapter 1.

References

Ashby, J. (1997) *Towards Voluntary Sector Codes of Practice*, York: York Publishing Services.

Berle, A. A. and Means, G. C. (1932) *The Modern Corporation and Private Property*, New York: Macmillan.

Carver, J. (1990) *Boards that Make a Difference*, San Francisco: Jossey-Bass.

Charity Commission (2000a) *Annual Report 1999–2000*, London: The Stationery Office.

Charity Commission (2000b) *The Hallmarks of a Well Run Charity*, Guidance Note CC60, London: Charity Commission.

Cornforth, C. (2001) *Recent Trends in Charity Governance and Trusteeship: The Results of a Survey of Governing Bodies of Charities*, London: NCVO.

Demb, A. and Neubauer, F. (1992) *The Corporate Board: Confronting the Paradoxes*, Oxford: Oxford University Press.

Donaldson, L. and Davis, J. (1991) 'Stewardship Theory or Agency Theory: CEO Governance and Shareholder Returns', *Australian Journal of Management*, 16, 1, 49–64.

Garratt, B. (1996) *The Fish Rots from the Head: The Crisis in our Boardrooms: Developing the Crucial Skills of the Competent Director*, London: HarperCollins.

Hampden-Turner, C. (1990) *Charting the Corporate Mind: From Dilemma to Strategy*, Oxford: Blackwell.

Handy, C. (1995) *The Empty Raincoat: Making Sense of the Future*, London: Arrow Books Limited.

Harris, M. A. (1994) 'The Power of Boards in Service Providing Agencies: Three Models', *Administration in Social Work*, 18, 2, 1–15.

Herman, E. S. (1981) *Corporate Control, Corporate Power*, New York: Cambridge University Press.

Herman, R. D. (1989) 'Concluding Thoughts on Closing the Board Gap', in R. Herman and J. Van Til (eds) *Nonprofit Boards of Directors: Analyses and Applications*, New Brunswick, NJ: Transaction Books.

Holden, L. (1996) 'Charities and Governance: A Study in Evolution', *The Charity Law and Practice Review*, 4, 1, 27–41.

Hung, H. (1998) 'A Typology or Theories of the Roles of Governing Boards', *Corporate Governance*, 6, 2, 101–111.

Hutton, W. (1997) *Stakeholding and its Critics*, Choice in Welfare No. 36, London: The Institute of Economic Affairs.

Keasey, K., Thompson, S. and Wright, M. (1997) 'The Corporate Governance Problem – Competing Diagnoses and Solutions', in *Corporate Governance: Economic and Financial Issues*, Oxford: Oxford University Press, pp. 1–17.

Kirkland, K. (1994) *The Good Trustee Guide*, London: NCVO.

Kooiman, J. (1999) 'Social–Political Governance: Overview, Reflections, Design', *Public Management*, 1, 1, 67–92.

Lewis, M. W. (2000) 'Exploring Paradox: Toward a More Comprehensive Guide', *Academy of Management Review*, 25, 4, 760–776.

Lorsch, J. W. and MacIver, E. (1989) *Pawns or Potentates: The Reality of America's Corporate Boards*, Boston: Harvard Business School Press.

Mace, M. (1971) *Directors: Myth and Reality*, Cambridge, MA: Harvard University Press.

Middleton, M. (1987) 'Nonprofit Boards of Directors: Beyond the Governance Function', in W. Powell (ed.) *The Nonprofit Sector: A Research Handbook*, New Haven, CT: Yale University Press.

Morgan, G. (1986) *Images of Organisations*, Beverley Hills, CA: Sage Publications.

Muth, M. M. and Donaldson, L. (1998) 'Stewardship Theory and Board Structure: A Contingency Approach', *Corporate Governance*, 6, 1, 5–28.

NCVO (1992) *On Trust: Increasing the Effectiveness of Charity Trustees and Management Committees*, London: NCVO.

NCVO (1996) *Meeting the Challenge of Change: Voluntary Action in the 21st Century*,

Report of the Commission on the Future of the Voluntary Sector, London: NCVO.

Lord Nolan (1995) *Standards in Public Life: First Report of the Committee on Standards in Public Life*, London: HMSO.

Lord Nolan (1996) *Second Report of the Committee on Standards in Public Life: Local Spending Bodies*, vol. 1, London: HMSO.

Nunan, K. (1999) *The Good Trustee Guide*, 3rd edn, London: NCVO.

Ostrower, F. and Stone, M. M. (2001) 'Governance Research: Trends, Gaps and Prospects for the Future', paper presented at the ARNOVA Annual Conference, Miami, Florida, 29 November–1 December.

Pfeffer, J. and Salancik, G. R. (1978) *The External Control of Organisations: A Resource Dependence Perspective*, New York: Harper & Row.

Plummer, J. (1994) *The Governance Gap: Quangos and Accountability*, London: LGC Communications.

Pollitt, C. (1993) *Managerialism and the Public Services*, 2nd edn, Oxford: Oxford University Press.

Pound, J. (1995) 'The Promise of the Governed Corporation', *Harvard Business Review*, March–April, 89–98.

Rhodes, R. A. W. (1994) 'The Hollowing Out of the State', *Political Quarterly*, 65, 138–151.

Roberts, J. and Styles, P. (1998) *The Relationship Between Chairmen and Chief Executives: The Search for Complementarity*, Working Paper, Cambridge: Judge Institute of Management, University of Cambridge.

Robinson, F., Shaw, K., Dutton, J., Grainger, P., Hopwood, B. and Williams, S. (2000) *Who Runs the North East ... Now?*, Durham: University of Durham, Department of Sociology and Social Policy. Available on www.dur.ac.uk/Sociology/nedemocracy.

Robinson, R. and Exworthy, M. (1999) *Two at the Top*, Birmingham: NHS Confederation.

Skelcher, C. (1998) *The Appointed State: Quasi-Governmental Organisations and Democracy*, Buckingham: Open University Press.

Skelcher, C. and Davis, H. (1995) *Opening the Boardroom Door: Membership of Locally Appointed Bodies*, London: LGC Communications.

Stoker, G. (ed.) (1999) *The New Management of British Local Governance*, London: Macmillan.

Tricker, B. (2000) 'Editorial: Corporate Governance: The Subject Whose Time Has Come', *Corporate Governance*, 8, 4, 289–296.

Wood, M. M. (1996) 'Introduction: Governance and Leadership in Theory and Practice', in M. M. Wood (ed.) *Non-profit Boards and Leadership: Cases on Governance, Change and Board–Staff Dynamics*, San Francisco: Jossey-Bass.

Part I

Who governs?

1 Who governs North East England?

A regional perspective on governance

Fred Robinson and Keith Shaw

Introduction

An emphasis on governance – and governance agencies – has rapidly become a central feature of contemporary studies on the 'architecture' of the British State. Within this literature there has been a strong focus on the *national* level. The ESRC's Whitehall Research Programme, for example, has charted the shift away from the Westminster model – in which a strong executive runs a unitary state – to a system of governance in which a range of non-governmental actors increasingly participate in public policy-making and delivery (Rhodes, 2000). As well as capturing the involvement of new structures, governance also refers to new processes and forms of co-ordination. For the Director of the ESRC Programme, governance refers to 'self-organising, inter-organisational networks, characterised by interdependence, resource-exchange, negotiation and significant autonomy from the state' (Rhodes, 1997). Recent studies of governance have also explored developments at the *local* level, emphasising the increasing fragmentation of institutional arrangements (Stoker, 1999), the continuing importance of local quangos (Skelcher *et al.*, 2000) or Local Public Spending Bodies (Greer and Hoggett, 2000), and the consequences for local democracy of the growth of new governance networks (Skelcher, 2000).

In this chapter we focus instead upon a *regional* context, exploring the landscape of governance in the North East of England. Such a focus is timely, given both the growing importance of new institutional arrangements at the regional level of English governance (Mawson, 1997; 1998) and the – increasingly high-profile – campaign for a directly elected regional tier of government in the English regions, including the North East (Tomaney, 1999). The approach adopted in this chapter aims to provide a comprehensive picture of the different layers and forms of regional governance and consequently reveals the complexities, contradictions and biases in the whole range of structures and processes of governance within a particular geographical area.

This account is based on our study, 'Who runs the North East ... now?'

(Robinson *et al.*, 2000). That study, the first of its kind in the UK, brought together detailed information about the complex array of organisations which manage and provide public sector services in the North East, looking especially at *who* runs them – who governs these bodies, how they attained their position and what interests they serve. Our analysis raises important questions about how we are governed and is also intended to provide citizens with the information they need to challenge organisations effectively. For, alongside the 'democratic deficit' (Weir and Beetham, 1999), there is a growing 'knowledge deficit' – most people have little knowledge or understanding of the structures and processes of governance. In our view, tackling that knowledge deficit is an important and necessary step towards building a more open, inclusive and democratic system of governance in which citizens can play an effective role in the running of their region.

The landscape of governance in North East England

The North East of England is a compact region of 2.6 million people. It is a region which has been through a painful and lengthy process of deindustrialisation resulting in high unemployment and deprivation. There is considerable dependence on public services, in relation both to the services they offer and the employment they provide. Indeed, a study for the trade union Unison indicates that the public sector accounts for nearly 30 per cent of jobs in the North East – a figure only exceeded in Northern Ireland (Unison, 2001).

Since the 1970s, the governance of public services has fragmented and there has been a shift from traditional forms of local government to a much more disparate 'local governance'. Alongside a leaner or 'hollowed-out' central and local government (Rhodes, 1994), there is now a bewildering collection of unelected, quasi-public organisations controlling and delivering public services funded by the taxpayer (Public Administration Committee, 2001). Such a change, which has also involved the development of a myriad of 'partnerships' that serve as alternative, collaborative structures of governance, has led Skelcher (1998) to refer to the emergence of the 'congested' state.

Through privatisation and the establishment of a plethora of agencies run by boards, central government has shed responsibilities, while local government has, unwillingly, been divested of responsibilities. In particular, local government's control of education has been substantially reduced, as has its role as a provider of social housing. In the North East, contracting-out of local authority services, through such mechanisms as compulsory competitive tendering, has been very limited (Unison, 2001), but may well develop much further under the 'Best Value' regime and public–private partnerships. Nevertheless, it needs to be emphasised that, despite this 'hollowing-out', the institutions of central and local government continue to be very important providers of public services and do have a major impact on the economy and society of the North East.

Both central and local government comprise democratically elected institutions. The North East has thirty MPs representing the region's constituencies in the House of Commons. Twenty-eight of them are Labour members, including the Prime Minister and several of his cabinet colleagues. Across the region there are twenty-five local councils, with altogether 1279 elected councillors, two-thirds of them Labour. There are also four MEPs (three Labour, one Conservative) representing the region in the European Parliament.

Important criticisms can certainly be levelled at the elected state, its operation and legitimacy. In the North East, central government is felt to be remote and insensitive to the region's problems; hence, there is some support for devolution of power to a regional tier of government (North East Constitutional Convention, 1999). Indeed, it can be argued that the region can never win, whoever is in power, since a Labour government takes its North East heartland for granted, while a Conservative government – with little political support in the region – largely ignores it. And local government is seen as lacklustre and has been emasculated by central government which controls, and pays for, much of what it does. Its credibility is also undermined by low turnouts in local elections, symptomatic of public indifference. In the 1999 local elections in the North East, only fourteen out of 432 wards had turnouts over 50 per cent, with Sunderland (19.2 per cent) having the lowest turnout in the region and the second lowest in Britain (Rallings and Thrasher, 1999). Elections for the European Parliament also produce low turnouts – only 19.5 per cent of the North East voted in the last European elections in 1999 – and that Parliament has, in any case, very limited powers.

Politics and, more specifically, representative democracy are hardly thriving in the North East. Politicians and their parties are neither popular nor much respected. Moreover, given the difficult economic experiences of the region – such as the recent closures of Siemens and Fujitsu – it is well understood that these institutions cannot control damaging global economic forces; they can, at most, alleviate the consequences.

However, at least from time to time the electorate has the opportunity to go to the polls and remove politicians. This is an important principle although, it has to be said, elections bring few surprises or upsets in a region so strongly wedded to one party and where people are disinclined to vote, other than in general elections. Nevertheless, this point of principle is widely considered to be important, indeed there is a certain pride in 'our democracy'. For many, it is fundamental, even if they do not vote, and is invoked right across the political spectrum.

But in the North East, as elsewhere in Britain, many public services – the services paid for by the taxpayer – are managed and provided by organisations which are *not* subject to local democratic control. There is a multitude of unelected bodies, governed by board members who are appointed by government ministers, or by other institutions, or who are selected by existing board members. Some of these are quangos, others quango-esque hybrids. Members of these boards cannot be removed by the electorate, however badly they are performing or however unpopular their actions. It is here where there is a serious 'democratic deficit'.

At the regional level, central government has established a form of regional governance which falls well short of devolved regional government. Regional Development Agencies (RDAs) were set up in the English regions three years ago to co-ordinate and secure regional economic development and regeneration (DETR, 2001). The RDAs claim to represent their regions, speaking and acting on behalf of the region, but they are appointed, not elected, bodies which therefore have no mandate to represent their supposed constituents. One NorthEast, the RDA in North East England, like the other RDAs across the country, is run by board members – all thirteen of whom have been appointed by the Secretary of State for the Environment, Transport and the Regions. They are answerable to the minister and, ultimately, Parliament – not to the region's people. However, at least the appointments process was more open, more considered and more meritocratic than had been the case, for example, of appointments to Urban Development Corporations in the 1980s. The selection of individuals to be appointed to the RDAs was conducted in various ways; in the North East, a panel was convened comprising the newly-appointed Chair, Dr John Bridge, senior officials from Government Office – North East and recruitment advisers from PriceWaterhouseCoopers. Over a period of nine months, the panel considered more than 100 candidates, then made detailed recommendations to the minister for his final selection and decision.

The lack of accountability within the new institutions of regional governance has, in a way, been recognised by the government which proposed the establishment of 'regional chambers' to work alongside RDAs. In the North East, the regional chamber, grandly titled the North East Regional Assembly, comprises forty-two local councillors, nominated by councils across the region (hence, thirty-four of them are Labour), together with twenty-one people from various organisations identified as 'regional stakeholders'. It is this body which enthusiasts for regional devolution would like to see directly elected.

The third element of regional governance is Government Office – North East, a group of civil servants from various central government departments who are based in Newcastle upon Tyne; their role is to represent central government in the region and oversee the delivery of government programmes. Power rests largely with One NorthEast and the Government Office, which both have a degree of autonomy in practice, but are accountable to central government, not the region's people. The

Regional Assembly, a partially indirectly elected body, has a weak role, virtually no resources, and a questionable mandate. This whole structure is evidently messy and confusing and, of course, difficult to challenge or influence (Robinson, 1999). As a recent review of the role of central government at the local and regional levels argues, 'there are too many Government initiatives, causing confusion; not enough co-ordination; and too much time spent on negotiating the system, rather than delivering' (Performance and Innovation Unit, 2000: 6).

Most people in the North East know nothing about these regional bodies and will not come into contact with them. Their impacts on the region are considerable, widely felt, even crucial, but the provenance of these impacts is unknown. By contrast, everyone comes into contact with *local* unelected bodies and uses their services, although most will have little or no knowledge of the ways in which these bodies are structured and run.

The vast majority of people use and rely upon the National Health Service (NHS), yet have little idea of how it is run. In fact, it is made up of quangos and quango-esque bodies. The NHS in the North East is overseen by a regional office (NHS Executive, Northern and Yorkshire Region), staffed by civil servants and has a regional chair, a non-executive member appointed by the Secretary of State for Health. At local level, there are six Health Authorities, which have a strategic function, and seventeen NHS Trusts running and providing hospitals and other services. The boards of all these bodies have a majority of non-executive members, appointed by the Secretary of State. In 1999, the government introduced Primary Care Groups (PCGs), that purchase health services for groups of GP practices, replacing the former 'fundholding' arrangements. The twenty-five PCGs covering the North East are constituted as sub-committees of the Health Authorities and are made up of members nominated by GPs, by community/practice nurses, the Health Authority and local authority Social Services. There is also a lay member, whose role it is to represent the local community.

Gradually, PCGs are becoming Primary Care Trusts, set up like the other NHS Trusts, with appointed non-executive members. In addition, there are now three Health Action Zones in the North East, in Northumberland, Tyne and Wear and Teesside, which target deprived areas with poor health status. The structure of the NHS is difficult for outsiders, such as patients, to understand, and is probably little understood by many NHS employees. Moreover, responsibility is diffused; no wonder it is hard to discover where the buck stops and so difficult for a patient to pursue a complaint against the NHS. And, without democratic control, local people have found it virtually impossible to put pressure on NHS bodies when they have restructured services and closed hospitals.

Alongside health, the other big service not noted for democratic control is education, and the democratic deficit is especially apparent in higher and further education. All educational institutions have governing bodies, but the different sectors of the system have different arrangements and structures. There are five universities in the North East; the two older universities (Durham and Newcastle) are governed by a council comprising staff, student union representatives and individuals from outside the university, mainly people with business and professional backgrounds. The newer (post-1992) universities (Northumbria, Sunderland and Teesside) are governed by boards, which include few staff members and are predominantly made up of local business people. There are also seventeen Further Education Colleges, seven Sixth Form Colleges and two City Technology Colleges in the region which are run by boards of governors and are independent of the Local Education Authority. All these bodies have a tendency to be self-perpetuating cliques; most governors are selected by the existing governors and very few are elected (the student union representatives are the main exception). Schools, nowadays with more powers delegated to them and less under the control of Local Education Authorities, are rather more democratic. Their governing bodies include several members elected by parents, but the majority of governors are appointed. As with the NHS, it is difficult to influence, let alone change, the policies and practices of educational institutions, particularly in the higher and further education sectors where business-like governing bodies are subject to very little democratic control. It is worth noting that colleges and universities are, in turn, beholden to the quangos (the Learning and Skills Councils and Higher Education Funding Council) that fund and regulate them and limit their autonomy.

Local police forces operate under a tripartite system of governance, with responsibility shared by the Home Secretary, local Police Authorities and chief constables. The Police Authorities have a duty to represent the local community and these statutory bodies draw up the police force budget, develop strategies and plans and appoint senior officers. There are three Police Authorities across the North East – Cleveland, Durham and Northumbria – each with a board of seventeen members, all of whom are appointed. Some are councillors nominated by local councils, some are magistrates chosen by the local Magistrates Court Committee and the rest are 'independent members' selected by the councillors and magistrate members in conjunction with the Home Secretary. Here again is a key local service – and a service which is quite frequently subject to criticism and complaints – which is not democratically controlled. Although Police Authorities are charged with representing the views of the local community, their very existence is unknown to the vast majority of local people.

In the late 1980s, the Conservative government essentially privatised the management and delivery of training schemes and enterprise development by establishing Training and Enterprise Councils (TECs), thus creating another layer of local governance. TECs were private-sector, but not-for-profit organisations, which operated under contract to central government. Their boards were not appointed by government, but the previous government did stipulate that two-thirds of their board members had to be from the upper echelons of the private sector. The five TECs in the North East were run by people who basically selected each other to serve on the board. These quango-esque hybrids were probably the least democratic, least representative and least defensible of the organisations providing publicly funded services. In April 2001 they were replaced by Learning and Skills Councils (four of them in the North East), responsible for overseeing post-16 education and training, including the Further Education sector. Their boards are intended to be more inclusive, with only 40 per cent of their members from business. But they are still appointed, not elected.

The great enthusiasm for partnership approaches, enabling different agencies and interests to work together, has had a substantial impact on contemporary governance in the North East. Throughout the region, numerous partnership boards have been set up to manage and deliver regeneration schemes (such as those funded by the Single Regeneration Budget) and to implement a wide variety of other government initiatives. In an attempt to bring some semblance of order to the increasing chaos of proliferating partnerships, the government has recently proposed the development of overarching Local Strategic Partnerships. Here again, there are likely to be problems of democratic accountability. A national survey of regeneration partnerships found, for example, that:

> SRB partnerships fall well short of the standards of transparency and accountability that would be expected of public service organisations ... in many cases members of the wider local community have inadequate levels of access to partnerships and their decision-making processes. Frequently partnerships fail to provide communities with both sufficient information regarding their activities and opportunities to influence those activities.
>
> (CURS, 1998: 61–62)

Most of the board members on these partnerships are nominated by the organisations involved in the programme or initiative. Community representatives on regeneration partnership boards are sometimes elected by the communities they are intended to represent, as is the case in several of the New Deal for Communities projects, but, very often, they are simply selected by the local authority which is primarily in control of the regeneration scheme (Robinson and Shaw, 2001).

The shift of power away from local government is perhaps particularly evident in the changing provision of social housing, stemming from the increased role of housing associations, now further expanding through major stock transfers from local authorities to existing or newly created associations. Housing associations are independent bodies, run by boards elected by their members (the nominal shareholders). However, the process of nomination is, all too often, not particularly open; there is also very limited representation of tenants and their interests. Housing associations are themselves accountable to a quango, the Housing Corporation, which funds and regulates them. This is quite different from local authority control of council housing with opportunities for change and influence through elected councillors.

In our study, 'Who runs the North East . . . now?' we also looked at the governance of arts in the region. There is a regional arts board, Northern Arts, which funds and supports arts in the North East and Cumbria, and Culture North East, a recently established 'Regional Cultural Consortium'. These bodies are run by unelected boards. A third of the board members of Northern Arts are councillors nominated by their councils and the rest are selected by the existing board. Culture North East comprises a chair appointed by the Secretary of State for Culture, Media and Sport and the other members are nominated by specified agencies and sectors in the region.

Our study did not, and obviously could not, cover all forms and aspects of governance in the North East. It focused on the main bodies active and based in the region and in positions of power, but beyond and outside the region are numerous boards, including national quangos, which have an impact. Within the region, there are other boards, some local authority joint boards running public services such as the Fire Service and Public Transport, a regional tourist board and numerous voluntary sector bodies contracted to provide public services. Nevertheless, the study did cover a good deal of ground and revealed the disparate and dispersed nature of governance and power. It also challenges the common assumption that public services are democratically controlled.

Accountability and openness

The institutions of central and local government are democratically accountable to the electorate, even though we recognise that their accountability is, in practice, far from perfect. They are also, more or less, open and are in fact bound by legislation safeguarding access to a considerable amount of information. The accountability of the various boards running public services is much less clear-cut and is usually convoluted and confused by multiple accountabilities. Most are far from open in relation to provision of information and access to their meetings.

The Nolan reforms and other changes introduced by the present government have made some of the quangos more open and, to a limited extent, more accountable to local people. All the local NHS quangos, for example, now have to hold their board meetings in public; up until recently, most NHS Trusts in the North East chose to meet behind closed doors. NHS board members are obliged to disclose their interests and enter these in a register available for public inspection. These bodies are directly accountable to government ministers, not the public; nevertheless, they are supposed to inform and consult with the public. Some make more of an effort than others and, of course, consultation is a limited approach to accountability.

Many of the other unelected bodies still do not allow members of the public into their meetings. The board of the new Regional Development Agency, One NorthEast, meets behind closed doors, as did the boards of Training and Enterprise Councils, and as do most of the governing bodies of educational institutions, most of the boards of Housing Associations, half the regeneration partnerships, and the boards of Northern Arts and Culture North East. Nowadays, most of the boards do make their minutes and papers publicly available – a practice new to most of them. That said, too many of them make little real effort to inform and engage with the public; in any case, these organisations often do not see themselves as accountable to local people even morally, if not formally, or simply take the view that local people would not be interested. And, the recent proliferation of a wide range of partnerships – what Skelcher (2000: 13) has referred to as 'tertiary' bodies – is likely to further complicate and frustrate accountability:

> Overall, the transfer of responsibility and power to tertiary bodies poses major issues both for the theory and practice of public governance and management. It removes centres of decision-making further from elected political structures, increasing their distance from citizens and often becoming invisible to public view.
>
> (Ibid.)

Fundamentally, what is lacking is a real belief in the importance of openness or an understanding that providers of public services ought to be accountable to the public they purport to serve. Unfortunately, this culture is not confined to the unelected bodies but is to be found also within the elected state. In the North East, paternalistic local authorities are not uncommon and some elected members are struggling to cope with the modernisation agenda which means, among other things, dialogue with the public and extensive, inclusive partnerships. It has been particularly instructive to see several local authorities in the region introducing cabinets which they decided would meet in private. They argued that this was an unimportant matter which was of no concern to the public; and some have implied that, in any case, open meetings would be a sham since deals would be done in closed meetings – as before. A number of the region's local authorities subsequently relented, and agreed to open their meetings, once they became aware of opposition strongly expressed by this – supposedly apathetic – public.

Who runs the North East?

It is a straightforward matter to find out the names, backgrounds and interests of MPs, MEPs and local councillors. This information is fairly widely available. After all, most politicians seek publicity and wish to be known to their electorate. It is much more difficult to discover who sits on the unelected boards. There is no central source of this information and, although many of these organisations now have their own websites, remarkably few of these sites provide *any* information about their governance. It therefore becomes necessary to contact these organisations and specifically ask about board members, as we had to do in our study. In addition, while almost all of these bodies have a publicly available register of board members' interests, access to this has to be requested and it usually has to be consulted at their offices. Very few have considered it necessary, or good practice, to publish information on board members' interests in their annual reports.

The simple answer to the question, 'Who runs the North East?' is: predominantly, middle-aged (or older), mainly middle-class men. About three-quarters of the people elected, selected or appointed to run the region's public institutions are men. Younger people (aged under 45) are largely absent from the formal decision-making structures and processes in the North East and younger women, in particular, have little involvement in running the region's institutions. In addition, few people from black or ethnic minority communities are involved in running the region's public services – though it is important to bear in mind that the North East has a small black or ethnic minority population. In view of the high incidence of disability in the region, a legacy of heavy industry, it is surprising that few disabled people are members of the boards of the unelected bodies, but there is a relatively large number of disabled people serving on local councils.

The people who run the region's affairs are clearly not representative of the diversity of the region's people (Table 1.1). This is the case in both the elected and unelected sectors. The MPs represent, but are not representative of, the region's population: twenty-six of the thirty MPs are male, most are in their forties and fifties, are university-educated and have professional backgrounds. Nowadays, few have 'working-class' backgrounds; some critics also point out that few have ever run a business. Like MPs, most local councillors – 76 per cent – are men and, moreover, twenty-three of the region's twenty-five council leaders are men. Most councillors in the North East are middle-aged or older: their average age is 56 and nearly 40 per cent are retired. A mere 3.3 per cent are aged under 35 and only 0.8 per cent are from an ethnic minority group (Local Government Management Board, 1998). Little wonder, then, that many younger people see local councils as stuffy institutions run by old men.

Table 1.1 Who runs the North East?

Body	Composition of the board
Parliament	Twenty-six of the North East's thirty MPs are male. Most are in their forties and fifties, are university-educated and have professional backgrounds.
Local government	76.6 per cent of councillors are men. The average age of the region's councillors is 56; only 3.3 per cent are aged under 35. Only two out of twenty-five council leaders are women.
NHS	43 per cent of non-executive appointees to Health Authorities in the region are women, 44 per cent on NHS Trusts are women and 41 per cent on Primary Care Groups. Some 6 per cent of members of both Health Authorities and PCGs are disabled.
Regional governance	Of the thirteen board members of One NorthEast (RDA), only three are women. Average age is 52. Only 12 per cent of the members of the North East Regional Assembly (Regional Chamber) are women. Two-thirds are councillors nominated from local authorities.
Education	Only one of the seventeen FE Colleges has a female Chair. Of the members of FE Colleges' governing bodies, 27 per cent are women, 2 per cent from ethnic minority communities, 24 per cent aged under 45. The governing bodies of universities are even less representative, with 19 per cent women and only 14 per cent under 45.
Police Authorities	73 per cent of the members of the region's three Police Authorities are men; almost all are aged over 45. Three of the fifty-one members are from ethnic minority groups.
Training and Enterprise Councils	Most members of TEC Boards are businessmen. Only nine of the seventy-two board members on the region's TECs are women. Three-quarters are aged 45 to 65. There are no ethnic minority members or people with disabilities.
Housing Associations (RSLs)	74 per cent of board members are men. Three of the sixteen housing associations surveyed had no women on their boards. Only 15 per cent were aged under 45.
Regeneration (SRB) Partnerships	68 per cent of the members of the boards of Regeneration Partnerships in the North East are men; 4 per cent are from ethnic minority groups, 1 per cent are disabled; 33 per cent are aged under 45.
Cultural bodies (Northern Arts and Culture North East)	67 per cent of the Northern Arts board are men; 50 per cent of Culture North East are men, 33 per cent of the Northern Arts board, and 40 per cent of Culture North East, are councillors.

Across almost all of the unelected sector in the North East the same pattern is repeated. Only three of the thirteen board members of One NorthEast are women and only 12 per cent of the members of the North East Regional Assembly are women – a reflection of the fact that senior councillors are almost all men.

Some 73 per cent of the members of the governing bodies of Further Education Colleges are men and three-quarters are over 45. The governing bodies of the region's universities are even less representative: 81 per cent are men, 86 per cent are over 45. Police Authorities (73 per cent men) and housing associations (74 per cent men) are the same. The Training and Enterprise Councils were predominantly made up of busi-ness*men*: only nine of the seventy-two board members on the region's TECs were women. There is very little or no representation of ethnic minorities or disabled people on these boards. It seems evident that, while organisations have developed equal opportunity frameworks for their full-time staff, consideration of these issues is underdeveloped with regard to the composition of their governing boards.

The one encouraging area is the NHS, where new targets and appoint-ment procedures set by the government have led to more women and people from ethnic minorities on the region's Health Authorities and NHS Trusts. Thus, 43 per cent of the non-executive members of Health Authorities are women, 44 per cent on the NHS Trusts. This shows that change is possible, if there is the commitment to make it happen.

That the North East is run mainly by older men is hardly surprising. The situation is similar elsewhere, though perhaps in this region male dominance is most marked, linked to the area's traditions of heavy male-employing industries and the associated political institutions. The domi-nance of men in the region's public affairs has changed little over time, while the machinery of governance has changed very considerably. Now, as in the past, men are in charge, but nowadays many more of them are 'middle-class' people with professional or business backgrounds. Indeed, appointment to boards in the North East region have tended to favour people who can bring in managerial or professional expertise or who are used to running a business. This is in contrast to the selection of 'ordin-ary' people who have the everyday experience of using public services or who have the 'capacity to understand the needs of diverse groups and to develop policies that reflect a wider public interest' (Skelcher and Davis, 1996: 14). As Greer and Hoggett (2000: 527) have noted of the boards that run Local Public Spending Bodies:

> Most have an essentially 'consumerist' orientation to their 'publics' rather than one based upon concepts of rights, citizenship, and social justice ... most are strongly managerialist and, despite efforts to open up board recruitment, are still governed primarily by what might be thought of as 'elite volunteers'.

There are still many councillors with 'working-class' backgrounds – though fewer than in the past – and some of them will be appointed or selected to serve on various boards. Overwhelmingly, however, the North East's public services are run by older, mainly middle-class men and this seems frequently to be regarded as inevitable; a normal state of affairs which cannot effectively be challenged and changed.

Public service and 'active citizens'

The fragmentation of governance and the incremental, *ad hoc* creation of new institutional arrangements in the North East have certainly removed and undermined local democratic control and resulted in complexity and public confusion about which organisations do what and who runs them. It has also led to real confusion about the concept of public service and the role of those 'active citizens' who run public institutions.

The individuals who serve on the institutions of governance in the North East – whether elected, selected or appointed – play an important part in the life of the region and help to ensure that services operate efficiently and effectively. It is right to recognise their commitment to public service. Many devote a substantial amount of time and effort to their work and take on major responsibilities. But are these 'active citizens' the right people to be running the region?

The lack of diversity among the group of people running the region is a problem. It undoubtedly restricts debate and limits understanding. As the Chair*man* (*sic*) of the Association of North East Councils recently put it: 'The proportion of women decision-makers in local government across the country, not just here in the North East, is woefully low. Women's views often take a back seat because they are so under-represented' (Councillor M. Davey, quoted in Robinson *et al.*, 2000: 158).

Diversity can mean that different points of view have a voice, have a platform. And this relates not only to women but to other groups, and not only to councillors (or, for that matter, council officers) but also to the unelected boards. The argument for diversity is not simply about equity; diversity also enhances the collective wisdom of an organisation, its responsiveness and its credibility. It may well result in better policy. It means also that the public may identify with an organisation run by people like themselves, including younger people and women. Older men have much to offer, of course, but do not have a monopoly of knowledge and wisdom. The promotion of diversity resonates with the emphasis in the First Nolan Committee Report on the 'stakeholder' (as opposed to the 'managerialist') approach to corporate governance, in which boards aim to incorporate a balance of skills, interests and backgrounds in order to promote debate and effective decision-making (Greer and Hoggett, 2000: 525).

However, there are significant barriers working against diversity, in particular the processes of selection. Within the elected sector, political parties (especially in the North East) have made little effort to bring forward a diverse range of candidates but, again, at least politicians have the legitimacy, albeit imperfect, of the electoral process. In the unelected sector, many of the 'active citizens' selected and appointed to boards have been chosen because they are known to existing board members, are considered safe choices, are supposedly among the great and good or are identified as 'people like us'. This produces boards which are essentially self-perpetuating cliques. As noted earlier, there is also a concern to appoint people with particular professional backgrounds, such as solicitors and accountants, or who have experience in running a business. While this emphasis can be justified within the 'stewardship model' of governance (see Introduction), in which the role of the board is viewed as adding value to the organisation by improving its top decision-making, it does run the risk of merely duplicating the existing expertise of the paid staff, rather than bringing in other interests and outlooks. It also tends to result in boards appointing a succession of similar people, another barrier to extending diversity.

However, there have been some changes in recent years. In the main quangos appointed by ministers, such as One NorthEast and the NHS bodies, the Nolan reforms have brought a welcome shift towards more transparent appointment processes, based more on merit and a concern to achieve diversity. But party patronage is an ever-present danger with quangos and the Commissioner for Public Appointments has recently raised serious concerns about the appointment of large numbers of Labour activists to NHS bodies in the North East (Office of the Commissioner for Public Appointments, 2000). The many other quango-esque organisations in the North East have been little affected by reform. They commit themselves to Nolan's 'seven principles of public life' but retain opaque selection processes. As far as we can tell, many of those organisations, such as governing bodies in higher and further education, for instance, or housing associations, rely heavily on the social networks of existing board members when recruiting new members to their boards.

This discussion takes us inevitably to the question: who *should* run the North East? Underpinning this are fundamental questions about the nature and scope of this kind of public service and the locus and distribution of power in the society. Looking at the unelected organisations of governance in the North East, however, it is evident that such questions have often hardly been considered, let alone resolved. There is a messy confusion of arrangements for appointments, all too often based mainly on established custom and practice rather than clear principles. It is uncertain whether the active citizens on boards are there as custodians of public services, managers, figureheads or political placemen. Their relationship with, and responsibilities to, the local community are unclear.

And confusions about public service are well illustrated and exemplified by different arrangements for remuneration, with some board members (and, incidentally, all politicians) being paid while others, who may also devote much time and effort, are unpaid (Klaushofer, 2000). At the heart of these uncertainties and confusions (as the Introduction notes) is the tension between 'stewardship' approaches, with their emphases on guidance, expertise and experience, and 'democratic' (or even stakeholder) perspectives which stress how board members are there to serve the constituency (or constituencies) or stakeholders they represent.

In our view, the basic issue is democratic control. Most, if not all, the unelected bodies should be replaced by elected ones as a matter of principle to provide the basis for accountability. Accountability to the local community is a key issue. These bodies can be accountable to local people at the same time as being held to account by central government and its agencies, in much the same way as are local authorities.

Administering a hefty dose of democracy should help to strengthen local accountability, ensure more openness and give greater credibility and legitimacy to those who run the region's organisations. It has to be admitted, however, that at present there is no evident enthusiasm for voting in the North East, as shown by the low turnouts in local elections. The region's rusty democracy needs, therefore, first to be revived and re-invigorated, beginning with local government. Real efforts need to be made to broaden participation in local government, in terms of greater diversity of candidates, innovation in voting methods and systems, and encouraging and enabling citizen involvement. Without the re-invigoration and renewal of existing local government, it is hard to make out a convincing case for bringing other bodies under local democratic control.

In several of the English regions there are campaigns for the establishment of regional government based on directly elected regional assemblies. The case is being put most strongly in the North East, spearheaded by the Campaign for a North East Assembly and the North East Constitutional Convention, with support from various other interests in the region, including the media. Much is being promised: it is argued that a regional tier of government brings democracy closer to the people; that a degree of regional autonomy would make for more effective policy-making; and that such an assembly could have power over the quangos and other unelected bodies. It remains to be seen whether such an assembly could deliver. What is clear at the moment is that such is the disenchantment with the political process in the region that generating broad popular support for regional devolution is very difficult. If a referendum on the issue was held now, it could well be lost – and few would bother to vote. Many would feel that a regional tier of government would just mean more 'jobs for the boys'.

For regional devolution to gain popular support and for it to make a difference, it would have to be different from existing local government.

The campaigners have begun to acknowledge that and have, for example, put forward ideas about the much greater inclusion and involvement of women in such an assembly (North East Constitutional Convention, 2000). But it is now essential that local government begins to reform itself, so it can, by its own example, make the case for greater local – and regional – democracy.

Conclusion

Governance in the North East of England is fragmented, confusing and largely detached from the people of the region. Within the elected sector, democracy is at a low ebb, characterised by inertia and decay. In the unelected sector, there is little accountability to local people and these organisations, hardly known to the public, are able to operate largely unquestioned and unchallenged.

In our view it is essential to open and democratise the unelected bodies, but it is evident that some quangos and quango-esque organisations will remain, and it may even be possible to justify the continuation of some of them. While they remain, they need to engage in reform. All should review their membership and seek ways of ensuring greater representativeness. The selection and appointment of board members should be open and transparent, with vacancies advertised and appointments subjected to a process of independent assessment. Meetings should be open to the public and media, and organised so as to encourage public attendance and participation. All these organisations need to seriously engage with the public, explaining what they do and taking seriously the views of local people who pay for and use their services.

The narrow range of people running the region's public services and the lack of diversity extend across both the elected and unelected sectors and constitute a major problem and weakness in the governance of the North East. If governance, and government, are to be revived, all sectors of the community need to be re-engaged with public services and be involved in running them.

References

CURS (1998) *Competition, Partnership and Regeneration: Lessons from Three Rounds of the SRB*, Centre for Urban and Regional Studies, Birmingham: University of Birmingham.

DETR (2001) *Strategic Development and Partnership Working in the Regional Development Agencies*, Regeneration Research Summary, no. 38, London: DETR. Available on www.regeneration.detr.gov.uk/rs/03800/index.htm.

Greer, A. and Hoggett, P. (2000) 'Contemporary Governance and Local Public Spending Bodies', *Public Administration*, 78, 3, 513–530.

Klaushofer, A. (2000) 'Putting a Price on Public Service', *Public Finance*, 27 October–2 November, 16–18.

Local Government Management Board (1998) *First National Survey of Councillors in England and Wales in 1997*, London: LGMB.

Mawson, J. (1997) 'The English Regional Debate: Towards Regional Governance or Government', in J. Bradbury and J. Mawson (eds) *British Regionalism and Devolution: The Challenges of State Reform and European Integration*, London: Jessica Kingsley.

Mawson, J. (1998) 'English Regionalism and New Labour', *Regionalism and Federal Studies*, 6, 158–175.

North East Constitutional Convention (1999) *Time for a Change: The Case for a New North East Assembly*, Newcastle: NECC.

North East Constitutional Convention (2000) *The Women's Forum Agenda for a Directly Elected North East Regional Assembly*, Newcastle: NECC.

Office of the Commissioner for Public Appointments (2000) *Public Appointments to NHS Trusts and Health Authorities*, London: OCPA. Available on www.ocpa.gov.uk.

Performance and Innovation Unit (2000) *Reaching Out: The Role of Central Government at Regional and Local Level*, London: PIU. Available on www.cabinet-office.gov.uk/innovation/1999/regions.

Public Administration Committee (2001) *Mapping the Quango State*, Fifth Report of the Select Committee on Public Administration, London: HMSO.

Rallings, C. and Thrasher, M. (1999) *Local Elections Handbook 1999*, Plymouth: Local Government Chronicle Elections Centre, University of Plymouth.

Rhodes, R. (1994) 'The Hollowing-Out of the State: The Changing Nature of the Public Service in Britain', *The Political Quarterly*, 65, 138–151.

Rhodes, R. (1997) *Understanding Governance: Policy Networks, Governance, Reflexivity and Accountability*, Buckingham: Open University Press.

Rhodes, R. (2000) 'The Governance Narrative: Key Findings and Lessons from the ESRC's Whitehall Programme', *Public Administration*, 78, 2, 345–363.

Robinson, F. (1999) 'Region and Community', *New Economy*, 6, 3,133–136.

Robinson, F. and Shaw, K. (2001) 'Regeneration Partnerships, "Community" and Governance in North East England', *Northern Economic Review*, 31, 4–19.

Robinson, F., Shaw, K., Dutton, J., Grainger, P., Hopwood, B. and Williams, S. (2000) *Who Runs the North East . . . Now?*, Durham: University of Durham, Department of Sociology and Social Policy.

Skelcher, C. (1998) *The Appointed State: Quasi-Governmental Organisations and Democracy*, Buckingham: Open University Press.

Skelcher, C. (2000) 'Changing Images of the State: Overloaded, Hollowed-Out and Congested', *Public Policy and Administration*, 15, 3, 3–19.

Skelcher, C. and Davis, H. (1996) 'Understanding the New Magistracy: A Study of Characteristics and Attitudes', *Local Government Studies*, 22, 2, 8–21.

Skelcher, C., Weir, S. and Wilson, L. (2000) *Advance of the Quango State*, London: Local Government Information Unit.

Stoker, G. (ed.) (1999) *The New Management of British Local Governance*, London: Macmillan.

Tomaney, J. (1999) *Home Rule for the North*, Urban and Regional Regeneration Bulletin, Newcastle: Centre for Urban and Regional Development Studies, University of Newcastle. Available on www.newcastle.ac.uk/curds/urrb.

Unison (2001) *Best Value – for Who: The Economic and Social Implications of Best Value in the Northern Region*, Newcastle: Unison.

Weir, S. and Beetham, D. (1999) *Political Power and Democratic Control in Britain*, London: Routledge.

2 Are quasi-governmental organisations effective and accountable?

Alan Greer, Paul Hoggett and Stella Maile

Introduction

Since the 1980s successive governments in the UK have entrusted the delivery of services and programmes to a range of organisations of different types, created from a variety of motivations for myriad functions and purposes, and referred to by a bewildering array of terms. Hood and Schuppert (1988a: 1) have used the term 'para-government organisation' to refer to 'all types of organisations other than core government bureaucracies which are used to provide public services'. The 'modernisation agenda' of the 'New Labour' government has arguably accentuated the trend towards the use of quasi-governmental organisations (quangos). The rhetoric has referred to a determination to keep the number of non-departmental public bodies (NDPBs) to a minimum, creating them only where appropriate and cost-effective. While it has been claimed that the number of NDPBs has been reduced by 10 per cent since 1997 (Cabinet Office, 2000a: iv), in reality, powerful new quangos have also been created. These include the Food Standards Agency, the National Institute for Clinical Excellence, and even quangos that supervise recruitment to other quangos such as the NHS Appointments Commission and the Commissioner for Public Appointments. New forms of partnership have also been established, such as Health and Education Action Zones, Employment Zones, Community Safety Partnerships, and those resulting from the New Deal for Communities, Single Regeneration Budget, and Sure Start initiatives (Benington, 2000; Skelcher, 2000).

Generalisations about quangos need to be made with care. Significant differences are found between sectors and also between bodies in the same sector, for example in their organisational histories and cultures, size and expenditure, and their ability to define their own objectives and outcomes. Two key dimensions of diversity are territorial coverage and relative autonomy from central government (see Figure 2.1). Quangos can be classified according to their 'closeness' to core government. Greve *et al.* (1999) develop a continuum stretching between departmental units, that are clearly aspects of government, and private sector companies. Between

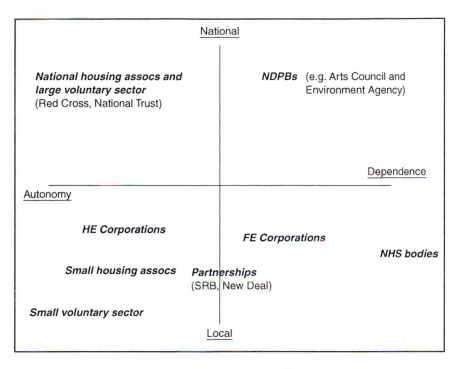

National

National housing assocs and
large voluntary sector
(Red Cross, National Trust)

NDPBs (e.g. Arts Council and
Environment Agency)

Dependence

Autonomy

HE Corporations

FE Corporations

NHS bodies

Small housing assocs   Partnerships
(SRB, New Deal)

Small voluntary sector

Local

Figure 2.1 Dimensions of quasi-governmental organisations

these end points there is a range of bodies which vary in their 'quangoness' from quasi-autonomous agencies of government, through NHS bodies and NDPBs to voluntary/charity bodies and semi-privatised organisations. However, the key dimension accounting for the actual diversity of these bodies is their 'practical' rather than formal/legal autonomy and we need to examine the context and history of each organisation to judge whether they enjoy autonomy or not. Essentially this means that we adopt a historical–institutional approach to the study of quangos (ibid.: 140). Thus factors such as the degree of dependence on government funding and the regulatory environment of the organisation are as important as constitutional status in determining the practical autonomy of quangos.

Organisations can also be classified according to whether their remit is local, regional or national. This covers national NDPBs such as the Arts Council and the Environment Agency (though they may also have a quasi-federal and regional structure) and 'local public spending bodies' (LSPBs). A widely accepted definition of these latter organisations refers to 'any local bodies operating under wholly or largely appointed or self-appointing boards that received public money to perform public functions or deliver public services' (Skelcher *et al.*, 2000: 10), for example, Further Education Corporations and Housing Associations. Such a broad and inclusive definition would also include virtually the whole of the UK voluntary sector, although here we are concerned only with large national voluntary organisations that spend public money to perform public functions.

For Skelcher, the use of quasi-governmental bodies was central to the managerialist inspired 'hollowing-out' of the state in the 1980s and 1990s. This was achieved through processes such as privatisation and by 'transferring responsibility for the management and delivery of public programmes from *primary* and *multi-purpose* governmental bodies to *secondary* and *single-purpose* agencies' (2000: 7, italics in the original). At the same time, however, greater central control has been exercised over policy formulation and implementation. More recently Skelcher argues that the hollowed-out state has given way to a 'congested state' that is characterised by organisational fragmentation, plural modes of governance, and a plethora of mediating 'partnerships', defined as 'organisational arrangements bringing together two or more agencies in pursuit of a public policy objective' (Skelcher, 2000: 9 and 12). These can operate at a tertiary level and 'manage, integrate and steer the activities of primary and secondary bodies – local authorities, health bodies, executive agencies and so on. More significantly, they may also engage in the development of policy and delivery of programmes on behalf of partners' (ibid.: 12–13).

That governments continue to see advantages in using quasi-governmental organisations raises two linked issues that provide the focus for this chapter. First, their use is often justified in terms of the need for effectiveness, summed up in the managerialist tenet that 'any public task will be performed more cheaply and effectively by bodies set at a distance from core government and following a business management model' (Hood and Schuppert, 1988: 12). However, there is scant evidence to support this contention and political considerations may still be important, for example, a desire to exercise control or, alternatively, an attempt to put central government at arm's length from political criticism (for a discussion of why quangos are used, see Cabinet Office, 1997: Chapter 2; Flinders and Smith, 1999; Greve *et al.*, 1999). Second, the use of quasi-governmental organisations has typically been an alternative to the use of core bureaucracies and democratically-based institutions such as local councils. As a consequence, there is a perceived need to ensure that they are in some sense held 'accountable', not least because they disburse, or control access to, significant amounts of public goods.

Drawing on these two considerations, this chapter argues that despite its variety, the quasi-governmental world is structured by a central tension between the need for boards to be democratic and accountable yet also provide effective governance and service delivery. The 'New Labour' government has promoted wider participation in board membership while at the same time pursuing the modernisation of service delivery through increased centralisation and uniformity. In working out tensions between performance and conformance (see Chapter 1), boards are driven by the need to ensure that they possess 'legitimacy for action', that is their right to operate and exercise power. Effectiveness requires a measure of flexibility and strategic/policy autonomy but this often conflicts with accountability requirements. Moreover, increasing central direction is justified in terms of policy delivery but threatens to erode the flexibility necessary for effectiveness. What organisations, and their boards, are both engaged in is a *legitimation process* that grounds their right to exercise power in a combination of some sort of public accountability and the efficient and effective delivery of their purposes. To this end, more sophisticated arrangements for accountability can be developed to incorporate the interests of stakeholders yet allow organisations maximum operational autonomy.

The empirical material on which this discussion is based was obtained primarily from two studies conducted by the authors into the internal governance of a variety of quasi-governmental bodies (focusing, for example, on organisational structures, the roles of boards, and the relationships between board members and senior executives). These were undertaken for the Joseph Rowntree Foundation in 1996, looking at housing associations, further education corporations, and training and enterprise councils, and for the Royal Society of the Arts in 2000, on national NDPBs, health boards, and large national voluntary organisations (see Greer and Hoggett, 1997a and b; 1999; 2000). This material is supplemented by drawing selectively upon the now extensive research on the governance of quangos (see, for example, Levacic, 1995; Committee on Standards in Public Life, 1996; Ferlie *et al.*, 1996; Clarke and Newman, 1997; Painter and Isaac-Henry, 1997; Rouse, 1997; Skelcher, 1998).

Fitness for purpose(s)

What are quasi-governmental organisations for?

Quangos can fulfil a variety of purposes – strategic, delivery, regulatory, representational, commissioning and advisory. A single institution such as the Environment Agency may be multi-functional, combining several different purposes. Many large national voluntary organisations are also highly complex and are involved in the provision of services and products as well as campaigning. Purposes can change over time. A member of the Environment Agency noted that its organisational purpose changed as it matured, moving towards acting as a champion of the environment rather than merely as a regulator. The chief executive of a voluntary organisation pointed out that it had begun as an 'enthusiastic child' and then had to be helped through its 'difficult teen years' in terms of being guided back to its core purposes and not trying to do more than it was equipped to do.

The purposes of organisations may be set out in a range of sources such as legislation, mission statements, constitutions and authoritative reports but may also have 'emergent' aspects. For example, the functions of the Radio Authority (an NDPB) are set out in the Broadcasting Acts of 1990 and 1996 providing, according to the Chair of the Authority, 'a clear and coherent framework for the activities of the organisation'. Whereas Health Trusts are primarily concerned with health care delivery, the purpose of Health Authorities has been defined as the provision of 'strategic leadership for health care' although with the advent of Primary Care Trusts they will concentrate on leadership, support and performance management (OCPA, 2000). However, it is arguably less clear what the purposes of the governing boards are, and whether the individual members on these are 'fit' for those purposes. There may also be a gap between the formal purpose of the board/board member and what actually happens in practice, perhaps linked to a lack of clarity about roles and responsibilities. What has emerged from interviews with members in several sectors is the suggestion that boards need to provide much more explicit statements of their purposes and objectives, both for the benefit of their members and on grounds of openness and transparency (see also Ashburner, Chapter 11 in this book). Nevertheless, three common purposes for all public and voluntary bodies are strategic leadership and giving direction (in some cases of policy development); stewardship and a locus of accountability for the executive; and to give expression to the interests of stakeholders.

Board recruitment, composition and the role of board members

In order to carry out their functions, organisations develop machinery for internal governance that may vary greatly between and within sectors (Greer and Hoggett, 2000). Typically they are steered by governing boards consisting of appointed members (usually non-executive) working, often voluntarily, on a part-time basis. Day-to-day operation is in the hands of a chief executive and senior management team. Different board members on different types of organisation may be required to provide different skills, capacities and expertise, depending on the purposes of the organisation. Some may contribute strategic thinking, some may be adept in the scrutiny of systems and procedures, and others reflect the interests of stakeholders. No single individual board member is expected to be fit for all purposes. It is the board of the organisation that needs to be 'fit' – what alternatively is referred to as the 'balance of the board'. The task in recruitment is to assemble a board with a suitable range of skills and experiences, although a generalist ethos still predominates in many sectors such as health (see Ashburner, Chapter 11 in this book; OCPA 2000: annex A).

Consideration of the qualities desirable in board members raises the thorny issue of board composition, linked to a critique of informal recruitment patterns ('old-boy' and political networks), and allegations of political bias in appointments (see Robinson and Shaw, Chapter 1 in this book). However, recruitment procedures have become increasingly standardised as a consequence of the general adoption of the Nolan principles (the influence of which has even extended to some large voluntary organisations). The House of Commons Select Committee on Public Administration (1999: para. 90) has advocated the removal of a large number of appointments from ministerial control and the extension to the quango sector of random selection, used, for example, for juries, has also been suggested (Wainwright, 2000). Many of the larger voluntary bodies studied are streamlining their internal governance arrangements, for example their committee structures and the way in which elections are used.

The importance attached to more open appointment procedures is rooted in a concern about the lack of diversity in board membership (see Robinson and Shaw, Chapter 1 in this book). The post-1997 government has been strongly committed to increasing the representation of women and people from ethnic minorities on governing boards, involving, for example, the formulation of action plans by individual departments (Cabinet Office, 2000b). Between 1992 and 2000 the proportion of women board members on public bodies (including the NHS) increased from 26 per cent to 33 per cent and those from ethnic minorities rose from 3.6 per cent to 4.4 per cent (Cabinet Office, 2000a: vi). However, many of these increases took place before 1997 and there are also wide differences between sponsor departments such as the Ministry of Defence and the Department of Health (ibid.: 169). There is some unease about 'political correctness' and 'tokenism' in the appointment process, in terms both of people having 'the right political credentials' (under both Labour and Conservative governments) and of gender/ethnic/age balance. Some interviewees expressed concern about an approach to selection that suggested 'we need one of x, two of y and one of z'. This did not deny the need for diversity but rather conceived of it in terms of the skills and talents brought by the members rather than their age, gender or ethnic origin.

Effective board membership raises questions of time commitment, remuneration, training and support. There remains a very strong attachment to the voluntary principle but increasing recognition of the need to consider how financial and other hurdles to a more diverse board membership might be overcome, for example, through income replacement schemes rather than direct payment. Discussions about skills, induction and training were often framed by the difficulties encountered in widening social representation, particularly in terms of the relatively poor training, employment and educational opportunities of under-represented groups.

Issues about the nature of boards are central to the tension between effectiveness and accountability. A lack of diversity in board membership can weaken the accountability of boards. At the same time dominant conceptions of effectiveness and efficiency can promote homogenisation in terms of the qualities thought essential in board members, particularly if conceived in narrow managerial terms. Several interviewees noted a tension between broadening the social base of participation and avoiding the incorporation of vested interests that might encourage a sectionalism that detracts from the purposes and effectiveness of the organisation as a corporate whole. The Arts Council for England, for example, changed its board structure in the 1990s because the old board was said to be too big, too involved with detail and riven by sectional rivalries between functional and territorial stakeholders. Members are now leading figures drawn from all fields of the arts, chosen for their ability to contribute creatively to strategy and policy development and are not expected to represent their fields of expertise. On the other hand, some members expressed concern that power had shifted too much towards the executive because members lacked the information necessary to fulfil their roles effectively.

Large national voluntary sector organisations also have to manage the tension between having appropriate internal governance structures (that promote the efficient and effective delivery of services) and the need to reflect the interests of its wide diversity of stakeholders. The British Red Cross, the Alzheimer's Society and the National Trust have all grappled recently with this dilemma when faced with the need to streamline their decision-making structures. Reflecting the diversity of the voluntary sector, there are a variety of means of representing interests. For example, the Alzheimer's Society tries to include users and carers in the decision-making process through focus groups and surveys. The British Red Cross has discussed the importance of responding more effectively to the needs of users. So in this sense strategy is tied to organisational goals and is increasingly 'needs-led' rather than provider driven. The National Trust has also been concerned with widening representation (at board level) partly because of a desire to move away from what are regarded as outdated notions of 'nation' and 'heritage'. On the other hand, a representative of Help the Aged noted that it is 'important not to allow particular stakeholder interests to influence the board, we have to encourage people to move beyond their own particular corner and look at the interests of the organisation as a whole'.

Nonetheless, it seems perfectly possible to broaden the composition of boards without compromising their quality in terms of skills and expertise. There is some evidence of a growing recognition of the need to provide a broader range of people with the opportunities and skills to participate, for example, by encouraging local employers to facilitate voluntary working. Indeed, such discussions are under way in organisations such as Business in the Community and the Greater Bristol Foundation.

Accountability and openness

The efforts made in recent years to make boards more diverse are a necessary, but not sufficient, contribution towards making boards more accountable. Questions of accountability and openness have been central to the debate about quangos in the UK (see Davis and Stewart, 1994; Weir and Hall, 1994; Skelcher *et al.*, 2000). Accountability, however, is multifaceted. Mulgan (2000) identifies a number of different usages of the term – the core process of being called to account, professional and personal accountability, accountability as control, accountability as responsiveness (including 'client focus'), and accountability as dialogue. It is important to distinguish political accountability from managerial and professional accountability. In recent years the apparatus of performance management has become the primary mechanism for operationalising managerial accountability. Professional accountability refers to the internalised norms that guide the behaviour of particular occupational groups. There are two dimensions of accountability for governing bodies, both of which need to be addressed. The primary focus here is on what might be termed 'political accountability', referring to how the governing body is called to account for its actions (linking to citizens, stakeholders including central government, and users). The second dimension – 'managerial accountability' – focuses on how the governing body can hold its officials/executive to account or internal governance (Greer and Hoggett, 2000).

For Mulgan, 'core' accountability in a democratic state involves issues concerning:

> how legislators can scrutinize the actions of public servants and make them answerable for their mistakes, and how members of the public can seek redress from government agencies and their officials. It leads to questions about different channels of accountability and their relative merits, about the balance between accountability and efficiency, and about distinctions between political and managerial accountability
>
> (2000: 556)

Following Mulgan, we wish to separate accountability from responsiveness and stress the core principle of 'holding the powerful to account through political and legal channels of external scrutiny and sanctions' (ibid.: 571). So at the core of accountability lies 'external scrutiny, justification, sanctions and control' (ibid.: 557), in other words, the capacity to hold another to account for actions (or inaction) undertaken. Sanctions are crucial to this. The capacity to hold another to account in turn depends upon the transparency of the actions in question and this leads us to a second core aspect of accountability, that is, 'giving an account for actions taken'. From this perspective, open government, including the provision of information, public access to board meetings and the extent to which actors are subject to scrutiny by consultative bodies, are a necessary but not sufficient condition for full accountability. Effective consultation does not in itself deliver accountability because consultative and advisory bodies lack power of sanction over the actors in question.

The post-1997 Labour government has been concerned with issues of transparency, openness, and attracting a wider range of people onto the boards of public bodies (Cabinet Office, 1997; 1998). While many of these proposals have not extended to the LPSB and voluntary sector (House of Commons, 1999: para. 57), many organisations themselves have taken steps to increase their transparency and increasingly make use of new technology such as Internet websites and emails. The Radio Authority, for example, provides an extensive range of information on its website, including the agendas and minutes of board meetings, consultation documents, and a register of members' interests.

Measures to increase transparency contribute to better accountability insofar as they increase public knowledge of the operation and performance of quangos. There does not appear to be any adverse relationship between effectiveness and greater transparency, except perhaps insofar as the latter falls short of the release of certain classes of information such as that deemed commercially confidential. If anything, it might be argued that the performance of organisations could be enhanced through greater openness. The chair of the Radio Authority, for example, is convinced that its general operation benefits from a presumption towards openness.

A key issue for political accountability is the nature of representation. Most of the members of quangos are selected on the basis of appointment rather than election. The suggestion that all board members should be elected is usually rejected because of its impracticality (see House of Commons, 1999: para. 62) although the idea of random selection (akin to that used in the jury system) has been mooted (Wainwright, 2000).

However, accountability in the sense of 'representativeness' can at least in part be achieved in ways other than direct election, for example through guaranteed places on boards for stakeholders and local councils. While the past twenty years have witnessed a significant downgrading of 'direct representation' (for example, the removal of local authority members from the boards of organisations such as further education colleges), the concept of 'representation as formally elected representative' still persists. Some newer members of health boards, many local councillors themselves, see their role as 'similar to that of a councillor, that is to hold executives to account, rather than sharing the collective responsibility of the board' (OCPA, 2000: 20). It has also been suggested that the development of 'partnerships' is a response to concerns about the lack of accountability of local public spending bodies (House of Commons, 1999: para. 64). Moreover, in some partnerships such as SRB and New Deal for the Community 'legitimation problems have been tackled through the introduction of mechanisms of participative democracy to enable user and community involvement'. However, practice varies and overall partnership arrangements remove 'centres of decision-making further from elected political structures, increasing their distance from citizens and often becoming invisible to public view' (Skelcher, 2000: 13).

NDPBs are formally accountable upwards to Parliament (in both a financial and political sense) through their sponsoring departments and ministers. The debate about the accountability of quasi-governmental bodies in the UK has 'primarily been confined to discussing the inadequacy of ministerial responsibility, describing a democratic deficit and developing alternative models of accountability to make quangos more responsive' (Cole, 2000: 34). Cole finds some evidence that these upwards arrangements are more effective than sometimes thought, but a 'control' approach to accountability is often criticised because it destroys the flexibility, user-friendliness and autonomy essential for effectiveness (Hood and Schuppert, 1988b: 253). It is more usually argued that alternative forms of accountability – usually horizontal or 'downwards' – need to be developed, for example, relating to 'peer groups', stakeholders and citizens. For Hood and Schuppert (ibid.: 258) a combination of user-group representation, the operation of markets and competition, and peer-group evaluation offers a 'much more real prospect' of keeping quangos under control 'than the core government regime of heavy audit, day-to-day political oversight and elaborate (often overloaded and ineffective) clearance procedures'. So perhaps what boards should be primarily concerned with is ensuring that a range of appropriate mechanisms are in place to ensure the accountability of the organisation.

Managerial accountability, reflected in the modern fetish for performance measurement and evaluation ('valuing what is measurable' rather than 'measuring what is valuable'), and indeed also in the attack on the self-regulating professions, works against 'horizontal' accountability arrangements. Arguments for greater 'self-policing' have re-emerged among board members across the variety of quangos, partly as a reaction to a perception that central inspection and audit have inexorably increased. In practice, many organisations such as NDPBs have both upward and downward accountability procedures. The Environment Agency, for example, reports up through the DETR but is also responsive to its other stakeholders through its network of regional committees. It also incorporates an element of representativeness in that the board combines a mixture of environmentalists, business people, academics and farmers.

In terms of 'representation', or at least some mechanisms for stakeholder influence, questions about performance are frequently linked to the issue of accountability in negative terms, for example, if the latter results in increased political interference and centralised control and direction. What is clear is that it is difficult to justify the existence of quangos 'which are subject neither to control in the form of effective "control" nor to effective alternative forms of control' (Hood and Schuppert, 1988b: 258). This brings us again to the central tension in the modernisation agenda between giving organisations the freedom to be effective while making them accountable, and/or the desire of governments to exercise control.

Effectiveness and the modernisation agenda

Much of the debate on quangos has previously been centred around issues of accountability and openness, but it is also necessary to pay attention to how such bodies operate and how they fit into the government's rhetoric about modernisation and the delivery of public services (Cabinet Office, 1999; Benington, 2000). There may be conflict between the need for organisations to provide effective public services (incorporating a concern for outcomes as well as outputs and processes), and the pressure for boards to be seen as transparent, representative and accountable. However, it would be a mistake to see such tensions as something new, for the earlier wave of quango studies (Hague *et al.*, 1975; Barker, 1982) also identified potential conflict between accountability and efficiency.

Effectiveness – whether defined in terms of policy advice, regulation or service delivery – is undoubtedly a fundamental requirement for boards. The ability of boards to achieve their purposes is linked to clarity of objectives, the construction and 'chemistry' of the board (a balanced and diverse membership), and to patterns of internal governance, including the key relationships between the chair and chief executive and between governing bodies and staff (Greer and Hoggett, 2000). Board members have to 'gel' with each other while allowing for the possibility of the 'creative tension' that can contribute to effectiveness. Nonetheless, even with the best possible individuals and overall chemistry/balance, board effectiveness can still be undermined by excessive central direction and an unresponsive external environment. Moreover, the plethora of arrangements that have been developed for 'performance measurement' do not give much real indication of the effectiveness of organisations or their boards. It has been suggested that outcomes, client needs and citizen opinion are 'a low priority' and that existing systems for performance measurement 'provide no additional incentive to measure client satisfaction' (Lawton *et al.*, 2000: 17; see also Talbot, 2000).

Contemporary concern with service delivery brings us back to the autonomy–diversity continuum outlined earlier. An organisation that is little more than an administrative arm of core government is more likely to have its purposes given to it. Health Authorities are encouraged to act strategically, but within an increasingly constrained policy framework set by government. One interviewee, close to the government's Health Secretary, was very clear that one of the primary purposes of NHS bodies was to implement national government policy in a strategic and responsive way. It can plausibly be argued that the centralising trend evident in the NHS has been accompanied by a weakening of local accountability (see Ashburner, Chapter 11 in this book). As Powell notes, 'existing trends seem to lead to the worst of all worlds: the disadvantages of central control, and local differentiation without any genuine local autonomy' (1998: 56). NDPBs, such as the Arts Council, enjoy some autonomy in translating broad parameters into applicable policies and strategies, perhaps because of awareness that 'creative' and 'centrally directed' are incompatible. Organisations such as Further Education Corporations are subject to statute, but the structures through which the board conducts its business and the appointment of officers are almost entirely matters for local choice. Voluntary organisations and charitable trusts traditionally have had a lot of freedom to define their own purposes and structures, although there are indications that their relative autonomy is being reduced with their increasing incorporation into government welfare policy as agents for service delivery. Our research on LPSBs in the mid-1990s revealed the paradox that independently constituted bodies had been created to act strategically in delivering government policies but were then constrained from doing so by a range of hands-off and hands-on controls that effectively curtailed much of their freedom of action (Greer and Hoggett, 1999). This is not simply a result of the way in which services such as education and health have become increasingly national rather than local over the last decade (constraining the space for local policy-making). Current government rhetoric speaks of the need to implement national priorities in a way that is responsive to local needs, but most services are now governed by such a comprehensive array of nationally prescribed indicators that the space for local responsiveness has all but disappeared.

The rhetoric of modernisation links the provision of high-quality public services with the institutional and procedural reform of organisations. Under the slogan 'modernisation and improvement' the Labour government is said to have 'mobilised a far-reaching programme of change and innovation in the organisational forms and cultures of the state, and in particular its relationships with citizens, users and civil society' (Benington, 2000: 3). Implementation tools (some of which may themselves be regarded as alternative mechanisms for achieving accountability) include listening to users, consumer choice, new forms of competition, development of new procedures and practices, incentives, and even the creation of new quasi-governmental arrangements such as the Action Zones for health and education. Moreover, government ministers are concerned 'that they pull the "levers" for change, but the wires feel slack and nothing happens at the end' (Benington, 2000: 4). This goes to the heart of the relationship between autonomy and central direction, raising the question of 'how much change should be driven from the national centre and how much developed by local managers and organisations' (ibid.).

Benington has argued that:

> effective leadership and public management is seen by the govern-
> ment as crucial to the success of the [modernisation] strategy because
> good leadership clearly makes a difference to the performance of an
> organisation, staff morale and motivation, public satisfaction and the
> ability to address change.
>
> (ibid.: 5)

The government has also identified the problems faced in building up effective leadership. It has encountered difficulties in getting recognition of leadership in the public sector, in getting strength in depth, 'turning competent professionals into good leaders', breaking down public–private barriers and developing a corporate approach, and helping organisations to 'select good leaders' (ibid.). Many of our respondents, however, were worried that the tendency for public sector reform to 'recentralise', and the contraction in the autonomy and flexibility enjoyed by boards, would actually make it more difficult to encourage good people to give their time to boards. On this view there will be increasing supply problems for quangos if they are treated as little more than the passive implementers of government policies and strategies, and are not given the autonomy and flexibility necessary for them to be effective.

Conclusion: legitimacy, accountability and effectiveness

Two main arguments are often advanced against the use of quangos generally (House of Commons, 1999: para. 23). First, that diversity means fragmentation and hence makes joined-up (or effective) service delivery more difficult. Second, their insulation from political pressures – perhaps deliberately so in the interests of effectiveness – contributes to their lack of accountability. To be effective, quangos must manage, without perhaps ever resolving, several contradictions and tensions. They 'constitute insti-tutional packages in which desirable features are accompanied by often unwanted but unavoidable side-effects' (Hood and Schuppert, 1988a: 15). Some of the central dilemmas include: being exhorted to act strategically by government while being simultaneously constrained from doing so; and the pressure to perform according to a set of centrally prescribed targets versus the need to foster distinctive competencies, reputations, missions and locally sensitive policies and practices. This chapter has focused particularly on the tension between the pressure to deliver ser-vices and programmes, on the one hand, and the need for democratic accountability and the capacity to represent the needs and experiences of service users and local communities on the other. As long as quangos are used there will always be tension between the need for them to operate effectively and the pressure to be transparent, 'representative' and accountable to stakeholders. In its evidence to the Public Administration Committee, for example, the Cabinet Office pointed to the need to strike a balance between 'transparency and the most effective operating methods for NDPBs' (House of Commons, 1999: para. 51). In our survey several interviewees across the range of organisations recognised the need for stakeholder representation, but also expressed disquiet about the impact of this upon the effectiveness of the organisation.

Perhaps what organisations and their boards are searching for is 'legitimacy for action' – the justification of their right to exercise power. The concept of legitimacy is important:

> not only for the maintenance of order, but also for the degree of co-operation and quality of performance that the powerful can secure from the subordinate ... The effectiveness of the powerful, in other words, is not just a matter of resources and organisation ... but also of their legitimacy.
>
> (Beetham, 1991: 29)

Legitimacy, then, contributes to the 'order, stability and effectiveness' of a system of power. Stability refers to the 'ability to withstand shock and failure because a solid level of support from its subordinates can be guaranteed', and effectiveness 'includes the ability of the powerful to achieve their goals because of the quality of performance they can secure from those subordinate to them' (ibid.: 33). Drawing on these insights, quangos gain their legitimacy not simply by operating to established rules, but also through considerations of both effectiveness and accountability. Effectiveness is clearly crucial for there is no point in an accountable organisation that does not work. Withdrawal of public consent as a result of the inability to deliver its core purposes can contribute to the delegitimation of a quango. On the other hand, when they hit difficult times in terms of delivering their purposes, organisations can draw upon reserves of legitimacy that have been built up through stakeholder representation and proper accountability and stewardship arrangements.

From our research it is clear that board members themselves are not preoccupied solely with effectiveness and that issues of representation and accountability remain central to their concerns. Indeed, as a senior member of an organisation dealing with complaints against the police pointed out, operational effectiveness required the presence of ethnic minority members on the board to give stakeholders confidence that their grievances would be fairly investigated. Despite the tendency (arguably) to prioritise the effective delivery of outcomes, most board members are exercised by the need for the boards to which they contribute to be seen as legitimate. This takes us back to the importance of stakeholder accountability and the management of recruitment to boards. Should board members be selected solely for their skills and expertise or is it also necessary to ensure the representation of stakeholders on boards, even at the expense of delivery capacity?

So board legitimacy derives both from the extent to which the organisation represents its stakeholders (including government) and is accountable to them, and from its performance. There is, then, a need for clear statements of missions and objectives that incorporate purposes, outcomes and the need to represent the whole range of stakeholders. An organisation may be successful in terms of service delivery yet have a negative public profile if its authority to act and to take decisions is questioned. If those board members running the organisation are perceived to be out of touch and/or unrepresentative, then the organisation's claims for legitimacy will be viewed with suspicion. The legitimacy of the Environment Agency, for example, depends not only on its success in managing flood protection as one of its purposes but also on its ability to demonstrate that it reflects the diversity of its stakeholders. If either farmers or environmentalists are not represented on the board, then the legitimacy of the board would likely be questioned by these stakeholder groups, making policy delivery all the more difficult. Similarly, a perception that the Arts Council favoured a particular art form, or even a particular region of the country, could bring its legitimacy into question by weakening confidence in its ability to distribute resources equitably.

Stakeholder representation is therefore vital in the legitimation of a board. However, it may not always be clear who the stakeholders of an organisation are, and there may be conflicting stakeholder interests that need to be balanced. There also remains considerable resistance, for example, among many of the board members we interviewed, to the idea of direct stakeholder representation on boards; and there are good reasons why interested parties are often not given places on governing boards, for example, avoidance of conflict between different sets of special pleaders.

So if stakeholder interests are not to be reflected primarily in board appointments, how should they be taken into account? There is a danger that the contemporary concern with modernisation, effective service delivery and performance measurement will marginalise considerations of accountability. More attention needs to be paid to the development of new and more sophisticated arrangements for local stakeholder or community representation that will at the same time not inhibit the effectiveness of organisations. There is a need for more 'experiments and research in systems of consultation ... which allow for more sustained and closer contact with members of the public affected by their work than is permitted through annual or occasional open meetings or publications' (House of Commons, 1999: para. 54).

To take account of the prevalent organisational diversity, the democratic reform of the quango sector would need to take many forms and there is no appropriate uniform model. Part of the sector could be placed under the control of elected local and regional authorities; other sectors such as health could be governed by directly elected functional authorities. Greater participatory democracy could be developed through stakeholder models of governance – embryonic elements of this can be observed in the education sector with elected parent, student and staff governors. These arrangements would have the advantage of incorporating the requirement for external sanction that is central to the core notion of accountability. Following the distinction made by Weale (1999), we suggest that democratic reform must seek to develop three different forms of representation: the representation of opinions through elected political parties, the representation of interests through stakeholder models and the representation of characteristics via election by lot and other models (i.e. the extent to which representatives 'mirror' the characteristics of the population they represent, for example, in terms of class, gender and ethnicity).

References

Barker, A. (ed.) (1982) *Quangos in Britain: Government and the Networks of Public Policy Making*, London and Basingstoke: Macmillan.

Beetham, D. (1991) *The Legitimation of Power*, Basingstoke: Macmillan.

Benington, J. (2000) 'Editorial: The Modernization and Improvement of Government and Public Services', *Public Money and Management*, April–June: 3–8.

Cabinet Office (1997) *Opening Up Quangos: A Consultation Paper*, London: The Stationery Office.

Cabinet Office (1998) *Quangos: Opening the Doors*, London: The Stationery Office.

Cabinet Office (1999) *Modernising Government*, Cm 4310, London: The Stationery Office.

Cabinet Office (2000a) *Public Bodies 2000*, London: The Stationery Office.

Cabinet Office (2000b) *Quangos: Opening Up Appointments 2000–2003*, London: The Stationery Office.

Clarke, J. and Newman, J. (1997) *The Managerial State: Power, Politics and Ideology in the Remaking of Social Welfare*, London: Sage.

Cole, M. (2000) 'Quangos: UK Ministerial Responsibility in Theory and Practice', *Public Policy and Administration*, 15, 3, 32–45.

Committee on Standards in Public Life (1996) Second Report, *Local Public Spending Bodies*, vol. 1, Cm 3270–1, London: HMSO.

Davis, H. and Stewart, J. (1994) *The Growth of Government by Appointment: Implications for Local Democracy*, Luton: Local Government Management Board.

Ferlie, E., Ashburner, L. and Fitzgerald, L. (1996) *The New Public Management in Action*, Oxford: Oxford University Press.

Flinders, M. and Smith, M. (eds) (1999) *Quangos, Accountability and Reform: The Politics of Quasi-government*, Basingstoke: Macmillan/Political Economy Research Centre, University of Sheffield.

Greer, A. and Hoggett, P. (1997a) *Patterns of Accountability within Local Public Spending Bodies: Steering Between Government and the Market*, York: Joseph Rowntree Foundation.

Greer, A. and Hoggett, P. (1997b) 'Patterns of Governance in Local Public Spending Bodies', *International Journal of Public Sector Management*, 10, 3, 214–227.

Greer, A. and Hoggett, P. (1999) 'Public Policies, Private Strategies and Local Public Spending Bodies', *Public Administration*, 77, 2, 235–256.

Greer, A. and Hoggett, P. (2000) 'Contemporary Governance and Local Public Spending Bodies', *Public Administration*, 78, 3, 513–529.

Greve, C., Flinders, M. and Van Thiel, S. (1999) 'Quangos – What's in a Name? Defining Quangos from a Comparative Perspective', *Governance*, 12, 2, 129–146.

Hague, D. C., Mackenzie, W. J. M. and Barker, A. (eds) (1975) *Public Policy and Private Interests: The Institutions of Compromise*, Basingstoke: Macmillan.

Hood, C. and Schuppert, G. F. (1988a) 'The Study of Para-Government Organisations', in C. Hood and G. F. Schuppert (eds) *Delivering Public Services in Western Europe: Sharing Western European Experience of Para-Government Organisation*, London: Sage, pp. 1–26.

Hood, C. and Schuppert, G. F. (1988b) 'Evaluation and Review', in C. Hood and G. F. Schuppert (eds) *Delivering Public Services in Western Europe: Sharing Western European Experience of Para-Government Organisation*, London: Sage, pp. 244–260.

House of Commons, Select Committee on Public Administration (1999) *Quangos*, Sixth Report 1998–99, HC 209 I and II, London: The Stationery Office.

Lawton, A., McKevitt, D. and Millar, M. (2000) 'Coping with Ambiguity: Reconciling External Legitimacy and Organisational Implementation in Performance Measurement', *Public Money and Management*, July–September, 13–19.

Levacic, R. (1995) 'School Governing Bodies: Management Boards or Supporters' Clubs?', *Public Money and Management*, April–June, 35–40.

Mulgan, R. (2000) 'Accountability: An Ever-expanding Concept?', *Public Administration*, 78, 3, 555–574.

Office for the Commissioner for Public Appointments (OCPA) (2000) *Public Appointments to NHS Trusts and Health Authorities: A Report by the Commissioner for Public Appointments*, London: The Stationery Office.

Painter, C. and Isaac-Henry, K. (1997) 'Relations with Non-Elected Agencies: Local Authority Good Practice', *Public Money and Management*, January–March, 43–48.

Powell, M. (1998) 'In What Sense a "National" Health Service?', *Public Policy and Administration*, 13, 3, 56–69.

Rouse, J. (1997) 'Performance Inside the Quangos: Tensions and Contradictions', *Local Government Studies* 23, 1, 59–75.

Skelcher, C. (1998) *The Appointed State: Quasi-Governmental Organisations and Democracy*, Buckingham: Open University Press.

Skelcher, C. (2000) 'Changing Images of the State: Overloaded, Hollowed-Out, Congested', *Public Policy and Administration*, 15, 3, Autumn.

Skelcher, C., Weir, S. and Wilson, L. (2000) *Advance of the Quango State*, London: Local Government Information Unit (LGIU).

Talbot, C. (2000) 'Performing "Performance" – A Comedy in Five Acts', *Public Money and Management*, October–December, 63–68.

Wainwright, M. (2000) 'It Should Be You', *The Stakeholder*, May–June, 32–33.

Weale, A. (1999) *Democracy*, Basingstoke: Macmillan.

Weir, S. and Hall, W. (1994) *Ego Trip: Extra-Governmental Organisations in the UK and their Accountability*, London: Democratic Audit, University of Essex and Charter 88 Trust.

3 Service users and charity governance

Michael Locke, Nasa Begum and Paul Robson

Introduction

'User involvement' has been taken during the past three decades as almost necessarily right and good for voluntary organisations, rhetorically anyway. This blanket approval of the concept, however, has obscured the problems of resolving what it means – or perhaps the many things that it might mean – and, more critically, the difficulties of effectively putting user involvement into practice.

In this chapter we review the development of user involvement in voluntary organisations in the context of the broader public policies moving in this direction and suggest the need to examine different intentions and models. In doing so, we draw on a programme of research for the past six years, working with voluntary organisations to enhance their user involvement.[1] We report on how our action research in selected charities has identified ways of clarifying the intentions for user involvement and working with users, staff and governing bodies to make progress.[2]

In voluntary organisations, user involvement has often – and we think too simplistically – been seen as a matter of users' membership of the governing body. We consider a range of issues in user membership of governing bodies, discussing how user membership is related to fundamental questions about the organisation and users' communities. Insofar as there is a key point in what we see to be a very complicated and highly charged arena, it is that the governing body is only one force among others in making or resisting progress.

Discussion of policy and practice about user involvement is clouded by the vagueness of both words 'user' and 'involvement'. Our work with service users and managers has revealed over twenty terms in common use to describe the people who use the services of voluntary organisations including:

> users, comrades, service users, service recipients, beneficiaries, clients, guests, participants, stakeholders, associates, members, residents, punters, tenants, friends, inmates, consumers, patrons, patients, customers, citizens, people who . . .

Likewise, 'involvement' can range from just using a service to participating in decision-making, and involvement in decision-making can range from receiving information about decisions made by others to holding control. We settled on the term 'user' as the most all-embracing and least hypothecated of the possibilities and on 'user involvement' as that in most general use, but we saw a major function of our research as to tease out different meanings and expectations and to draw out their implications for action.

The political context

We have described the movement towards greater user involvement as a 'tide of change' in that a number of currents were moving in the same direction – national government policies, professional theory, the 'user movement', and voluntary organisations' thinking (Robson *et al.*, 1997). However, voluntary organisations were also caught up in cross-currents from the pressures of the 'contract culture' and the legal environment (Locke *et al.*, 2001).

The Conservative Government (1979–1997) promoted the involvement of users in decision-making through its commitment to market forces, seeing users as consumers but also seeking to reduce the part of local authorities in providing services. The Griffiths Report (1988) split the roles of 'purchaser' and 'provider', focusing social services, health and other statutory agencies on identifying needs and buying in services to meet those needs from voluntary and commercial organisations. This change, legislated through the NHS and Community Care Act 1990, created what is usually called the 'contract culture' and encouraged voluntary organisations to bid to provide services at least partly on the strength of their user involvement. Alongside this, social services and health authorities were expected to consult users in planning community services.

Converging on this public policy was the demonstration from the disability movement (Campbell and Oliver, 1996; Oliver, 1996) about the ways in which traditional charities, as much as statutory services, were part of a disabling process for users. Parts of the user movement have demanded for some time that traditional voluntary organisations should become user-led (Morris, 1994). Alongside this, concepts of popular democracy gathering strength from the pressure groups of the later 1960s helped shape the development of many voluntary organisations and of ideas of community development, featuring the importance of empowerment (Barnes and Walker, 1996).

The validity of this case was recognised both by social workers (e.g. Beresford and Croft, 1993; Beresford and Harding, 1993) and by social services and health authorities in purchasing services, influenced also by the influx of business management precepts about customer care (Taylor, 1996). Thus, public services did reform within themselves to increase user involvement (Goss and Miller, 1995). Alongside this, as purchasers, authorities put user involvement among the criteria for contracts (Flynn, 1996).

However, the requirements of the contract culture produced some contradictory pressures for executive control which tended to marginalise lay people (Howlett and Locke, 1997). This was echoed among agencies as purchasers by a tension between buying responsive local community services versus playing safe with bureaucratically secure national organisations. Although purchasing authorities saw voluntary organisations as vehicles for user involvement, Kumar (1997) found voluntary organisations were not always as good at involving users as assumed.

Thus, while user involvement can be described as a tide of change, the environmental pressures for voluntary organisations were not consistent. For instance, the government was attempting to reproduce market relationships throughout welfare provision whereas the user movement was arguing for full citizenship.

The legal context

The voluntary organisations we are concerned with in this chapter are constituted as charities. Charitable status has been the keystone of the voluntary sector and a stumbling block of user involvement. In England and Wales the registration and supervision of charities are the responsibility of the Charity Commission, while in Scotland, without a Charity Commission, the Inland Revenue recognises charitable purposes. The Charity Commission in England and Wales exercises a supervisory function on behalf of the state and the public, and has been encouraged during this period to take a more active role in supervising charities (Harrow and Palmer, 1998).

The basis of charity law is the separation of the role of members of governing bodies defined in charity law as 'trustees' from the users defined as 'beneficiaries'. Trustees are accountable in law for the 'proper administration' of the charity: they have a duty to ensure that money and other assets (endowments, donations, grants or income from fees and trading, etc.) are applied in the interests of the beneficiaries as set out in the charity's objects. In so doing, trustees must have no personal interest and avoid a conflict of interest (see below). They are required to be business-like in maximising and administering assets on behalf of others.

For generations, it was broadly accepted that these principles prohibited users from being trustees. Charity law also places a heavy responsibility upon trustees in that their liability is personal and unlimited; trustees have been told in many training courses that if they fail in their duties their bank account or house are at risk. The Tumim Report (1992) shocked first by its revelation of how many trustees did not realise they were trustees and then by the focus on the force of the liabilities.

However, the dominance of the traditional charitable structure eased away. In some charities, on a case-by-case basis, the Charity Commission permitted some beneficiaries (users) to be appointed or elected as trustees. The Commission issued advice in a standard letter to individual organisations that the number of users should not exceed a third but was more liberal with self-help groups (see below). Nonetheless, the basic point of charity law was held that trusteeship is concerned with 'proper administration' rather than representation.

The Charity Commission responded further to the pressures by instituting a consultation on users as trustees. Some organisations having experience of users in a majority on the governing body, such as the Royal National Institute for Blind People (RNIB), found the issue uncontentious, but a few resisted strongly. Housing associations, in particular, argued that current users should not be able to risk future prospects and should not therefore constitute more than one-third of a governing body.

In 2000 a new note of guidance was published (Charity Commission, 2000) recognising charities could increase their user membership of governing bodies, although it played safe by proposing one-third as the norm. Moreover, it featured a long discussion about dangers of conflict of interest in relation to user trustees – a victory of legalism over experience. Although the Charity Commission's guidance was cautious and the implications of the conflict of interest might be a deterrent, it accepted that organisations could, if right for them, have users in a majority on governing bodies.

Responses in the voluntary sector

Historically voluntary organisations were founded on a philanthropic model which was reflected in the traditional legal position, just outlined: organisations were formed by people who were being charitable in the everyday sense and helping unfortunates quite unlike themselves. There was very little intention or expectation that beneficiaries would or ever could be trustees.

However, increasingly from the late 1960s onwards some charities were created by carers, who then formed or comprised a section of the governing body, and, although they were not literally the beneficiaries, they were, in some senses, users of services and blurred the dividing line between trustees and beneficiaries. More radically, self-help or mutual-aid groups emerged, founded by people with a common experience or need, and they were registered as charities; members, who are also the beneficiaries, ran the organisation themselves, and as they grew in size and status some members/users became the governing body, taking on trusteeship.

The traditionally structured philanthropic organisations adapted to the changes in the political context. A review by voluntary sector leaders stated that 'users are vital stakeholders' in voluntary organisations and that 'their rights are central to the future role of the sector and their involvement is crucial' (Commission on the Future of the Voluntary Sector, 1996). ACENVO (Association of Chief Executives of National Voluntary Organisations, now minus 'National' as ACEVO) formed a working party on user involvement and produced some guidelines on good practice for chief executives (Taylor, 1999). There was also a recognition among some service-providing organisations that their 'market share' might be threatened if purchasing agencies preferred organisations with greater user involvement or if users themselves chose those organisations.

Key developments in the sector were the ways in which two major national organisations with traditional charitable legal structures, Arthritis Care and Mencap, reformed themselves into bodies where there was either a majority or substantial user involvement in formal governance. Arthritis Care transformed itself from having a governing body dominated by professional expert and medical opinion to one controlled by people with arthritis (see below). Mencap – perhaps most challenging of all in relation to dominant ideology – created a structure of governance in which people with learning disabilities were represented by occupying a minimum of one-third of places on a new national assembly. Elections to the assembly are on a one-person, one-vote basis with 11,000 members eligible; standards were set for the production of election material to ensure accessibility. Seven members of the assembly are elected to the board of trustees, which is completed by the chair and three co-opted trustees.

In a different direction, some small and medium-sized organisations, under pressures of the contract culture and grant-making bodies, moved towards structures which strengthened executive management.

The broad picture was of voluntary organisations introducing policies and measures to increase user involvement. In an exploratory survey of 200 voluntary organisations providing social welfare services in 1996, we found twenty-four out of forty-two responding organisations had users on the governing body (Robson *et al.*, 1997). However, many frustrations were reported from users and from staff trying to implement user involvement.

Action research

We began our research programme in 1995 with the question, if the movement towards user involvement is so clear, why was it proving so difficult to implement? When we initially surveyed chief executives of voluntary organisations, three-quarters believed that voluntary organisations and users themselves were attempting to increase user involvement (Robson *et al.*, 1997). However, we found a lack of agreement about what it was for; many believed users were not interested in formal representation in governance but only in the quality of services.

There is much evidence from which we conclude that there is no one best way in general nor for any specific organisation to increase service user involvement (Lindow and Morris, 1995; Hasler, 1997; Hope and Hargreaves, 1997; Robson *et al.*, 1997; Robson *et al.*, 1998). Pressure for change may come from internal sources (e.g. existing users, some staff) or external sources (e.g. organisations of users, funders, comparison with similar organisations, changes in the capacity of people with certain conditions, the policy environment). Wherever the pressure comes from or whatever the particular arguments, the process of change would, as we analysed the problem, be individual to a particular organisation: there were no off-the-shelf solutions.

Therefore, having reviewed the issues and carried out a broad survey, we designed an action research project. We worked with twelve organisations to plan the particular measures of increasing user involvement appropriate to them and, in a next stage, to implement those plans in four organisations. We proceeded on the working assumption that greater clarity about the goals of user involvement for each organisation and its users was a prerequisite for effective implementation.

Central to this process is clarifying whether user involvement is viewed as a matter of 'consumerism' or 'democracy'. The distinction between 'consumerism' and 'democracy', developed from Beresford and Croft (1993), distinguishes between:

- users as consumers and focus on matters such as information about services, market research, needs assessment, evaluation of services, complaints procedures and so forth;
- users as citizens and focus on participation and representation in formal and informal decision-making.

Thus, while, for instance, it might be argued that a person's greatest concern would be to receive the desired and appropriate service, there is a world of difference between having that service selected by a professional and choosing it yourself.

One line of argument is that organisational effectiveness should come before everything else: considerations of who should control an organisation would not be relevant; what matters is quality of service. Furthermore, some suggest that users would not have the skills or experience necessary to govern organisations. On the other hand, it is argued, who could know better than users what they want and need? Furthermore, some suggest that, especially where the user group has traditionally been disempowered, the exercise of democratic rights or fulfilment of citizenship should take priority over management expertise.

The meaning of user involvement has generated much argument in organisations, often revealing intellectual and practical dichotomies between users and professional staff. Users expect more direct decision-making power on an everyday basis. On the other hand, staff and trustees expect to use their expertise to make what they see as good decisions or – as charity law – to conduct its 'proper administration'. The challenge from users provokes a constant re-evaluation of professionalism, and the professionals may feel undervalued by the users. So, a starting point is to discuss what the organisation and its users see as the goal.

In seeking to clarify goals for organisations, we set out a spectrum featuring the range of terms in use (see Figure 3.1). The left-hand side indicates that users have the power in controlling or managing the organisation, whereas to the right-hand side users are informally consulted or informed. The middle columns suggest varying degrees of involvement, without defining whether that is through formal governance machinery or through management communication systems. The main distinction now is commonly crystallised as the difference between being an organisation of 'a group of people' or 'for' them.

Governing bodies

It is often assumed that if a voluntary organisation wants to seriously involve users in the running of the organisation, then one or more users should be members of the governing body, but it is not necessarily so. This may be an effective method of involving users, but it can also be fraught with problems if not carefully thought through – and it is not right for all organisations and users.

One consideration is the model of governance in use in the organisation, echoing the distinction between consumerism and democracy (see above). One model, closer to consumerism, would see the system of

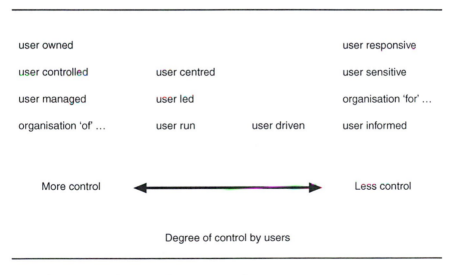

Figure 3.1 User involvement: the spectrum of terms

governance as a neutral set of structures and processes which are designed to ensure that the organisation operates within its constitution, within the constraints of external regulators and within the best interests of the organisation. Its legitimacy is derived from charity law and from its formal accountability, and it justifies decision-making as the objective assessment of information in the interests of proper administration. Board members need to be detached, rather than emotionally involved. This relies on the theoretical underpinning of the 'compliance' or 'traditional' model discussed in the Introduction. In practice this model often does not exist in pure form. The governing body may be seen as 'stewards' of resources while some of their number, especially in service-providing charities, are likely to have been recruited for their medical or other professional expertise, in line with a 'partnership' model of the board.

Alternatively, the governance system may be seen, in a democratic perspective, as a mechanism for different interests to negotiate and bargain over priorities, policy and resource allocation. It is explicitly a political process through which different interests, internal and external, attempt to have a part in control of the organisation. Thus, while it does not negate the requirement of charity law for 'proper administration', in practice this may seem secondary to 'representation' and resolution of sectional interests. The focus of user involvement – or the question of where it is worth putting energy – may depend on which view of governance predominates in the organisation.

A second consideration is the nature of the organisation and its services. For instance, in a centre providing day services for homeless people, previously a user had sat on the management committee, but the dominance of some individuals and problems of dealing with committee procedure and dual roles were seen to create difficulties. With a transient population, people elected at one time might not be supported by the users a few months later. However, this organisation recognised the right of people to have a say in decisions affecting them, and sought methods to enact it, including: a staff member to act as a link between users, staff and committee; monthly visit by a trustee; a member of staff and a trustee to meet with users one week before committee meetings to discuss users' views on agenda items; and a slot on every committee agenda for user issues.

By contrast, the National Schizophrenia Fellowship restructured the composition of its board of trustees to achieve greater user representation. Unlike Arthritis Care, they chose a quota system so that 30 per cent of elected trustees are people who have direct experience of mental health problems. Previously, the constitution allowed for any carer or relative or person with mental health problems to be elected, and its origins as a support group for carers and relatives meant all the elected trustees came from that group. Internal reforms still left the lack of a significant voice for users, and formal provision for membership of the governing body was needed to secure the desired user involvement.

In our research we have sought to analyse key issues for each organisation, so as to offer pointers to interventions aimed at increasing user involvement in governance. Here we focus on five general issues:

- locus of power;
- appointment process;
- resources in user communities;
- resistance;
- membership and ownership.

Locus of power

On the surface, it may seem reasonable to assume that the power to control a voluntary organisation rests with the governing body. However, experience shows that, while the formal authority may be with the governing body, control over some or even all decisions may be located elsewhere. As widely recognised, the power of governing bodies in all stages of decision-making may be reduced by both informal networks and processes and by the information and options presented by chief executive or other staff. Moreover, even within the governing body, power is not distributed equally.

These problems are likely to be exacerbated for user representatives in that they may raise issues and questions not perceived as relevant by other board members or they use language which does not fit the dominant discourse of expertise or 'proper administration'. More pessimistically, some board members may be prejudiced about users and either unconsciously or deliberately discount their contribution.

Even in boards with a large majority of users or self-help groups, there can be problems like this. Governing bodies may become engrossed in organisational and technical matters and lose touch with their grassroots members. Larger self-help groups are likely to employ professional staff to support the self-help activity. In some cases, the professional staff become 'expert' and have the time, skills and resources to form alliances with other organisations and politicians, with the consequence that members and their elected governing body lose oversight and control.

Many organisations have found that representation of service users on their governing bodies is not necessarily the first step towards greater user involvement. The Alzheimer's Society, the Leonard Cheshire Foundation and United Response have all successfully initiated programmes with substantial funding to develop user involvement, which starts at the grassroots. The primary focus of these projects is building the capacity of users to take part in decisions about the services they use at both personal and policy levels. Capacity building is centred on personal development for users including skills (e.g. communication or staff selection) and know-how (e.g. decision-making methods or direct payment systems). Skills and knowledge together can lead to increased confidence. Another aspect of capacity building is developing a collective voice, so that users as a body can influence services, organisations and whole areas of public policy. The three projects all have a remit to examine the accessibility of existing decision-making processes to users and to suggest changes to increase it. However, while a focus on enabling individuals and groups of users to influence decisions that affect them is important, it is equally necessary for organisations to adapt their processes and structures.

The Cedar Foundation provides services for disabled people in Northern Ireland. It explored the feasibility of developing individual membership as a way of democratising user involvement, which had previously focused on feedback about specific services. Our work with the Cedar Foundation's management and service users revealed that involvement could be enhanced not by promoting individual membership but by improving mechanisms for users to participate in service development and planning and quality assurance. Consequently, setting up an organisation-wide user forum became a key objective. This is not to say that users of the Cedar Foundation's services should not be trustees. In fact, we discovered disabled individuals who were willing and able to play a role at that level. However, evidence from nearly 20 per cent of users indicated that they desired other means of involvement, that belonged to them and were run in ways that suited them, before they began to contribute to governance processes.

There are questions to explore in any organisation about what kind of power or influence users on a governing body have; it is not just a question of being there. Tokenistic involvement, where users are present but do not have power or influence, may undermine policy to involve users.

Appointment process

A first step in becoming a member of a board is to find out how the process of appointment or election operates. However, in many organisations the process is far from transparent. Often, there are systems of 'guided democracy' in which candidates preferred by existing trustees or senior managers are 'elected' or appointed.

Where trustees and managers agree that one or more users should be on the board, they can encourage individuals through the election process. Where a board has provision for co-opted members, this method is often used, either because it is quicker or perhaps because an election would not result in user representation or possibly that the election process might open up conflict.

A compromise between open election and co-option is designation of one or more places for users on the board as what can be termed a 'protected minority'. These places have to be filled by election but a qualification for nomination is that the individual is a service user.

A key consideration is the extent to which positive action should be taken to get users on the board. On one hand, it may appear unfair or patronising to suggest that users should receive assistance such as designated places or co-option. On the other hand, it may be argued that users are in an inherently disadvantaged position within charities. As discussed above, they are traditionally intentionally excluded from becoming trustees. On these grounds, positive action is a means to ensure that all those who should take part in governance can.

In the past ten years at Arthritis Care, measures to prepare and encourage users as trustees and an overhaul of the board structure were combined with the development of a pool of users who could be candidates for election. The first round of open elections then resulted in a change from a board of over forty-five trustees, of whom one or two had personal experience of disability, to a board of eighteen, a majority of whom were people with arthritis. The measures put in place included: producing job descriptions and specifications of the skills and experience needed to contribute to the governing body; inviting candidates to describe how they could contribute; providing induction, support and training to enable all board members to fulfil their responsibilities. The policy for all Arthritis Care's committees at the national, regional and local level states: 'Overall, it is desirable that a majority of the board's members should have personal experience of arthritis themselves.'

Resources in user communities

The extent and pace of increases to user involvement are influenced by the availability of user-led support structures. These structures can take many forms and can be internal or external to the voluntary organisation. A useful comparison can be drawn between the fields of disability and homelessness. There is a twenty-five-year tradition of independent organisation by disabled people modelled on civil rights principles. A network of groups campaign and provide support for disabled people promoting the social model of disability.[3] The disability movement has systematically criticised voluntary organisations not already controlled by them as unrepresentative and demanded increased influence for disabled people (e.g. Oliver, 1996). The movement has also encouraged and supported disabled service users within those organisations to press for change.

Younger members of Arthritis Care formed their own internal group that adopted the social model of disability as a guiding principle and demanded that the whole organisation should do the same. Contact between those within Arthritis Care and the wider disability movement gave their campaign impetus and also practical support and ideas, e.g. a pool of disabled trainers to run courses on self-management and raise awareness for people with arthritis.

In contrast, it is only in the past few years that homeless people have begun to form groups that are run by homeless people for homeless people and that focus on *their* agenda. However, this is a young network of people with rapidly changing circumstances and is therefore unable to offer leadership and support on the same scale as the disability movement can to its constituency. As a result, homeless people who try to gain influence in organisations providing services for them are often isolated.

In summary, a strong user community provides role models, collective experience, advice, advocacy, scrutiny, legitimacy and a supply of people who are willing and able to contribute to governance. Nevertheless, the membership of user groups is rarely homogeneous, and disagreements about objectives and/or tactics can serve to limit support to users who are attempting to increase their influence.

The functions of user groups internal to charities include consultation, shadow decision-making, advisory, social, therapeutic, consciousness-raising, political campaigning and personal development. The range of reasons for users to want to get together can also lead to difficulties. Where a user group appears to lack focus, this is often because they are under-resourced (Drake, 1994).

The importance of bottom-up developments from service users is crucial to sustainable development of user involvement at any level and particularly on the board. However, our action research shows that bottom-up change has to be met by an opening-up of opportunities from the top, for there to be a shift in control. User groups and networks are dependent on the leadership's attitude and the purse-strings within the voluntary organisation as well as on the existence of a wider user movement.

Resistance

Some people and organisations resist greater involvement of users, even after policies have been promulgated. We have referred already to some processes of resistance such as tokenistic appointments, restricted decision-making processes or lack of practical support. Arguments against greater user involvement in both principle and practice are commonly cited.

There is a feeling, not uncommonly off the record, that user involvement is just a fashionable ideology, 'political correctness'. Allied to this, may be a more explicit criticism that user involvement is promoted for its own sake, as an end in itself, rather than as a means to improved organisational performance. And the cost in time, money and effort is a reason given to justify inaction on the issue.

It is difficult, as we have recognised, to formulate a clear vision of an organisation's governance incorporating greater user involvement, and this may suggest that it would be bound to be tokenistic or ambiguous. Likewise, positive action to ensure users become trustees or have more influence in other ways is attacked as unfairly discriminatory or patronising.

Some managers in a survey (Robson *et al.*, 1997) stated that they felt users would be unable to contribute because of their medical condition or their fatigue or emotionalism. This view is reflected in general ignorance and indifference, primarily born out of unfamiliarity, and leading to disabled people's social exclusion (Leonard Cheshire, 2000).

People in organisations may resist change because it involves a loss of something with which they are familiar or because it is perceived as a threat, openly or subconsciously, to their professional or political status.

Concerns about conflict of interest dominated the Charity Commission guidance on users' trustees and have also been a preoccupation of managers and their advisers (Hudson, 1995; Charity Commission, 2000). Users, it is feared, cannot separate personal from corporate interests or are too emotionally involved. Moreover, users involved in governance are perceived as unrepresentative because they cannot know the views of all users, because they only represent current and not future users or because they become 'professional users'.

However, resistance to change can be viewed as an inevitable and useful part of a process. The arguments provide feedback about the values and attitudes prevalent in an organisation, and that can help in planning change. Our action research has shown when an organisation embarks on a change programme, people will need to work through what the changes mean for them and make sense of them as they move on. Greater user involvement is more a journey than a change to a predetermined end-point. Thus, while resistance may focus on present trustees and managers simply holding on to power, it may be more helpful to focus on practical steps rather than on rapid changes in people's beliefs. A change of culture for an organisation from one of paternalism to becoming user-led is possible but is likely to take at least five years, or perhaps a decade.

Membership and ownership

Where a voluntary organisation has a membership, this can provide a mechanism for user involvement within a process of democratising the organisation. For Mencap, the incorporation of its users into the governing structures was part of a complex national policy to develop a strong membership.

If users can join as members, they gain a right to take part in aspects of the organisation, including participation or representation in general meetings and in election of at least some members of the governing body. However, membership power is limited. If it is dominated historically by a particular group, then new groups such as users can find it difficult to influence decisions despite their formal position. Moreover, the governing body as trustees of the charity have ultimate responsibility under charity law, not a general meeting.

Scope introduced one-person, one-vote in a move similar to that of Mencap to get away from a governance structure that did not involve disabled people in positions of influence. Its new membership system was put to the test in late 2000 when members reacted to an announcement at an AGM of widespread cuts and narrowing of the focus of the organisation; the leadership was pressured to delay implementation to enable more consultation and time for alternatives to be set up where services were to be closed.

Membership systems in voluntary organisations are sometimes dormant. A small number of members may carry out the functions such as voting for trustees and attending annual general meetings as mere formalities. There may be confusion about who is and is not officially a member. In one disability organisation, the annual general meeting is regularly attended by over 150 people comprising users, supporters and staff; some are official members but there is no visible difference in the participation or behaviour of members and non-members; it appears that all present to some extent see themselves as belonging to the organisation even though not members.

Questions about membership lead to questions about 'ownership' – whose organisation is it? It may be popularly supposed that a voluntary organisation belongs to its members, who may include users. However, charity law separates the two aspects of ownership: the use or 'enjoyment' (in legal terms) rests with the beneficiaries but the control rests with the trustees, not with the members. Asking 'who owns this organisation?' can assist analysis of an organisation's relationships with users. Ownership, in this analysis, is not just a legal issue but a moral sense with rights and responsibilities (Robson, 1995).

In some organisations, the answer will be that it is the users' organisation or that it can become their organisation. In other organisations, there may be more than one claim to ownership: carers or other communities may deserve or need to share in ownership; staff or other professionals may be seen as entitled to be in partnership with users. However these questions are answered for particular organisations, we argue that service users are at least among the legitimate owners of voluntary organisations which exist to benefit them, and from ownership flows entitlement to control as well as to use, though in some cases this may be a share in control.

Thus, this analysis moves towards the stakeholder model where governance structures and processes provide ways of representing and resolving a variety of interests.[4] However, study of user involvement complicates the models as discussed in the Introduction. First, despite this emphasis on stakeholding, where users are in control, it may be more helpful to focus on issues of agency and compliance: user trustees may have to deal with problems of how to get professional staff to act in the interests of users. Second, increasing user involvement may not be in tension with improving organisational performance: it should be a means of enhancing organisational effectiveness. Above all, the development of user involvement is a journey where principles and practice must interact: you cannot just adopt a model and expect it to work.

Conclusion

It is now broadly accepted that charities providing services or campaigning for improvements in services or policy should involve their intended beneficiaries, their users, in decisions about those services and campaigns. Different pressures and arguments flowed together from the policy environment, professional practice and from the demands of the user movement. The traditional view of charity has, to some extent, stood out against this tide of change but has been modified in law and in many voluntary organisations' policies. However, research with a range of charities has demonstrated that there is no one way to provide greater user involvement and that acceptance of the principle of involvement does not lead to a simple set of practical measures.

The evidence discussed in this chapter indicates the need for a contingency approach to developing user involvement in governance. We suggest that prior to focusing on particular measures to involve users, organisations and their communities need to consider what they are trying to achieve and why. Some may be based on a belief that service users should be in control or may see users as partners in the enterprise. Others, more managerially orientated, may consider services or campaigns could be more effective with feedback or input from users.

With more clarity about the reasons for increasing user involvement, organisations, combining users, staff and trustees, can develop appropriate methods. The best methods for any particular organisation will be contingent on the specific context and internal factors. For example, if a governing body has a predominantly rubber-stamping role, then getting users on the board is unlikely to lead to any great influence. Nonetheless, increasing users' influence in other aspects of governance may help shift the governing body into a more active role or may help cope with its residual legal and symbolic stewardship – and either development might be right in the circumstances.

User involvement as a project helps us to realise that the governing body in an organisation is only one force among others in making or resisting progress and only one aspect of governance.

Notes

1 We are grateful to the Joseph Rowntree Foundation for their financial and human support through the three phases of this research. We are grateful to all the organisations and people with whom we have worked in this project and also to the students on the MA Voluntary Sector Studies and MA by Work-Based Learning at University of East London who developed studies in their own organisations and communities.
2 We make clear that we undertook this research with a commitment to increasing involvement of users in decision-making.
3 The social model of disability states that it is disabling environments and attitudes that prevent disabled people from participating fully in society rather than their individual physical impairment or medical condition.
4 It does not follow that a stakeholder should share in governance: purchasers and funders may be stakeholders but relate differently to the organisation than through governance structures and processes. When we explored who constituted stakeholders for chief executives/co-ordinators of local voluntary organisations, we found that the local authority as funding body was seen as the main stakeholder (Howlett and Locke, 1997).

References

Barnes, M. and Walker, A. (1996) 'Consumerism Versus Empowerment: A Principled Approach to the Involvement of Older Service Users', *Policy and Politics*, 24, 4.

Beresford, P. and Croft, S. (1993) *Citizen Involvement: A Practical Guide for Change*, Basingstoke: Macmillan.

Beresford, P. and Harding, T. (eds) (1993) *A Challenge to Change: Practical Experiences of Building User-Led Services*, London: National Institute for Social Work.

Campbell, J. and Oliver, M. (1996) *Disability Politics: Understanding Our Past, Changing Our Future*, London: Routledge.

Charity Commission (2000) *Users On Board: Beneficiaries Who Become Trustees*, London: Charity Commission.

Commission on the Future of the Voluntary Sector (Deakin Report) (1996) *Meeting the Challenge of Change: Voluntary Action Into the 21st Century*, London: National Council for Voluntary Organisations.

Drake, R. (1994) 'The Exclusion of Disabled People from Positions of Power in British Voluntary Organisations', *Disability and Society*, 9, 4.

Flynn, N. (1996) 'A Mixed Blessing? How the Contract Culture Works', in C. Hanvey and T. Philpot (eds) *The Role and Workings of Voluntary Organisations*, London: Routledge.

Goss, S. and Miller, C. (1995) *From Margin to Mainstream: Developing User- and Carer-Centred Community Care*, York: Joseph Rowntree Foundation.

Griffiths, R. (1988) (Griffiths Report) *Community Care: Agenda for Action*, London: HMSO.

Harrow, J. and Palmer, P. (1998) 'Reassessing Charity Trusteeship in Britain? Towards Conservatism, Not Change', *Voluntas*, 9, 2, 171–185.

Hasler, F. (1997) *In the Right Hands: Changing Control and Culture in a Disability Organisation*, London: Volprof, City University.

Hope, P. and Hargreaves, S. (1997) *User Involvement: Principles and Practice for*

Involving Users in the Design and Delivery of Public Services. Framework in Print, 20 Shawclough Drive, Rochdale, Lancs OL12 7HG.

Howlett, S. and Locke, M. (1997) 'Governance in the Voluntary Sector and the Reciprocal Relationship in the Governance of Localities', in *Proceedings of the 3rd Researching the Voluntary Sector Conference,* London: National Council for Voluntary Organisations.

Hudson, M. (1995) *Managing Without Profit: The Art of Managing Third-Sector Organisations,* London: Penguin.

Kumar, S. (1997) *Accountability in the Contract State: The Relationship Between Voluntary Organisations, Local Government and Service Users,* York: York Publishing Services.

Leonard Cheshire Foundation (2000) *Committed to Inclusion? The Leonard Cheshire Social Exclusion Report 2000,* London: Leonard Cheshire.

Lindow, V. and Morris, J. (1995) *Service User Involvement: Synthesis of Findings and Experience in the Field of Community Care,* York: York Publishing Services.

Locke, M., Robson, P. and Howlett, S. (2001) 'Users: at the Centre or the Sidelines', in M. Harris and C. Rochester (eds) *Voluntary Organisations and Social Policy in Britain: Perspectives on Change and Choice,* Basingstoke: Palgrave.

Morris, J. (1994) *The Shape of Things to Come: User-Led Social Services,* London: National Institute for Social Work.

Oliver, M. (1996) 'User Involvement in the Voluntary Sector: A View from the Disability Movement', in Commission on the Future of the Voluntary Sector, *Meeting the Challenge of Change: Voluntary Action into the 21st Century: Summary of Evidence and Selected Papers.* London: National Council for Voluntary Organisations.

Robson, P. (1995) 'Who Owns Voluntary Organisations?', in *Proceedings of 2nd Researching the Voluntary Sector Conference,* London: National Council for Voluntary Organisations.

Robson, P., Locke, M. and Dawson, J. (1997) *Consumerism or Democracy? User Involvement in the Control of Voluntary Organisations,* Bristol: Policy Press.

Robson, P., Locke, M. and Devenney, M. (1998) 'Increasing User Involvement in the Governance and Management of Voluntary Organisations: Setting Agendas for Change', in *Proceedings of the 4th Researching the Voluntary Sector Conference,* London: National Council for Voluntary Organisations.

Taylor, M. (1996) 'The Future of User Involvement in the Voluntary Sector: A Contribution to the Debate', in Commission on the Future of the Voluntary Sector, *Meeting the Challenge to Change: Voluntary Action into the 21st Century: Summary of Evidence and Selected Papers,* London: National Council for Voluntary Organisations.

Taylor, M. (1999) *Preparing for the Future: Involving Users in the Running of Voluntary Organisations,* London: Association of Chief Executives of National Voluntary Organisations.

Tumim, W. (1992) (Tumim Report) *On Trust: Increasing the Effectiveness of Charity Trustees and Management Committees,* London: National Council for Voluntary Organisations.

Part II

What do boards do?

4 What influences the strategic contribution of boards?

Charles Edwards and Chris Cornforth

Introduction

This chapter considers the factors that affect the contribution that boards make to organisational strategy in public and non-profit organisations. It draws upon a research study into the behaviour of public and non-profit boards and the relationship between board members and management (Cornforth and Edwards, 1998).

The idea of boards adding value through their contributions to organisational strategy features both in descriptive and prescriptive accounts of board roles. In descriptive accounts of boards in the private sector, this strategic role is often seen as being in conflict with the control role (Taylor, 2001). As noted in the Introduction, there is a concern that a board focus on 'conformance' will be at the expense of its contribution to 'performance'. Other chapters in Part I have described the tensions between the role of public and non-profit boards in advancing organisational effectiveness, in synergistic partnership with management, and their roles in ensuring democratic accountability, transparency and adherence to government policy and performance. Many prescriptive accounts of public and non-profit board role prioritise this value-adding strategic role (Carver, 1990), as do many prescriptions for private sector governance (Pound, 1995; Garratt, 1997).

Empirical studies of what strategic role public and non-profit boards actually play, and if and how these tensions impact on them, are rare. Accounts of board behaviour have also been criticised for their over-reliance upon one source of data, usually the perceptions of board members, and lack of any independent confirmation of actors' accounts (Peck, 1995). The study reported upon in this chapter adopted a case study methodology drawing on three different sources: observation of meetings, actors' accounts and board documents. Four organisations were studied: a school and a further education college from the public sector, an overseas development agency and a community-based organisation from the voluntary sector.

The chapter first discusses what is meant by the term 'strategic contribution' in public and non-profit governance, and whether and how this can be distinguished from operational and policy contributions. It outlines the framework used to conceptualise how various factors – context, inputs and board processes – influence what boards do, elaborating on the wider institutional influences upon boards. After summarising the research methodology, the chapter presents some findings about the different strategic contributions of boards. A concluding discussion suggests how the strategic contribution of boards is shaped by the regulatory environment, the particular history of governance, the orientation and competencies of key board members, and the way the board is organised and run.

Strategic contribution

There are two principal problems with defining boards' strategic contributions to organisations. The first concern the fuzziness of the boundary between operational detail and strategic focus. As Greer and Hoggett (1997) have pointed out, in practice members of boards find it harder to distinguish between the two than is implicit in prescriptive literature.

It is not only that the two can be difficult to distinguish, but our understanding of strategic issues may come from exposure to operational detail, albeit necessarily on a selective basis, as Rochester notes in Chapter 6. In small public and non-profit organisations, such as schools or local charities, comprehension of the boundaries between strategic and operational management may be limited. In larger organisations, many senior managers may see strategic management as a main element of their own management role. A division between directors' and managers' functions based upon the former as strategic decision-takers and the latter as implementers, is both simplistic and anachronistic in a modern managerial culture. More pertinent are the boundaries within the strategic management function between what managers and board members do. Clarifying and implementing these boundaries may involve more work by managers than simply supplying board members with copies of operational papers to 'receive', 'note' or 'approve'. To identify and present to the board what is strategically significant in operational information, reports and activities requires time, skill, board input and a high degree of trust between board members and senior managers.

The second definitional problem is more specific to the public and non-profit sectors and concerns the distinction between 'policy' and 'strategy'. Greer and Hoggett (1999) have argued that it has been simplistic just to substitute the term strategy for policy, as many have tried to do. They point out that strategy derives from the discourse of how organisations position themselves competitively while policy derives from the public purpose discourse about giving substance to collective values. Thus in a college, concerns about curriculum quality and relevance or about outreach work with disadvantaged communities would be matters of policy.

Whereas possible mergers with or take-overs of other colleges, or diversifying using subsidiary companies to win contracts in discrete market niches, would be matters of strategy. In practice, again, the boundary is blurred: pursuing an initiative that builds upon a reputation for good special needs education combines both. Greer and Hoggett (1999) note that as UK public policy affecting what different local public spending bodies do has become more centralised, and as the environment in which these bodies operate has become more marketised, so the discourse of strategy has become predominant.

Caution is therefore required when asserting that public and non-profit boards should focus on making strategic contributions. This can over-simplify what is operational and apparently not worthy of board attention. Strategic contribution is a contested term: how boards interpret it depends on perceptions about the very purpose of quasi-autonomous public and non-profit organisations. For the purposes of the case study research, board papers and discussions that incorporated assessments of organisations' overall resource and capability strengths and weaknesses, their relative performance and their options and priorities for future development were interpreted as being strategic.

Determinants of board outputs

Figure 4.1 presents an input–output model for conceptualising boards' strategic contributions. This develops the work of Dulewicz *et al.* (1995), who use the term 'tasks' to denote the outputs of what a board actually does. Their framework concentrates on inputs – who is on the board – and processes, for example the way in which the board defines its roles and responsibilities, the way board business and meetings are conducted. The main difference in our model is the addition of context, which both constrains and enables organisational action.

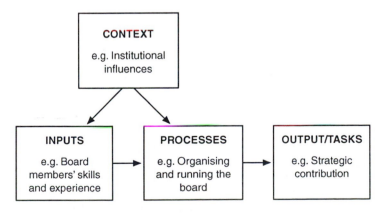

Figure 4.1 Influences on board outputs

ition to strategy is defined as an *output* of a board's involve-
organisation. The inputs and processes that shape board
themselves shaped by the *context* in which organisations and
operate. Actions within organisations, and in this case within
ot take place within a vacuum, but are highly situational (Pettigrew and McNulty, 1995), for example, the legal regulations surrounding governance and board constitution are important influences on board behaviour. Organisational action also has to be understood in its historical context. Previous board actions may shape how the board defines its role, the norms of board behaviour and how board members interpret the issues that face them.

The environmental context of organisations may place demands on them in two ways. First are economic and technical demands that stem from the market or quasi-market in which organisations operate. Second, there may be social or cultural demands that require organisations to behave or operate in certain ways. The second of these particularly affect board behaviour in non-profit organisations. The new institutional theory of organisations (DiMaggio and Powell, 1991a; Scott *et al.*, 1994) is helpful in trying to understand the cultural and social influences on boards.

A central idea of institutional theory is that organisations are shaped by the institutional environment. Over time various ideas and practices gain legitimacy and become the accepted or taken-for-granted way of thinking and doing things. The ideas become institutionalised; they take on 'a rule like status in social thought and action' (DiMaggio and Powell, 1991a: 9). Acceptance of these ideas by powerful bodies in society, such as the state and the professions, is usually an important part of this legitimation process. Hence, organisations are not just shaped by the need to be efficient and effective (as stressed in functional theories), but by 'cultural elements' of the environment, that is 'taken for granted beliefs and widely shared rules that serve as templates for organising' (ibid.: 26–27).

DiMaggio and Powell (1991b) distinguish three ways in which institutionalisation may occur, through *coercive, normative* and mimetic *institutional* pressures. Coercive pressures refer to the ability of some organisations to impose rules on others, for example, government laws and regulations. Government requirements on how the audit function is carried out by further education college boards, or Charity Commission requirements for organisational reporting, are both examples of coercive pressures. They affect the type of people boards recruit, what they devote their time to and what they perceive their priorities and function to be, all of which have an impact on the extent and type of strategic contributions that boards make to their organisations.

Normative pressure stems from wider cultural influences such as social norms and values, which may be transmitted through processes such as socialisation and professional education and training. The pressure from management writers and consultants for boards to focus on the strategic at the expense of the operational, or from politicians for boards to be more representative of their local communities, are examples of normative pressures that can affect boards' strategic contributions.

Mimetic pressures occur through the desire to copy other organisations. If an organisation is uncertain how to act, it may copy another that it thinks has found a successful or legitimate way of dealing with the situation. This is particularly evident in the widespread borrowing, by public and non-profit boards from the private sector, of notions of what governance requires.

Institutional theory suggests that, over time, common institutional pressures result in organisational forms and practices in particular organisational fields converging or becoming isomorphic. However, this thesis has been criticised for being overly deterministic and inadequately explaining organisational variety. One promising way of dealing with this problem is the idea that society comprises many institutional orders which are potentially contradictory (Friedland and Alford, 1991).

The idea of institutional contradictions is central to understanding some of the approaches that boards take, or do not take, to develop their strategic contribution, and the tensions they then encounter with their other perceived board roles. Various institutional pressures have helped to shape current thinking and norms about boards, with board members drawing upon these different and often contradictory sets of ideas in interpreting their own role and the role of their board. This helps explain variety among boards, and why boards often face difficult tensions and dilemmas.

Researching practice

The study looked at practice in both the voluntary and public sectors. The four organisations chosen for study allowed for differences in sector, size, board and composition. The four cases were:

- a local voluntary organisation (LVO);
- a small national voluntary organisation (NVO);
- a local education authority school;
- a regional further education college.

Table 4.1 shows the key features of the four cases.

The research drew upon the following sources:

- Structured observations of board and sub-committee meetings. These were observed over a cycle, i.e. two board meetings and the intervening meetings of sub-committees. The researchers logged the content, source and level of agenda items, the detail of board–manager

Table 4.1 Key features of the four cases

	Local Voluntary Organisation (LVO)	Local primary school	National Voluntary Organisation (NVO)	Further Education College
Main service(s)	Homes and support for domestic violence victims	Primary education	Overseas development services, education and lobbying	Post-school, vocationally oriented youth/adult education
Size	£⅓ m budget p.a., 6 homes, 2 advice centres, phoneline	£⅔ d m budget p.a., 15 teaching staff, 400 pupils	£¼ m budget p.a., 7 staff, national membership	£25 m budget p.a, 1400 staff (300 FT teaching), 4 sites
History	Est. 1970s Originally a collective	Long established	Est. 1970s Former co-operative Founder recently left New co-ordinator	Incorporated 1993 Ex-local authority controlled
Funding	Grant and premises aid from local authority and housing associations; rents	State funded. Local authority delegated 85 per cent of budget to governing body	Donations, rents, grants	Mainly through state's Further Education Funding Council (FEFC) student-related block grant
Legal structure	Co. Ltd by guarantee and registered charity	Local authority school National curriculum and inspection requirements	Co. Ltd by guarantee and registered charity	Independent within FEFC regulatory and inspection parameters
Management	Strong CE	Head teacher plus deputy	Emerging formal management structure	Principal and senior management team. Matrix responsibility and faculty structure
Governance	Board met every 6 weeks 6 Directors, + 'attending representatives' from local organisations, 2–3 informal sub-committees	Full governing body met once a term 4 elected parents, 2 teachers, 5 local authority apptd, 4 co-opted and Head 4–5 sub-committees	Board met 4/5 times p.a. Local group members elect 7 trustees 5 sub-committees	Board met 6 times p.a. 3 co-opted, 8 independent, 1 nominated, 2 elected staff, and Principal 3+ sub-committees

interaction, the quantity and quality of supporting information, and the nature of board action and behaviour.

- Semi-structured interviews with key managers and board members. Between eight and ten taped interviews of an hour or more were conducted in each organisation
- An analysis of board documentation and information systems. Copies of all the papers which board members received before and during the meetings observed, were collected and studied, as was formal documentation relating to the remit and regulations of particular committees.

The findings

The type, extent and quality of boards' strategic contributions varied across the cases. In both the local voluntary organisation (LVO) and the school, this contribution was slight. Greater contributions were made at the national voluntary organisation (NVO) and the college. This contribution is examined in more detail below, drawing out the influence of institutional factors, board inputs and processes.

Principles, policies, power, practices

Local voluntary organisation (LVO)

Strategic contribution

There was little distinction made in the LVO between either strategy and policy or strategy and operations. Most of the board business observed was concerned with current preoccupations of the chief executive (CE). Although these could be deconstructed externally to include strategic, policy and operational dimensions, in interviews such dimensions did not feature in either managers' or board members' perceptions of their respective roles. There was no delineation between, for instance, the board's role in establishing overarching values, standards or objectives and the management's role in delivering these and being held to account to the board for such delivery.

The board had little involvement in formulating or overseeing strategic management. When the chair of the board was asked whether the board had any involvement in either producing or setting the framework for the LVO's business plan, her response was: 'I don't think the CE did involve anyone actually, you will have to ask her. I wasn't involved in it. I think [the CE] mainly did it on her own.'

In practice, the board performed three main functions. It acted as a link to important stakeholders in the LVO's environment and as such was used by the CE as a source of information and advice. It was also used occasionally by the CE as a backstop to take decisions that might be difficult or controversial, for example, a problem over the pay of a particular person. Finally, it performed a limited compliance role, overseeing the work and finances of the organisation. However, there was a recognition that it often acted largely as 'rubber stamp' in this capacity.

Context

This slight strategic contribution owes much to four normative pressures that are not uncommon in determining board roles in UK voluntary organisations. The first is the perception of a board as a 'supporters' club', of people whose support, contacts, funding connections and specific skills can be tapped into free of charge by voluntary organisations. From this perspective the primary role of the board is to support the organisation and those that run it, rather than to drive strategy.

The second is the relative autonomy of voluntary organisations compared with public sector organisations. The LVO is essentially an operational service deliverer, set up to meet some local needs, with its organisational strategy limited to its perpetual need to secure its financial base.

The third is a reaction, perhaps over-reaction, to a collective and anti-hierarchical tradition prevalent in the UK voluntary sector in the 1970s and 1980s. The LVO had been part of that tradition, with staff, volunteers and trustees operating together in confused structurelessness. The current CE had put an end to that tradition, but she still associated board involvement in management as a dilution of her management role and/or as a threat to the clarity of decision-making in the organisation:

> You could have a group who were ... chummy chummy ... [and] go on away days and get to know each other, live in each other's pockets maybe and who may function well as a group, but who may be even less use than they are now to the organisation ... Because ... it may be dangerous as well because at the moment they will have their own opinions. They won't have been influenced by anybody. There won't have been any lobbying because that doesn't happen here.

A fourth contextual factor is the relative lack of awareness of governance issues in many UK voluntary organisations (NCVO, 1992). There is a board because there has to be; it meets to do the business it is required to and it might as well be filled with useful and pleasant people. However, there is little thought devoted to whether it performs its duties well or to whether governance is an opportunity to add value to the organisations' work. This in part stems from a tradition of voluntarism, whereby people with time and goodwill, rather than with expertise or experience, make up many local voluntary organisation boards. Although the LVO had recruited board members with useful contacts and expertise, they still

tended to view their responsibilities in a fairly limited, reactive and supportive way.

Inputs: board experience and skills

Most board members had been identified by the CE from the ranks of
organisations and professions with which the LVO worked: the police,
social services, a solicitors' practice, community organisations, etc. Little
attention was paid to any relevant experience of strategic management or
governance. As a board member reported:

> I think sometimes, some people feel a bit out of their depth. I've cer-
> tainly felt confused when I didn't understand what things meant and
> what the real significance of things was ... Possibly not having enough
> knowledge to challenge or tease out more of what comes from [the
> CE] perhaps.

Processes: organising and running the board

As discussed earlier, strategic contributions do not just happen. They
require the appropriate amount of information provided at the right time
to the right people, and meetings in environments that foster strategic
awareness and decision-making. The way the LVO board members were
serviced and organised was not conducive to a strategic role. Very selective
and limited information was supplied by staff to board members.

> We Board Members ... who are not part of the organisation, are so
> dependent on [staff] for the information and the understanding of
> what is going on, that it is almost like guiding and ratifying what they
> are proposing rather than much initiative coming from us.

The school

Strategic contribution

The board lacked confidence in its capacity to influence the direction of
the school. It was sandwiched between a seemingly endless stream of policies from government and a hard-to-challenge professional staff knowledge of how the school delivered policies. A glimpse of a policy
contribution observed – the school had to formulate an anti-bullying
policy – revealed more about the dependence of the board upon government policy guidelines and upon head teacher's decisions, than about its
ability to make real policy choices. No participant interviewed identified a
governance role involving the school's 'competitive' strengths and weak-

nesses in relation to neighbouring schools. The board would probably have concerned itself with relative organisational defects had a decline in enrolments and a poor inspection report brought the issue to the fore. However, in the absence of a self-confident strategic or policy role, observations confirmed extensive and often repetitive board coverage of day-to-day issues.

Both governors and senior staff saw the main role of the board as one of compliance – keeping an eye on how the school was run, and a check on the power of the head teacher. To a lesser extent they also played a political role, bringing some local accountability and involvement. There was little evidence of the board seriously affecting how the head teacher decided the school should spend its money or organise its activities. Both staff and governors respectively seemed to recognise that in reality the governors made little direct impact on the school's strategy:

> If you've got a good Head, a good Deputy Head, good teaching staff, that has a hundred times more impact than whatever the governing body is like.

> I've read some of the introduction to governors' booklets and stuff and it seems to me that they're presenting something more than we actually do. I think the School is, to a large extent, the Head and the Deputy, followed closely by the staff that's there. I don't know enough to know how much we could change the direction or the ethos of the School.

Context

Various contextual factors help to explain the limited involvement in policy or strategy. One is the limited freedom of action that UK school governing bodies have for strategic choice. They are subject to coercive pressure through extensive control and regulation by both central and local government. A second factor is normative: a traditional disinclination to seeing school governance in managerial terms. This is reflected in the language of education: good professional teachers become head teachers (not principals, directors, managers or CEs). Teaching is a profession and governing bodies have tended to see their role as 'not to interfere' with teaching and pastoral care issues. Instead, school boards can be seen as expressions of 'political' accountability, even though the emphasis of accountability has shifted from political parties to parents. The governing body's representative role – together with its associated local accountability, communication and involvement – was the one that the head and governors most identified with and saw as the body's main contribution to the school. This emphasis was reflected in the state's view of school governing bodies (DfEE, 1996):

Governing bodies are accountable to those who established the School and also to parents and the wider community for the way in which it carries out its functions ... although [governors] are not delegates, the governing body reflects the community it serves.

Inputs: board experience and skills

School boards may represent parents and communities at the expense of bringing in strategic management expertise and experience. The pool for such expertise is often limited in the small communities that primary schools serve. Like many others, this school experienced difficulty in attracting governors at all, let alone those with strategic management skills.

Processes: organising and running the board

The way board meetings were serviced and run also limited the governing body's capacity to make a strategic contribution. Agenda items for meetings were not prioritised; information that was presented was partial and not organised to inform strategic choices. Meetings consisted largely of limited scrutiny of a long list of items, many dealing with matters of operational detail.

> We get the agenda, and with the agenda we get all the minutes of the previous meetings. We get any papers that have come from County. We get all the draft policies. I think it wasn't so much the fact that we get those, but then we all get them again for the full governors' meeting. But then, if you haven't sat on the Curriculum Committee, you need to know what those policy documents are. So we do get wads of it to wade through. I've got four folders upstairs, of governors' stuff.
>
> (school governor)

The background and experience of most governors made it difficult to challenge how the governing body was run. Most governors had not served on other boards and had limited management experience, and any training they received as governors focused mostly on their statutory duties. As a result, they had few alternative models of governance to draw upon.

The NVO

Strategic contribution

People at NVO board meetings did discuss policy: whether the NVO should be involved in this service in that country, or how it should frame its relationships with partners. The NVO evidently valued the autonomy that a voluntary organisation has to shape its own objectives and values. There was very little discussion of the NVO's strategic position *vis-à-vis* other overseas development charities, although there was an awareness of what other organisations were doing and considerable interaction with them. The board recognised a tension between strategic and operational issues.

The NVO board made a greater contribution to strategy than at the LVO or the school. It discussed the long-term direction of the organisation and its mission, what to evaluate in overseas projects, future plans and priorities. However, an acknowledged weakness of the board was that it frequently got drawn into operational issues, and consequently not enough time was spent on longer-term strategic issues:

> Directors' meetings are very cluttered with a lot of stuff which is why I would be happy to get a lot of the nitty gritty out of it, because we don't really have time to consider things and to make decisions that are long term. I think that's why we shy away from them so that we can worry about short term things.
>
> (trustee)

Overall, the main roles the board played were ensuring compliance and short-term planning.

Context

Of all four organisations, there was least separation between board member and staff roles at the NVO. Various historical influences were behind this. The NVO was originally run by volunteers, only taking on paid staff some time later. There persisted a philosophy of collective working, with both voluntary board members and staff involved in decision-making. Although the NVO was reviewing its governance and management after the arrival of a new co-ordinator, the absence of a clear management structure meant that board members still tended to focus on short-term operational issues.

> I think we get involved too much in the nitty gritty, that's a big theme at the moment ... but that's part of the problem of having people

who come up as volunteers and been doing it, and now they want to do more.

(trustee)

Inputs: board experience and skills

NVO trustees were elected from the organisation's membership, although the existing board often identified candidates whose election was not contested. It was recognised that there was often a trade-off between candidates' local activism record and their management expertise:

> The way the board is formed ... it is totally unrealistic to expect to have those type of people (i.e. people with governance skills) sitting around in the membership waiting to sit on your board. I think you only get that type of people if you are co-opting people on, and then you lose the interest bit and the dedication bit.

(staff member)

Processes: organising and running the board

Board and sub-committee meetings tended to drift towards operational issues and spend little time on broader issues of policy or strategy. This reflected the way board meetings were organised and run. As with the school, meetings typically had between fifteen to twenty items on the agenda. Items were not usually prioritised so it was difficult to distinguish important from more routine issues.

> I don't think board meetings work terribly well. I think we are not very good at organising our time. I think we need to be much more disciplined in meetings ... And actually really restrict what people talk about at meetings, that we don't go over, talk through blow-by-blow accounts of things.

(trustee)

The lack of structure or of clear focus to the agenda lead to 'operational drift', whereby meetings became bogged down in the detail of more routine and familiar items that arose. People were more comfortable dealing with operational issues rather than the uncertainties and dilemmas that surrounded long-term strategy-making or evaluating how the organisation was doing: 'The board tends to repeat previous discussions at sub-committees ... people want to justify what they have done' (trustee).

The college

Strategic contribution

The board wanted the college to deliver the most suitable educational services for the population of the community it served. Yet, as discussed under inputs below, the background of the most dominant board members was not in educational policy but in strategy in the competitive, management sense. Board members in both meetings and interviews conformed to a discourse of organisational success similar to that used in a business environment.

Although FEFC processes and policies consumed a huge, and resented, volume of board time, the board managed to create and protect space to focus on strategic issues. Typically one away day per term was set aside to tackle strategic matters free from the normal board agenda. The board was seen, positively, as playing an increasingly strategic and important role by both senior staff and governors:

> not day-to-day decisions, but I think the long-term decisions that affect the nature and style of the College, I think this is a role for the board.
>
> (governor)

> They're enhancing [this organisation] insofar as I now feel that they have the self-confidence to sack me. Now that is actually very significant.
>
> (CE)

The board was also playing a more important role in examining how the performance of the college could be improved and acting with senior management as a driver for strategic change. However, it recognised that this role needed to develop further and that, conforming to the competitive strategy discourse, it was hampered in this by its lack of comparative information about performance:

> the area where we're not getting enough information and we're not knowing what's happening is in the area of the college's results, comparative success with other colleges and the measure of achievement.
>
> (governor)

> I would like to see the high level numbers, which we've never been presented with because the information hasn't been available up to now . . . I'm not interested in the nitty gritty detail, but what I would like to know is . . . what it is costing to run the faculty, what number of students are there for the amount of money that we are spending . . . the results

of ... faculties in terms of educational achievements and what their view is on what resources they are going to need for the next few years.

(governor)

The board also actively and carefully scrutinised and questioned management proposals and had an audit committee that oversaw detailed investigations of the college's financial systems and procedures. It also acted as a link to some important customers and stakeholders. However, the board was less clear about how to operationalise its accountability to the broader community.

Context

All three types of institutional pressures had helped to shape the nature and role of the board. Coercive pressure in the form of government legislation required colleges to recruit people with business experience to serve as governors. Legislation had also forced FE colleges to compete with other educational organisations and to face closure if student demand or satisfaction fell to unacceptable levels. These changes had helped to create a normative climate in which the idea of the college as a business, and a more managerial view of governance, had gained increasing resonance at the expense of one that emphasised local political accountably. Many governors felt comfortable in this climate, given their business backgrounds. The selection policy of the board reflected and reinforced this climate:

> We are seeking to fill those [vacancies] with industrial members rather than otherwise, so there is a clear feeling that we need more weight on that side to help us survive the future. It's an increasingly cold, business-like financial environment.

(CE)

There were also mimetic pressures, whereby the college's senior management wanted to mimic what it saw as role models: successful businesses. The principal wished his college to be seen as businesslike by his peers and the presence of senior business executives on his board was a matter of some pride to him in FE circles.

Inputs: board experience and skills

The selection of board members for their management expertise and experience contributed to the board's strategic contribution and its capacity to influence strategic decisions. The board's ability to question management drew on relevant experience:

We're far more pro-active, we're asking an awful lot of questions . . .
the staff now expects us to ask questions and be critical and want to
know why we're doing it and how we're doing it and see how it fits
with the pattern. We're taking a fair amount of advice from outside
and we're also feeding back from our own organisations.

(governor)

[The corporation is] bringing together a diverse group of people who
have in common that they've operated at a senior level in another
organisation and creating as a result of that a sort of chemistry that
challenges, excites, motivates and persuades the college to look outwards and to identify best practice, to bring on board best practice . . .
I honestly think they would go down the drain if they didn't have the
Corporation.

(governor)

The college's greater capacity to recruit senior managers than in the other
cases was perhaps because of its much greater size and status as an organisation. It was also not constrained by the need to elect external members.

Processes: organising and running the board

The board's strategic capacity was enhanced by how it was organised and
run. Members did the following:

*   made selective but significant efforts to be involved with and under-
    stand the college's work, for example, holding occasional meetings
    with staff and students, and shadowing managers on particular tasks;
*   conferred with each other and with senior managers outside formal
    board meetings;
*   delegated more operational matters to sub-committees it had confi-
    dence in;
*   held occasional strategy away-days clear of ordinary agenda matters.

Yet the board was also hampered by the sheer weight of rules and direc-
tives from the FEFC about its operations and processes: 'We have too
heavy agendas, too many rules about what we can do and what we can't do
– it constrains us' (governor).

Conclusion

The study revealed a range of contextual, input and process factors affecting how public and non-profit boards interpreted and practised their strategic roles. The school and LVO boards made only slight strategic con-

Table 4.2 Factors in the boards' strategic contribution

	Context	Inputs – board experience and skills	Process – organising and running the board	Tasks – strategic contribution
LVO	Network of supporters Charity regulations	Directors chosen for support/contacts, not governance expertise	Reactive Little and poor information Involvement constrained by CE	Slight; approval of CE plans/actions
School	Tradition of political/local accountability Active state regulation	Keen parents elected/apptd Shortage of people with expertise CE has monopoly of expertise	Reactive Unstructured agendas Information overload Dependence on CE	Slight; some policy discussion Operational drift
NVO	Membership organisation Tradition of collective working and member involvement Charity regulations	Board elected Tension – activism vs. expertise Occasional use of co-options to bring in expertise	Unstructured agendas Information overload Staff/Trustee boundary issues	Moderate: board role in planning and performance review Tendency to operational drift
College	From political to managerial model Active state (FEFC) regulation	Appointed board members bring in: Management skill/experience Intervention skills	Management of formal and informal processes Information provision changing	Increasingly significant

tributions, the NVO and college boards more substantial ones. Table 4.2 summarises these findings from the four cases.

The interplay of contextual factors was complex, with organisational factors (such as size and history) mixing with wider coercive, normative and mimetic institutional pressures. The state has an important coercive and normative influence on governance through its policies, legislation and guidance. Legal responsibilities emphasise non-profit boards' compliance role – checking propriety and legality, safeguarding assets and organisational mission, and accounting for expenditure. Unsurprisingly the compliance role was dominant in all four organisations. This was particularly true in the school, where the compliance role squeezed out more strategic considerations. This was not due to any distrust of the staff – as implied by agency theory – but to a fear of not adequately performing their legal duties of checking and ratifying policies. This was compounded by traditions in school governance emphasising parental involvement and political accountability, with professional educationalists and the state monopolising anything bordering on the managerial or strategic.

History also constrained the other boards' strategic contributions. The LVO's previous life as a collective meant that the CE was fearful of a board's potential capacity to compete with her control of strategy. At the NVO, the board had traditionally been a vehicle for involving volunteer members in the organisation and the development of its strategic role could not be at the expense of that tradition. At the college, there was constant reference to a pre-incorporation history of, essentially, political boards. However, the introduction, through the state, of greater market pressures and of more board members with business experience had created a climate where a more managerial view of governance prevailed. As a result, the board, in a conscious attempt to counter its history, saw strategy as part of its role, and was better equipped to deal with strategic issues.

However, even the college board experienced a tension between its conformance and performance roles. The more the state tries to use boards as vehicles for controlling the quality and consistency of public services and of procedural propriety, the more it reinforces the compliance role of governance. The danger is that this can swamp boards' strategic role. If government wants the boards of public and non-profit organisations to play a greater role in strategy, then it may need to ensure that it does not over-burden boards with other requirements.

To differing degrees, various process factors limited the effectiveness of boards' strategic contributions, particularly agenda-setting processes and the way meetings were run. At the school and the NVO board meetings had long unstructured agendas, with little prioritisation. Longer-term strategic issues were squeezed off agendas or given inadequate time. Various factors contributed to this process. First, it reflected some lack of clarity over the role of the board versus the role of management, so the board dealt with many items that might have best been dealt with elsewhere. Second, there was ambiguity between the chair and senior managers over who should manage the agenda, which meant that neither did the job effectively. Third, there was a lack of appreciation of the importance of good meeting practice.

Another process problem was poor board-level information: sometimes too little, sometimes too much. Board members complained of the amount of information they had to deal with, in particular items arising from sub-committees, yet there was also a lack of information needed for strategic contributions. There was certainly a lack of information to enable boards to consider their organisation's performance compared to other similar organisations.

A key input factor was the level of governance process skills among boards: many board members experienced problems in carrying out their roles. Especially on the boards of the smaller organisation, members had received little training in, or lacked experience of, discriminating between significant and routine information. Or of when and how to ask the right questions and be simultaneously both supportive and constructively critical of management proposals. There was little evidence of board members prioritising strategic issues for discussion. Some members made no contribution outside of formal meetings, even in circumstances when informal counsel outside of a meeting appeared a more effective form of intervention. These deficiencies reflected the lack of relevant governance or management experience among board members, the main exception being the college board. This was exacerbated by the lack of appropriate training: where board members had attended training courses, these tended to focus primarily on boards' legal responsibilities.

Together these contextual, process and input factors constrained the strategic capacity of public and non-profit boards. As long as governments retain control of policy through tight regulatory and performance management regimes, it may be difficult for public boards to develop their strategic contributions in the policy sense of the term. Developing strategic contributions in the competitive sense may also be difficult. Such contributions conflict with how many public and non-profit board members perceive their roles. And they may require a different level of board inputs and processes than is currently found in public and non-profit boards, especially smaller ones.

Notwithstanding these constraints, boards might enhance their strategic contributions through periodic review with senior management of their respective roles with regard to governance, and of the composition, processes and performance of their boards. For instance, re-thinking agenda management or structuring board 'away-days' to add real strategic value could reduce the tendency to 'operational drift'.

However much change individual organisations could make to their processes and inputs, they would still face challenges, in developing strategic contributions, that have their origins in conflicting and deep-rooted institutional pressures. It may, for example, be unrealistic to expect many lay boards, rooted in voluntarist, democratic and supportive traditions, to be deeply involved in strategy. Making strategic contributions may require public and non-profit boards to make difficult choices and trade-offs with other important governance roles and traditions.

References

Carver, J. (1990) *Boards that Make a Difference*, San Francisco: Jossey-Bass.

Cornforth, C. and Edwards, C. (1998) *Good Governance: Developing Effective Board-Management Relations*, London: CIMA Publishing.

DfEE (1996) *Guidance on Good Governance*, London: WEE Publications Centre.

DiMaggio, P. J. and Powell, W. W. (1991a) 'Introduction', in W. W. Powell and P. J. DiMaggio (eds) *The New Institutionalism in Organizational Analysis*, Chicago: University of Chicago Press.

DiMaggio, P. J. and Powell, W. W. (1991b) 'The Iron Cage Revisited: Institutional Isomorphism and Collective Rationality', in W. W. Powell and P. J. DiMaggio (eds) *The New Institutionalism in Organizational Analysis*, Chicago: University of Chicago Press.

Dulewicz, V., MacMillan, K. and Herbert, P. (1995) 'Appraising and Developing the Effectiveness of Boards and Their Directors', *Journal of General Management*, 20, 3, 1–19.

Friedland, R. and Alford, R. R. (1991) 'Bringing Society Back In', in W. W. Powell and P. J. DiMaggio (eds) *The New Institutionalism in Organizational Analysis*, Chicago: University of Chicago Press.

Garratt, R. (1997) *The Fish Rots from the Head: The Crisis in our Boardrooms*, London: HarperCollins.

Greer, A. and Hoggett, P. (1997) 'Patterns of Governance in Local Public Spending Bodies', *International Journal of Public Sector Management*, 10, 3, 214–227.

Greer, A. and Hoggett, P. (1999) 'Public Policies, Private Strategies and Local Public Spending Bodies', *Public Administration*, 77, 2, 235–256.

NCVO/Charity Commission (1992) *On Trust . . . Increasing the Effectiveness of Charity Trustees and Management Committees*, London: NCVO.

Peck, I. E. (1995) 'The Performance of a NHS Trust Board: Actors' Accounts, Minutes and Observation', *British Journal of Management*, 6, 135–156.

Pettigrew, A. and McNulty, T. (1995) 'Power and Influence In and Around the Boardroom', *Human Relations*, 48, 8, 845–873.

Pound, J. (1995) 'The Promise of the Governed Corporation', *Harvard Business Review*, March–April, 89–98.

Scott, W. R., Meyer J. W. and Associates (1994) *Institutional Environments and Organizations: Structural Complexity and Individualism*, Beverly Hills, CA: Sage.

Taylor B. T. (2001) *From Corporate Governance to Corporate Entrepreneurship*, Henley Working Paper 0111, Henley: Henley Management College, UK.

5 The financial role of charity boards

Jenny Harrow and Paul Palmer

Introduction: 'trusting the trustees'?

Voluntary boards face a dilemma when making financial decisions that arise from the legal framework under which boards operate. The legal framework requires trustees to act together, taking collective responsibility for decisions, arguably at their most critical in relation to organisations' financial resources. This presupposes board members have a shared understanding of, and implicitly, shared expertise in reaching those decisions. Yet, in practice, expertise is often unevenly distributed and some board members' reliance on their more financially literate colleagues can imbalance this collective responsibility model. Dependency relations may thus develop on boards between financial specialist and non-specialist colleagues, as well as between boards and their paid staff. Paradoxically, in order to attract trustees, organisations may downplay the degree of financial understanding required by each trustee. Boards therefore face a continuing dilemma, as they are simultaneously encouraged to develop their financial expertise while valuing the contributions of non-specialist board members.

This chapter examines boards' financial decision-making when faced with this dilemma. The collective responsibility model of board decision-making has operated together with cultural norms filtering out criticism of boards, since board members are 'unpaid volunteers doing complex work, under difficult circumstances' (Jackson and Holland, 1998: 162). However, this tolerant approach now appears to be disappearing, and at a time when expectations of user involvement in the sector, including board membership, are also growing (Locke *et al.*, 2001). As Abzug and Galaskiewicz (2001) note, boards may be 'crucibles of expertise or symbols of local identities'. In a period of conflicting pressures, 'trusting the trustees' on voluntary boards itself becomes an important governance issue.

Three arguments underpin this chapter. First, that the collective responsibility model may be at variance with many boards' practice, because of differential skills, interests and time pressures among board members. Second, that the prescriptive approach to boards' financial decision-making promoted from within the sector, offering a trust- and team-based approach, provides an equally idealised governance picture, which may create unrealistic expectations of practice and diminish boards' sense of achievement. Third, that the development and direction of accounting regulations for charities will focus boards' attention on risk aversion rather than risk taking.

The first two arguments suggest that operational realities in non-profit boards are such that considerable divergence from 'official' pronouncements on board functioning may occur. For some organisations, divergence from the 'official' norm (for example, board members wholly reliant on their staff for financial strategy) may enable the organisation to keep going. In others, tacit agreement between trustees that only some will contribute to the detail of financial decision-making may ensure retention of trustees with other relevant backgrounds and skills. This perception of board functioning as being less than perfect need not be regarded as a basis for sectoral criticism. Rather, it reflects a pragmatic streak in non-profits, aimed at 'getting the work done'; and a degree of robustness in organisational processes, despite operating outside the official blueprint. In some small organisations especially, this may reflect a fight for survival, when external prescriptions seem an irrelevant burden.

In such situations, it seems imperative for board members to be trusted to come as near to conformance with legal requirements and governmentally or sector-prescribed 'best practice' as is compatible with the organisation's local environment, and operating contingencies. However, an increasingly demanding accounting regime points to boards accepting the diminution of public trust, and in return, operating conservatively and cautiously, subject to greater external control and regulation.

This chapter extends agency theory by casting trustees as 'agents' (as well as representing 'principals'), subject to review and control of their behaviour. The perspective is supported by the Charity Commission's view of its role as deliverer of a charity sector, operating to publicly set standards and meeting the public's interests. In the widest sense, then, the public may be seen to 'own' charities, in addition to subsidising them through tax relief. This view of trustees as agents, and thus the focus of scrutiny, may be contested on two grounds. First, where trustee boards see themselves as essentially private bodies (notably some trusts and foundations), where external scrutiny is seen as unwarranted. Second, where trustees subscribe to a partnership working style with the organisation's managers, blurring the lines of organisation responsibility while jointly working towards organisation goals. Here, trustees operate more in accordance to stewardship theory ('trustees and managers behaving well') than with agency theory ('trustees and managers behaving badly'). However, the view of trustees as agents accountable to a wider public seems set to continue and is confirmed by the announcement of yet further funding, to give the Charity Commission a 'keener regulatory edge' (NGO Finance, 2000: 1).

Boards' financial decision-making: the case for control

Public disaffection with charities as a lever for change

Public concern regarding charity probity and efficiency provides one rationale for increasing the regulation of charities. Mayo (1999: 5) states: 'trust in charities is at an all time low'. In 1998, a MORI poll for the Charity Commission found 74 per cent of the 'general public' agreeing that 'there needs to be tighter control over the laws governing charity affairs'. It is difficult to know whether declining public confidence has arisen from an improved regulatory focus on charities; or from increased awareness of charity failures. Either way, the Charity Commission's role as regulator for charities in England and Wales is complex; with apparently heightened public expectations for the Commission to intervene in charity affairs. For example, its 1999/2000 Annual Report presents survey findings showing a widespread public perception that there are 'too many charities'; with the implicit assumption that the Commission could and should 'do something' in response.

The regulatory role of the Charity Commission

Of the estimated 500,000 voluntary organisations, approximately 180,000 come under the supervision of the Commission.[1] While by number of organisations, the Commission is a minority regulator, by organisation income it is more significant, with registered charities having a combined income of £24 billion; and tax concessions estimated at over £1 billion (Randall and Williams, 2001). The nature of charity activity as a voluntary act, often deriving from people's passionately held beliefs, may make that regulatory role difficult; evidenced, for example, in disputes with charities' founders. Acting simultaneously as regulator and adviser, the Commission's recent focus has been on charity performance 'improvement'. In its 1999/2000 *Annual Report*, its objectives include to 'improve the governance, accountability, efficiency and effectiveness of charities' (Charity Commission, 2001: 1). Hitherto known for its rare use of intervention powers, this is changing as its monitoring and investigative activities gain in prominence, and funding for this increases.

Commission inquiries – 'what boards do and do not do'

It is from the reports of the Commission's inquiries that some of the complexities of 'what boards do' in relation to financial decision-making emerge. The Commission's assessment of the most problematic areas are those of fundraising, trustee benefits and charities' relations with trading subsidiaries. The 1999/2000 report shows inquiries among 255 charities investigated resulting in the protection or repayment of over £25 m of charitable money, at risk of embezzlement or misuse. Past examples range from the overtly fraudulent (a founder running an organisation alone, inventing an entire trustee group) to the simply struggling (an organisation needing help to wind up, where original trustees had died and none found to replace them, leaving one remaining trustee and a dormant organisation). Publication of inquiry outcomes on the web includes reference to the 'wider learning' arising; although the extent of dissemination of this learning, and its recognition within organisations, are uncertain.

The Commission's inquiry into Integrate Services, a charity providing services for people with disabilities, represents a governance landmark, given its publication in full on the web. Here, allegations included financial irregularities and misappropriation by the (named) chief executive, assets applied outside the charity's purposes, and concern over administrative systems. The inquiry resulted in closure and another charity taking over its work. Though the trustees are not named in this inquiry, the level of detail now being provided has the potential of becoming a trustee 'name and shame' register.

From charity monitoring work, boards' sins of omission and commission are highlighted, including the widespread failure by 50 per cent of charities to provide Annual Returns and Accounts within a ten-month period; the discovery of an example of wrongful trustee remuneration; the payment to a solicitors' firm where one trustee was a partner and the subsequent repayment to the charity of some £40,000. Yet the question of where trustee remuneration *is* seen as appropriate (even if not legal) is, ironically, highlighted elsewhere in the report. Reviewing its public consultation on the topic, the Commission reports 'some sympathy' among respondents, for the view that trustees 'should be paid for any professional work they provide for the charity, on top of their work as trustees' – perhaps the ultimate financial governance tangle.

Changing accounting and reporting regulations

The clearest sign of governmental intervention in strengthening the boards' role as financial controller is shown in developments in charity accounting regulations, the 'Statement of Recommended Practice' (SORP). From a slow start, following Bird and Morgan-Jones' (1981) report on charity accounts, showing wide variations in practice, the pace of change has quickened, and the demands on disclosure increased. The introduction of the SORP in 1988, providing a common framework for charity accounts, appears to have been largely ignored by the sector. In 1995, regulations requiring a common framework operating on fund accounting principles, became mandatory for all charities with an income over £250,000. In 2000, the revised SORP's title, 'Accounting and Reporting by Charities', indicated a further shift in board control; with the new requirement for trustees to provide 'confirmation that major risks facing the charity have been identified and steps taken to mitigate them'.

The implications of these requirements are permeating trustee briefings run by chartered accounting firms with specialist charity units, and are seen as wide-ranging. One firm reports that the risk management statement requirement from trustees is 'the sting in the tail'; a requirement that 'is relatively onerous and should not be taken lightly by any charity' (Buzzacott, 2001). Another regards this as a 'spillover' from the pressures for governance improvement in the for-profit sector (Haysmacintyre, 2001). As a result, boards are likely to become more risk adverse, adopting an increasingly 'custodial' approach to decision-making (conserving funds, acting cautiously and possibly less innovatively), as suggested by Harrow and Palmer (1998).

Control and an agency theory approach to boards' financial decision-making

Such interventionism is in line with an agency theory perspective, where organisation relations are characterised by high monitoring and low trust levels (Jensen and Meckling, 1976; Waterman and Meier, 1998). As discussed in the Introduction, agency theory, assuming divergent interests between a firm's owners and managers, imposes controlling mechanisms on managers, who may be expected to act first in their own best interests; one of the 'economic approaches to governance ... which depict subordinates as individualistic, opportunistic and self-serving' (Davis *et al.*, 1997: 20). Mayer *et al.* (1995) restate agency theory as the unwillingness to be vulnerable; and the formalisation of risk assessment reporting in the revised SORP regulations supports the growing primacy of agency theory as the prevailing view of governance, where financial decisions are concerned.

The application of agency theory in studies of non-profit organisations has been limited. Olsen's (2000) work is a striking example, relating to boards of private universities in the USA and their need to monitor managers. His prescriptions for board practices contrast to those widely advised in UK contexts, such as limiting board tenure:

> [L]ong tenured boards are less likely to ... feel under the control of the existing management team and therefore able to do a better job of monitoring. Management, being more closely watched and assisted, is able and willing to do a better job of bringing resources to the institution.
>
> (Olsen, 2000: 293)

The Introduction highlighted the difficulty in applying an agency perspective to governance in public and non-profit bodies, because of ambiguity in identifying the principals or owners; in the case of charities, the founders, trustees, beneficiaries or members. The Charity Commission's over-riding aim, 'to give the public confidence in the integrity of charities', suggests some sort of indirect 'ownership' of charities by the public generally (Charity Commission, 2001: para. 1). Carver (2001: 55) notes that in such organisations 'ownership may be more akin to the "moral" ownership of social contract than it is to a kind of legal ownership'. A public 'ownership' view of charities could further support an agency theory perspective in framing the prevailing governance regulations, even though the manifestly private nature of trustees' choices in taking on such obligations might challenge this. The longer-term implications for boards of an agency-based approach remain to be seen. While agency theory does not specify total control of agents, it is possible that some trustees, burdened by the pressures of decision-making in their charity's best interests, may prefer to operate in the risk-averse context imposed by the latest SORP regulations, and actively *choose* agency governance prescriptions.

Boards' financial decision-making: the case for trust

Complexity, practicality and generosity demanding a trust-based approach to governance

The very complexity and diversity of issues encompassed within boards' financial decision-making make the case for their governance structures to incorporate trust-based features. The resource implications of not doing so, both for regulator and regulated are open-ended, and trust-based approaches may (if they work) be more cost-effective. The complexity of boards' financial role can be seen by examining their core tasks: they must ensure that there are proper policies and procedures in place governing their financial responsibilities, notably their exercise of budgetary control in relation to expenditure, financial and physical assets, human resources costs, and income generation. Yet their central task – seeing there is sufficient cash and keeping to budget – is only a small part of their work. This is likely to include wider strategy formulation and financial objective setting, effective fund management, optimising resource use and safeguarding assets (see Palmer, 2001).

The complexity of boards' work is further illustrated by research exploring board roles which suggests that financial aspects thread through all board activities; and not just those which have an overtly financial focus. For example, Jackson and Holland's (1998: 160) research that identified 'six dimensions of board competency' makes no separation between financial responsibilities and those relating to boards' other domains. On a practical level, this degree of complexity suggests that there may be limited value in those trustee training programmes which concentrate on the acquisition of overtly financially oriented skills, somewhat akin to quasi-accounting technician courses. In a period when pressures on recruitment and retention of trustees are unremitting, particularly for smaller charities (see Chapter 10, and Cornforth, 2001), it seems both churlish and possibly downright dangerous to imply that these highly prized board members are *not* trustworthy (the perspective taken when trustees are themselves seen as agents).

The very heterogeneity of the voluntary sector, containing bodies with a myriad of organisational purposes, activities, styles of working, histories and plans, points to a further rationale for highlighting trust in board members as a cornerstone of the sector's practice. That is, that the cost of doing otherwise may become prohibitive. While the Charity Commission reports its safeguarding funds of around £25 million in the sector annually, its own costs are rising fast towards this figure. Self-regulation, therefore, as the outcome of trusting boards to act responsibly, while acting flexibly, may have the added benefit of costing less than externally imposed regulatory systems.

One outcome of stringent self-regulation may be the elusive but important notion of an organisation's reputation, as a safeguard against errant behaviour and a guarantor of appropriate practice. That reputation may reside variously in trustees, other volunteers, staff, organisational history or notable beneficiaries. Boards may be expected to know that their organisation's reputation is a valuable if intangible commodity, with which they are entrusted and which opportunistic, irrational or inappropriate decision-making will endanger. Thus, Ortmann and Schlesinger (1997: 102) explore 'reputational ubiquity' in non-profits and for-profits alike, considering it 'important to note that reputation might still be a superior enforcement mechanism given the alternatives (principal–agent enforcement)'. There is a lack of research to confirm or challenge this argument. Nor does there seem to be research to explore the degree to which hitherto 'reputable' organisations recover from reputation loss and whether and how their internal control systems are modified or changed. On balance, it seems that reliance on retaining an organisation's 'good name' is a necessary but not sufficient means of controlling trustees or their managers.

Above all, however, the case for 'trusting trustees' may be made based on respect for trustees' generosity, as special types of volunteer. If altruism, and a desire for 'service' without gain (except perhaps of the reputational kind) are accepted within society as trustees' prime motivators, then it is both reasonable and rational to expect 'good' behaviour from these 'good' people. Such paragons may be in short supply, being the view of one respondent in Harris and Rochester's (2001: 10) research on governance in the Jewish voluntary sector: 'serving on a voluntary body was something that nice people used to do but they don't seem to do it any more'. An alternative perspective on the struggle to recruit and retain trustees, however, is to express communal gratitude that there are still 'so many' prepared to take on these roles; and thus to expect a resulting high standard of trustee behaviour. Some key factors motivating board membership may themselves supply the springs for the enduring reliability of trustees' work. For example, Harris and Rochester (2001: 7) suggest 'the importance of family connections in motivating the participants in the study came through very clearly in the data'; this 'going beyond drawing them in . . . to remain involved – often for long periods – and to take the position of chair . . . frequently an onerous . . . commitment'.

It is unclear as to the extent of familial connections among charity trustees. At worst, these may lead to nepotism, or more often a sense of 'inherited duty' in relation to board membership, so that trustees who 'inherit' a family 'seat' may become distanced from or even indifferent to the charities on whose boards they serve. At best, however, such family traditions represent the very essence of the 'stewardship' notion of trusteeship, and the value of further research on their degree of influence in sustaining the good practices of boards, in faith community organisations especially, is indicated.

The prescriptive literature on boards' work

One mechanism to help sustain trust in boards is for them to undertake regular processes of self-review or assessment. The extensive prescriptive literature from within the voluntary sector, setting out measures and models against which board members, collectively and individually, may assess the extent of their 'good practice' provides for this (see, for example, Kirkland, 1994). The rather worryingly titled *Fit to Govern: A Ten Point Health Check for Organisations* (NCVO, 1992b), for example, provides a comprehensive overview of board and organisation practice, including 'capacity to govern', 'stakeholder participation' and 'financial health'. The last item in particular begs a whole series of questions, not least that 'the board as a whole is competent in taking financial decisions'. From a different perspective, the Association of Chief Executives of Voluntary Organisations' (ACEVO) *Model Code of Conduct for Trustees* (ACEVO, 2000) provides another 'gold standard'. These two examples have value where they confirm the intricacies of board responsibilities. Yet the standards of board behaviour which they advocate may be recognised by many trustees as so idealised as to be unattainable. Given trustee recruitment problems, it is important that trustees should not see themselves or their organisations as totally inadequate against such prescriptions. A public acceptance of possible board fallibility, bound up with the notion of board members as volunteers, may act as an antidote to board members' perceptions of inadequacy, when measured against such prescriptions.

This prescriptive literature also often promotes an implicit professional-isation of boards' work (for example, with the case for appraisal systems for boards). The question arises, however, as to what effect these prescriptive models have had on boards' work. Where, if at all, are there known cases of boards being improved by these models or damaged by subsequent resignations? Does their existence promote or inhibit discussion on board functioning? Jackson and Holland (1998: 161) cite Ashford (1989) in suggesting that self-assessment yields inaccurate results, in particular since 'most boards have vague and inconsistent expectations of trustee performance'. The extent to which such approaches have improved board governance and members' dispositions towards their multiple roles is an important, if contentious, research topic in its own right, which has not been adequately researched.

Trust among trustees and the applicability of stewardship theory

This prescriptive literature conforms to the legal view of boards, where members are expected to act jointly and are equally liable for decisions. Although blandishments to a wavering would-be member on the lines of 'don't worry – you won't have to sit on the finance sub-committee' may be made, trustees are unable to delegate responsibility for their decisions to their 'finance sub-committee' colleagues. Yet, given the variations in financial backgrounds and interests likely among trustees, implicit delegation of this sort is highly likely to take place.

The degree and nature of this dependency are a key finding in some empirical research on boards and financial issues, discussed below. Promotion of a 'corporate' view of boards may be to miss how, where and why board members reach the financial decisions which they make, that is *within* boards, there will be 'leaders' and 'followers' on financial issues especially. For this implicit delegation to work well, it can be argued that members as individuals have to trust each other; as well as trusting any staff they employ. A widespread criticism of boards is that they recruit 'in their own likeness' (see NCVO, 1992 and Cornforth, 2001 for trustee profiles). Yet to do so may be a necessary pre-condition for establishing trust – or at least confidence – among board members. 'To what extent do you trust your fellow trustees?' is a question which the authors have never asked trustees directly in any of their research programmes but it is one that may need to be asked, if the realities of financial decision-making among voluntary boards are to be better understood.

In making a case for trust rather than control (or mistrust) of trustee boards to underpin regulatory systems, the literature on stewardship theory is apposite. Here, the personal needs of individuals are met by the shared achievement of goals. The Introduction denotes this as a 'partner-ship model', where specialist board members add particular value and joint manager/board working relations are characterised as team activities. For Davis *et al.* (1997: 20), stewardship theory 'depicts subordinates as collectivists, pro-organisational and trustworthy'. However, public misgivings seem unwilling to allow for the vulnerability and ambiguity that partnership may bring. Possibly, stewardship theory may make for complacency as well as trust. The contrast is at its most clear when Davis *et al.* (1997: 24) argue that 'a steward's autonomy should be deliberately extended to maximise the benefits of a steward, because he or she can be trusted ... indeed control can be potentially counterproductive'. It remains to be seen whether the Charity Commission's increased regulatory stance, and the latest SORP requirements, have this effect.

Financial decision-making by boards: some empirical research findings

Trustees' reliance on the professional standards of paid staff

Research studies in the UK voluntary sector illustrate the expected complexities of boards' financial role, challenging the notions of collective decision-making and the regulator's expectations (as depicted in the growing trustee guidance and 'good practice' literature from the Commission) that trustees will be pro-active in their decision-making. Gambling and Jones (1996: 41), for example, concluded that the annual reports and accounts of charities, on which the initial SORP reforms had concentrated, were 'only as good as the administrative systems which underpin them'. Their research in eighteen organisations of varying sizes and purposes found 'no examples of total ignorance' among trustees of their role, in contrast to the landmark NCVO study (NCVO, 1992), where trustees' lack of awareness of their roles was highlighted. The diversity of names given by charities to their committees and sub-committees dealing with finance was identified as potentially misleading for external observers (and perhaps for some trustees themselves).

Importantly, Gambling and Jones found trustees tending to 'place little reliance on their personal participation in budgetary control exercises; many feel entitled to rely on the professional standards and care of the auditors and senior paid officials' (1996: 43). This raises the question as to the extent to which this 'entitlement' drew on well-placed trust, unwise complacency, or was, more pragmatically, the result of pressures on trustee time and the assessment that 'seniority' of staff validated their information and advice. That board members do internally differentiate in financial leadership terms is suggested by these researchers' own differentiation by their references to the 'senior trustees' whom they interviewed.

Trustees' management information needs in small charities

A similar pattern of dependence on paid staff or fellow trustees was identified in research on trustees' management information needs in small charities (Harrow *et al.*, 1999). Survey research among sixty trustees of five charities, working in child care and disability fields, showed trustees' use of management information was highly dependent on its prior provision by paid staff. There was little evidence of trustees seeking out management information, or scrutinising it to examine the organisation's performance, though all were active and thriving. Trustees reported feeling neither over-burdened with information, nor 'in the dark' as a result of the financial management information they received. They rated that information as 'very effective', though lacking organisational support (such as internal audit) to assess that information's integrity and rarely looked to wider sources for comparisons of their charities' performance. Nor did trustees express a willingness to increase the amount of information which they received; since this might 'adversely affect their input into the charity' (Harrow *et al.*, 1999: 166). This was interpreted by the researchers as trustees seeing their roles primarily in terms of upholding the organisation's mission and values, rather than detailed scrutiny of its performance.

Subsequent case study research in three of the organisations confirmed how trustees view and use the management information supplied to them. The lack of pro-activity from trustees led the researchers to depict them as '*reactive reviewers*' of management information rather than 'active users' or inquirers (Harrow *et al.*, 1999: 167). Similarly Otto (Chapter 7), found the chairs of voluntary organisations playing a largely reactive role. In one organisation, information was screened to be commensurate with trustee expertise. The chief worker provided financial information according to 'what I feel they should know, what they would want to know, and what they ought to know' (Vincent *et al.*, 1998: 349). Widespread trust between board members and between board members and their paid staff was reported. This was further confirmed by the tendency to enrol new trustees, those who were friends of existing trustees, because of their familiarity with board members as well as with the charity's work.

Effective board–management relations

It is possible that the emphasis in the above study was too strongly on the *formal* management information with which trustees worked. Cornforth and Edwards (1998: 45) in case study research on effective board–management relations in public and voluntary settings, draw attention to the extent to which informal contacts and organisational access can enhance board effectiveness. In one voluntary organisation, they found that informal relations between one board member and the CEO led to the former's acquisition of 'significant information' about the organisation's management 'beyond that contained in formal meeting papers'. This board member occupied a dominant position on the board, because of her perceived knowledge and expertise. The board tended to rely on her judgement concerning financial and management issues. This study also confirmed the heavy dependence by the board on information supplied by paid staff; in this case, the finance officer, who reported that 'If I was one of them, I'd want to know more but they aren't very finance oriented' (Cornforth and Edwards, 1998: 59). Here the degree of dependence by trustees on the viability of the organisation's internal financial systems was also such as to imply, if not board compla-cency, then a 'looking away' from the realities of the situation; with the finance officer describing the situation as 'a rather blind trust' in her. Findings in these cases suggest also the existence of dominant coalitions within boards in relation to financial decision-making where groups within the group take the lead; though the extent to which such coalitions exist and are relatively stable or shifting provides a further issue for research.

With their research pointing to expertise as a crucial factor affecting the quality of board members' contribution to financial issues, Cornforth and Edwards identify the need for boards to make greater efforts to recruit and make use of accountants and other financial management spe-cialists. For this to be achieved, the debate about trustee remuneration may need revisiting. Wise puts the case pragmatically: 'the payment of remuneration would significantly increase the willingness of *suitable man-agers* to serve as trustees' (2001: 56; italics in original). In such situations, however, levels of trust at personal levels among boards may be increas-ingly substituted by trust between board members as professionals, perhaps with an associated expectation of boards increasingly challenging their key employees.

Small organisations and their variety of funding regimes

In a study on the impact of funding regimes on the survival of small volun-tary organisations over a ten-year period, a range of expected and unex-pected financial decisions by boards were revealed (Alcock *et al.*, 1999). Sixteen case studies, in London and Sheffield, explored boards' survival in the context of three prevailing funding regimes: where organisations had one major funder; where they had major and minor funders; and where they had funding from a variety of bodies. However, no one funding regime proved more likely than another to sustain the organisations; and other contingencies, most prominently the leadership skills of the chief (often lone) paid worker, were key indicators of organisational survival. This was at its most evident in one service-providing organisation, whose temporary key worker had revived the organisation's fortune, despite – or perhaps because of – major and significant gaps in her board. She commented: 'Our partners and funders ... expect a treasurer's signature and want a personal relationship with one ... [but] no treasurer is better than a bad one' (Alcock *et al.*, 1999). The option of 'trustee-free' organisations (see Harrow and Palmer, 1995) does not exist for charities but it is possible that there are many more small organisations managing or struggling with such gaps in trustee ranks (and some of them doing well).

Boards displayed a variety of interesting responses to risk. Thus an arts organisation rejected professional advice for the installation of cameras to deter thefts in its bookshop as contrary to the organisation's ethos, being likely to deter the community from entering the bookshop. By contrast, financial growth rather than loss was the trigger for a trustee board to close down an organisation, just as it finally achieved its decade-long goal of statutory funding. Here, the dramatic rise in demand for the organisation's services, combined with an unfortunate melting away of volunteer help, pressurised the board to closure, to the evident shock within its community and anger of its paid worker. Ironically, the then chair later reflected that the *arrival* rather than *loss* of funding was the source of change: 'it is possible that if we had not had this funding, we would still be thriving' (Alcock *et al.*, 1999: 35). In both cases, it could be argued that while trustees were not necessarily 'behaving badly', they could be seen as behaving unpredictably and in the latter case, against the grain of public expectations of virtuous, even noble, boards, expected to 'carry on' in difficult circumstances.

Financial decision-making in boards: group or individuals' decisions

The behaviour of individuals on boards, as leaders and as followers, warrants further examination beyond the growth of typologies of trustees' approaches to their roles, which give only a starting point to such exploration (see Harrow and Palmer, 1998). Currently the authors are undertaking pilot research on trustees' responses to organisational 'crises', where these have a marked financial component, drawing on Eitel's (1999) work. The research examines, first of all, the relative prominence of board members as individuals or as a corporate body; and second, the impact if any of qualified finance specialists as trustees or trustee advisers, on the direction of the board's decision-making. This approach is based on the designation of the trustees as 'agents' for the wider public benefit, as well as principals, monitoring the work of others. Using purposive and then snowball sampling techniques to identify organisations, the authors are using participant observation methods, supplemented by trustee interviews. A total of ten case studies is planned.

The following summaries from the case studies completed so far illustrate two of the 'crisis' scenarios. In 'case A', the fortuitous recruitment

of an accountant on the trustee board of a declining professional
association, who when 'spotted' by the President, and diverted to a new
income-generating committee rather than the inevitable 'finance sub-
committee', led to organisation 'turnaround', within two years. Here, the
accountant was pleased to have been cast in a positive role, having
dreaded the 'cost-cutting' role which he felt sure board members expected of him. In 'case B', board and staff failures occurred in a youth
organisation, arising largely from historical closeness between the organisation and the church which founded it, and worsened by the treasurer's
absence through ill health. Failure to comply with the rules governing
access to expected EU funding, and mispayments from church rather
than organisation funds, led to an emergency trustees' meeting where the
bank manager offered to arrange temporary overdraft facilities, if under-
written by personal guarantees from the trustees. The Bishop, as chair of
trustees, wrote his cheque on the spot and his fellow trustees followed suit.

This pilot research illustrates a variety of leadership and followership
patterns on boards and a variety of board responses to the inputs of financial specialists, including emphasis on issues of trust and challenges to
boards to demonstrate their 'trustworthy' credentials. Thus, case A illustrates that the recruitment of finance specialists onto boards will not
necessarily produce expected outcomes; or what might be described as
'mainstream' accountant behaviour. In case B, extrication from a 'well-
meaning mess', through a leadership intervention that was critical but still
relatively low-risk, raises questions on the extent to which charity trustees
in England are personally funding charities' shortfalls and debts. This
area requires research attention in its own right, despite likely problems in
gaining access. The major contrast here is with practices on many US
boards, where board members' personal giving and their organisation
supervision are linked. This is illustrated by a case in a Florida college,
where wealthy board members, who 'did not ask enough questions about
the school's finances', themselves funded an endowment shortfall of
approximately $16 million (NCNB, 2000).

Conclusion

This review of 'what boards do' in relation to financial decision-making
has illustrated board members' dilemmas, as the regulator seeks high
levels of board responsiveness to increasingly formalised guidance; and as
prescriptive practice models critique those boards' activities. The tensions
facing boards are exemplified in decisions which may be regarded as
unexpected or out of line with 'good' board practice, for example, insti-
gating peremptory organisation closure or rejecting professional advice
where this conflicts with a wider organisation ethos. Despite the limited
empirical research base, one conclusion which may be drawn is that
boards' financial decision-making continues to show a wide range of

board behaviours. These may be divergent from, as well as convergent with, prescriptive decision-making frameworks and the regulator's perception of good practice. This is not to argue that some trustees set out deliberately to avoid the regulatory framework which surrounds them (though some may do so). Rather, that the diversity within and across the non-profit sector is a limitation on achieving standardised board practices and preferences, where financial decisions are concerned.

The application of stewardship theory to boards' financial decision-making offers a perspective on board practices that is both attractive and realistic. Its assumptions of mutual trust between organisation players provide an appropriate value base from which to sustain an apparently shrinking trustee pool. It recognises implicitly the heavy demands of trusteeship, which may be handled to some extent by close working with, and dependence on, organisations' senior managers. It requires that trustee motivations are respected not doubted and suggests that where overall trustee numbers are declining, those 'staying on' are making even greater contributions than hitherto. The disparate nature of – and disparate needs of – organisations across the non-profits spectrum points to the importance of achieving a balance between trust and control-oriented regulatory frameworks. The one emphasises the immense personal contributions made by trustees, the other the legitimacy of external attention on trustee and organisational practices. Yet no blueprint for achieving such balance exists; and its necessary accompaniment, accepting the failures of boards from time to time, seems increasingly out of tune with these monitored and audited times.

With the England and Wales regulator wedded to a 'one size fits all' approach to charity governance, boards' financial decision-making seems therefore increasingly likely to conform to an agency-theory driven governance model or at least to give the impression of it. This is bound to increase even further those pressures on boards with significant trustee recruitment problems. It raises questions as to what pressures might be brought to bear on this approach to regulation, if boards began to resign *en masse,* for example, following boards' compliance with the new risk assessment requirements. One practical barrier standing in the way of this scenario appears to be the very large extent to which organisations fail to submit their accounts and reports to the regulator! While this may be seen an unlikely scenario, a variation, the gradual drift away by board members, causing problems of lack of continuity and leaving gaps in organisational knowledge and memory, will be more difficult to track. It may also be more damaging, continuing to give the impression that boards are generally functioning well.

An ever-strengthening appreciation and 'pushing' of the financial specialist as trustee carries another governance dilemma. This is, how to enforce a fully corporate and shared board 'view' of financial decisions, when such prized trustees will come with skills that are designed to set them apart from fellow trustees, and may receive (if not expect) a high degree of board member deference? If this deference becomes further enshrined in prescriptive materials, then at best, the need to pay attention to the degree of internal trust between board members may be more fully recognised. Furthermore, the unrealistic expectations that all board members are fully cognisant of the details of financial decision-making will be opened up for debate. The irony of professionalising boards, while blocking their remuneration, is further heightened given wider society debates in which professionals' roles and power over decision-making are now widely challenged. Agency theory may sit uneasily with much of the voluntaristic spirit that is lauded in and vital for the sector; but its apparent ability to protect trustees and secure a public recognition of acceptable practices in charities makes it most likely to become the only governance 'show in town'.

Note

1 Figures taken from p. 1 of the Charity Commission's main website, www.charity-commission.gov.uk, accessed May 2001.

References

Abzug, R. and Galaskiewicz, J. (2001) 'Non-profit Boards: Crucibles of Expertise or Symbols of Local Identities', *Non-profit and Voluntary Sector Quarterly*, 30, 1, 51–73.

ACEVO (2000) *Model Code of Conduct for Trustees*, Harrow: Association of Chief Executives in Voluntary Organisations.

Alcock, P., Harrow, J., Macmillan, R., Vincent, J. and Pearson, S. (1999) *Making Funding Work: Funding Regimes and Local Voluntary Organisations*, York: York Publishing.

Ashford, S. (1989) 'Self-Assessments in Organisations', *Research in Organisational Behaviour*, 11, 133–174.

Bird, P. and Morgan-Jones, P. (1981) *Financial Reporting by Charities*, London: ICSA.

Buzzacott Co. (2001) *Risk Management and the Revised Charity*. London: SORP.

Carver, J. (2001) 'A Theory of Governing the Public's Business: Redesigning the Jobs of Boards, Councils and Commissions', *Public Management Review*, 3, 1, 53–72.

Charity Commission (2001) *Annual Report, 1999/2000*, available from: website: www.charity-commission.gov.uk/annualreport.htm

Cornforth, C. (2001) *Recent Trends in Charity Governance and Trusteeship: The Results of a Survey of Governing Bodies of Charities*, London: National Council for Voluntary Organisations.

Cornforth, C. and Edwards, C. (1998) *Good Governance: Developing Effective Board–Management Relations in Public and Voluntary Organisations*, London: The Chartered Institute of Management Accountants.

Davis, J. H., Schoorman, F. D. and Donaldson, L. (1997) 'Towards a Stewardship Theory of Management', *Academy of Management Review*, 22, 1, 20–48.

Eitel, D. F. (1999) 'How Public and Non-Profit Boards Communicate During

Crisis', paper presented at Third International Research Symposium on Public Management, Aston Business School, Aston University, Birmingham, 25–26 March.

Gambling, T. and Jones, R. (1996) 'Financial Governance of Charity', *Management Accounting*, 74, 41–44.

Harris, M. and Rochester, C. (2001) *Governance in the Jewish Voluntary Sector*, Research Report No. 1. 'Planning for Jewish Communities' research programme, London: Institute for Jewish Policy Research.

Harrow, J. and Palmer, P. (1995) 'Some Alternative Agendas for Charity Governance', paper presented at Association of Chief Executives in National Voluntary Organisations, National Conference, June.

Harrow, J. and Palmer, P. (1998) 'Reassessing Charity Trusteeship in Britain? Towards Conservatism Not Change', *Voluntas: International Journal of Voluntary and Non-profit Organisations*, 9, 2, 171–186.

Harrow, J., Palmer, P. and Vincent, J. (1999) 'Management Information Needs and Perceptions in Smaller Charities; An Exploratory Study', *Financial Accountability and Management*, 15, 2, 155–172.

Haysmacintyre (2001) *Charity Briefing: The Risk Assessment Process and SORP 2000*, Southampton House, 371 High Holborn, London WC1V 7WL.

Jackson, D. K. and Holland, T. P. (1998) 'Measuring the Effectiveness of Non-profit Boards', *Non-profit and Voluntary Sector Quarterly*, 27, 2, 159–182.

Jensen, M. C. and Meckling, W. H. (1976) 'Theory of the Firm: Managerial Behaviour, Agency Costs and Ownership Structure', *Journal of Financial Economics*, 3, 305–360.

Kirkland, K. (1994) *The Good Trustee Guide*, London: The National Council for Voluntary Organisations.

Locke, M., Robson, P. and Howlett, S. (2001) 'Users: At the Centre or on the Sidelines?' in M. Harris and C. Rochester (eds) *Voluntary Organisations and Social Policy in Britain: Perspectives on Change and Choice*, London: Palgrave.

Mayer, R. C., Davis, J. H. and Schoorman, F. D. (1995) 'An Integrative Model of Organisational Trust', *Academy of Management Review*, 20, 709–734.

Mayo, E. (1999) *Fundraising Costs*, London: Director of Social Change.

National Centre for Non-profit Boards (2000) *Board Member Online*, 9, 10 December. Available online at: www.ncnb.org.boardmember/case.

NCVO (1992a) *On Trust: Increasing the Effectiveness of Charity Trustees and Management Committees*, London: National Council for Voluntary Organisations.

NVCO (1992b) *Fit to Govern: A Ten Point Health Check for Organisations*, London: National Council for Voluntary Organisations.

NGO Finance (2000) *Commission to Clamp Down on Late Filers*, Charity Information Service, November: 1.

Olsen, D. E. (2000) 'Agency Theory in the Not-for-Profit Sector: Its Role at Independent Colleges', *Non-profit and Voluntary Sector Quarterly*, 29, 2, 280–296.

Ortmann, A. and Schlesinger, M. (1997) 'Trust, Repute and the Role of Non-profit Enterprise', *Voluntas*, 8, 2, 97–119.

Palmer, P. (2001) *The Good Financial Management Training Guide*, London: National Council for Voluntary Organisations.

Randall, A. and Williams, S. (2001) *Tax and Charities*, London: Jordans.

Vincent, J., Palmer, P. and Harrow, J. (1998) 'Trustee Decision-Making in Small Charities', *Nonprofit and Voluntary Sector Marketing*, 3, 4, 337–352.

Waterman, R. and Meier, K. J. (1998) 'Principal–Agent Models: An Expansion?', *Journal of Public Administration Research and Theory*, 8, 2, 173–203.

Wise, D. (2001) 'Would the Payment of Market Rates for Non-Executive Directors Strengthen Charity Governance?', *International Journal of Non-profit and Voluntary Sector Marketing*, 6,1, 49–64.

6 The role of boards in small voluntary organisations

Colin Rochester

The heterogeneity of the voluntary sector

On both sides of the Atlantic the role and behaviour of the unpaid boards that govern the activities of non-profit and voluntary sector organisations have been an early and enduring preoccupation of the scholars who specialise in the study of the third sector (Kramer, 1965; Zald, 1969; Harris, 1989). The result has been a substantial body of literature which underlines the importance of governing bodies; exhibits a high degree of agreement about their key functions or roles (Widmer, 1993; Harris, 1996); highlights problems with the successful implementation of the board role; and provides us with explanatory theories for the frequency with which boards fail to carry out their key functions successfully (for example, Kramer, 1985; Middleton, 1987; Harris, 1989, 1993; Herman, 1989; Wood, 1992).

The weakness of this body of literature, however, is that it tends to treat issues of governance as generic. The nature of the board's role and the issues faced in implementing it are seen as essentially the same, regardless of variations in the size or function of non-profit and voluntary sector organisations or of the environments in which they operate. One recent study (Harris, 2001), however, has noted that the experience of board members in local agencies varied significantly from that of their counterparts in national organisations. A recent survey by Cornforth and Simpson (see Chapter 10 in this book and Cornforth, 2001) found that the ability of charities in England and Wales to recruit and support board members was related to their size. More generally, there is a growing acknowledgement of the heterogeneity of the third sector (Klausen, 1995) and an appreciation that the differences between organisations within the sector may be of similar importance to the differences between them and organisations in the other sectors.

Much of this debate has focused on the differences between two kinds of voluntary organisation. On the one hand, there are the well-resourced, formally organised and staff-led 'big battalions' that have 'accounted for significant numbers of paid employees and made major contributions to the economy' (Salamon, 1998: 89). On the other are the multitude of 'grassroots associations' (Smith, 1997a; 1997b) which are small, relatively informal and entirely or largely dependent on the voluntary work of their members. These two very different kinds of organisation can be seen as the opposite ends of a spectrum in between which we can find a range of organisational forms with varying levels of formality and professionalism (Rochester and Billings, 2000).

It is the opening premise of this chapter that the nature of the governance role and the ways in which it can be successfully implemented will differ according to the characteristics of the voluntary organisations concerned. This will be explored by looking at how the challenge of developing and maintaining an effective board is experienced and addressed in small or 'micro' voluntary organisations which can be seen as 'on the cusp' between grassroots associations and fully-fledged formal voluntary agencies (Rochester, 1998).

The empirical basis for the discussion is a study undertaken by the author and colleagues at the London School of Economics' Centre for Voluntary Organisation between November 1997 and June 1998 in two areas of England. The overall aim of this project, which was funded by the Lloyds TSB Foundation for England and Wales, was to understand the distinctive characteristics of small agencies in order to provide those who manage and lead them with suggestions about appropriate ways of achieving greater effectiveness. Primary data was collected through semi-structured interviews and focus groups involving the senior staff members and leading board members of twenty-six voluntary agencies with no more than the equivalent of four full-time paid staff. Further interviews were conducted with people who administered funding programmes which assisted small agencies and those who worked with them in a developmental or consultancy role (Rochester, 1999; Rochester *et al.*, 1999).

The chapter will review some of the central findings of the study about the nature of small agencies of this kind, concentrating on the problems associated with what we have called the 'liability of smallness'. It will then look more closely at their experience of recruiting and sustaining an effective governing body; the problems they have encountered in carrying out the work expected of the board; and the nature of the relationship between the board and paid staff. After discussing the ways in which small voluntary organisations have been able to respond to these problems and challenges, the chapter will conclude by suggesting how our understanding of governance can be improved by reflecting on the experience of this particular sub-set of voluntary sector organisations.

Small agencies and the liability of smallness

The agencies studied had a number of features in common. The first of these was, of course, their size. All of them employed at least one member of staff to carry out some of the operational activities of the agency. They were not purely voluntary associations in which the work of the organisation is entirely dependent on the unpaid labour of its members. Very few of them, moreover, came close to our 'ceiling' of the equivalent of four full-time employees. The modest scale of their paid staff resources was reflected in the size of their incomes; the average figure was just under £50,000 per year.

There were, however, some significant variations in the study population. Organisations had been selected to provide as wide a cross-section as possible of different kinds of activity and user groups within the broad field of social welfare. There were variations in the length of time they had been active. The newest was three years old while the oldest had been established twenty-eight years before the study took place. And, while the majority of them were completely 'free-standing' bodies, a significant minority were branches or affiliates of national organisations.

One of the starting points for the study was a belief that the size of small agencies was a matter of choice: that their smallness was not the result of lack of time to get bigger nor the consequence of a failure to grow. With a small number of exceptions the organisations in the study had no ambitions to become larger. It was true that most of them would have preferred a modest increase in their resources but this was seen as providing the means of enabling the organisation to function more comfortably at its existing level of operation rather than creating the conditions for expansion. There were two broad reasons why our informants preferred to preserve the smallness of their agencies. The first of these was that their size was appropriate to the nature and scale of their activities. The manager of a day centre for older people with mental health problems felt she could run the project on the basis of a detailed knowledge of each of the users and their carers, which would not have been possible in a larger organisation. The second reason was a belief that small voluntary organisations had a value of their own and a distinctive contribution to make to the quality of life and collective living conditions. In other words, they had a particular kind of 'expressive dimension' (Mason, 1995) which was as important as their ability to achieve instrumental goals.

The decision that the agency should remain small in order to retain its 'fitness for purpose' and expressive dimension was, however, not without its difficulties. Despite the fact that more than half of the organisations studied had been in existence for ten years and a significant minority had survived for twice that period, one outstanding theme in our study findings was the *vulnerability* of small local agencies. This had both an internal and an external dimension.

Internally the small agencies studied were heavily dependent on the work and commitment of a small number of key individuals. In almost every case the principal role was played by the most senior – sometimes the only – member of the paid staff. Other key people included honorary

officers such as the chair or the treasurer, other members of the governing body and, in some cases, one or two of the organisation's volunteers.
Much of the work of the agency was carried out by a core of people of this
kind – maybe four or five in the larger organisations but as few as one or
two in the smallest – while other people were involved to a far lesser
extent. The key people tended to 'do everything' from driving the
minibus or emptying the dustbins to writing grant applications and lobby-
ing the local authority.

Many of the people who had accepted these heavy responsibilities for
the work of the agency were happy with the extent of their commitment
and enjoyed the variety of the activities in which they were involved.
Senior staff, in particular, willingly made a contribution considerably
above the requirements of their job descriptions or terms of employment.
On the other hand, there were clear risks for the agency when the loss of
one or two key individuals could have far-reaching consequences. And
there were costs for the individuals concerned. In many of the agencies
studied we came across people who had maintained this high level of personal commitment over a number of years but there were clear signs that
this could not be sustained indefinitely. And when individuals felt the
need either to scale down their activities or, more commonly, to give them
up altogether, their decision was often accompanied by feelings of guilt
and failure.

The tendency for the work of the agency – and its survival – to be concentrated in a small number of hands was in a number of cases strengthened by the operation of a cycle which led to a diminishing number of
people taking an increasing share of the workload. An inner group
emerged as people who were seen to have the skills, knowledge, enthusiasm or time volunteered or were persuaded to undertake tasks for the
agency. If they carried out the tasks reliably – and if they derived some satisfaction from doing so – they would be entrusted with other and more
important activities. As their experience and confidence grew, they took
on more and more of the work. In the long run they could find it increasingly difficult to reduce the load. Those outside the inner circle were
reluctant to take over partly because the time commitment had become
significant and partly because they felt that they lacked the knowledge and
experience of those in the inner group. When some of the active minority
eventually left the agency, those who were left tended to find it easier to
take on additional responsibilities rather than to persuade other people to
join the inner group. And the more they did, the greater the disincentive
for potential new members who balked at the workload. In extreme cases
the active members struggled on until, exhausted or 'burned out', they
were forced to drop out and create an organisational crisis.

Externally small agencies were financially vulnerable. Many of them
were heavily dependent on funding from a single source, usually local
government. Typically these funding arrangements were short term and

subject to an annual process of review and renegotiation. At a time of reorganisation of local government and constrained local authority budgets the annual negotiation was a time of high anxiety especially since it was common for the results of the process not to be known until very close to the end of the current funding period. Other sources of income could be unpredictable; one agency with an enviable track record of raising funds from charitable trusts found its income from this source had shown a marked decrease in 1998–99 for no apparent reason. As well as uncertainty about future income, small agencies also tended to have little 'slack' in their budget and very few had significant reserves. As one of our interviewees expressed it, they were operating 'on a knife edge'. In some cases the fragility of their finances meant that small agencies had to make difficult choices such as whether to pay the volunteers' expenses or put petrol in the minibus.

This vulnerability of small agencies had several consequences. In the first place they found it difficult to adopt a long-term or strategic perspective. Uncertainty about future funding undermined long-term planning while the need to take care of everyday operational and support activities left little time and energy for the agency's leaders to develop a strategic view. A second 'liability of smallness' was the restricted range of expertise and skills the small agency could deploy. The knowledge and experience of the small number of active individuals involved were finite and the small scale of the operation gave little scope for employing people with specialist skills. At the same time the agencies' resources of time and money were rarely enough to enable them to make good these deficiencies by accessing external sources of information, advice and training. The same constraints were the key factors in another common problem for small agencies – their isolation. Establishing and maintaining links with other organisations working in the same field, statutory agencies, intermediary bodies and funders were seen as time-consuming activities which had to take second place to the over-riding need to provide services.

The experience of governance

Board composition

With some exceptions the small agencies in the study had experienced difficulties in the recruitment of board members. They found it difficult to attract people to the governing body and those they did manage to recruit lacked expertise and experience. This is consistent with the findings of Cornforth and Simpson's survey of governing bodies in charities in England and Wales (see Chapter 10) that the problem of recruiting board members was commonest in the smallest organisations. A number of explanations were offered for this problem. Small agencies had comparatively low profiles and there was little in the way of prestige to be gained from membership of their boards. They lacked extensive networks through which to identify and approach potential board members by word of mouth, the most common method of finding new trustees. The staff and existing members lacked the time to undertake effective recruitment. And there were powerful disincentives in the shape of the amount of 'hands-on' work that board members could be expected to undertake and the precariousness of the finances for which they would be responsible.

Many of the agencies were also experiencing problems in retaining the board members they had recruited. One interviewee referred to a 'transient' membership. While that can be seen as an extreme case, the comparatively rapid turnover of board members was a common experience. In some cases the problem was due to frequent changes of nominee on the part of organisations who were represented on the board. This lack of continuity was seen as a major problem by several interviewees: 'they change so quickly we don't have a consistent way of running the organisation'. In others it was associated with the very active operational roles played by a minority of the board members. These activities brought a degree of involvement with and knowledge of the agency's work which was simply not available to other board members who became disillusioned with their comparatively peripheral involvement and dropped out. The existence of a 'dominant coalition' or 'inner board' in voluntary sector boards is not uncommon, but the gap between the active minority and the relatively passive members in the small agency could be widened by the extent to which the former took on operational roles. In some agencies the board was heavily dependent on the work of a very few stalwarts who had been involved since the earliest days of the agency's life and who – often unconsciously – tended to discourage newer recruits.

Some board members were described as 'apathetic' and 'lacking motivation'. This lack of commitment was shown in their feeling that attending board meetings was the extent of their responsibilities and, often, their failure to meet even that limited requirement by attending regularly. It was also associated with the criticism that governing bodies were unaware of their roles and responsibilities and knew little about the agency and its work.

On the other hand, a number of interviewees from the small agencies studied had few anxieties about recruitment and were much happier about the quality of their board members. One had drawn most of its governing body from the volunteers who were involved in the agency's work (plus a few members with relevant expertise). They were, in the staff member's view, 'totally Agency X focused' and did not have the problem of 'wearing two hats'. The result had been a stable membership and a consistently high turnout at meetings.

The board's roles and responsibilities

In some of the agencies there was a lack of clarity or agreement about the board's role. If we use the theoretical framework set out in the Introduction of this book, this ambiguity can be explained in terms of tensions between controlling and partnering the paid staff and between conformance and performance roles. One interviewee succinctly summarised these issues: 'Is the committee there to run the agency, manage the staff or act as a representative body? How far should it leave the management of the agency's work to the (paid) Co-ordinator?'

In other agencies, interviewees felt that there was a common view of the board's *role*. In most cases this tended to be seen as working in partnership with the paid staff and focused on performance rather than conformance. The concern in these agencies was directed towards the ability of the board to carry out its *functions*. Harris (1996) has provided a valuable digest of the functions which have been identified in the literature as key to the work of the board. These are:

- being the point of final accountability for the actions of the agency;
- being the employer of staff;
- formulating policy;
- securing resources;
- acting as a 'boundary spanner'.

There were specific issues and problems for the governing bodies of small agencies in addressing these functions. There was little evidence of the board *acting as the final point of accountability* for the actions of the agency's staff and volunteers or for the use it made of its resources. Accountability was seen largely in terms of providing increasing quantities of very detailed information to the agency's major funders and, as such, was taken to be a task principally carried out by the senior member of staff who alone had the time and knowledge to undertake it. Boards also relied 'on the co-ordinator to keep a weather eye on health and safety, insurance, etc., and let the committee know what they need to know'.

The extent to which the board could be said to be the *employer of staff* varied from agency to agency. Some had written employment policies and procedures, for example, detailed terms and conditions of service, arrangements for supervision and appraisal, grievance procedures and so on. It was far from clear, however, that these written prescriptions were 'owned' by the board; they had often been drafted by the senior member of staff or one or two board members in response to demands from funders rather than developed with a view to regular or systematic use in the management of the organisation. Other agencies had not found it necessary to commit more than a few basic principles to paper. Whether or not the written polices existed, there were often unclear expectations of the paid staff; the boundaries of staff roles were rarely well defined; staff were not expected to produce detailed work plans or to have their activities monitored and their performance evaluated. And they were not provided with support and supervision on a regular, formal and structured basis.

The third ascribed role for the board – *formulating policy* – was pursued only fitfully and in connection with limited areas of decision-making by boards in the majority of cases. Important decisions were made about the scale and scope of the services to be delivered, the number and kinds of staff to be employed and the principles governing the involvement of volunteers. These were, however, often reactive – taken in response to problems that had presented themselves and on the advice of the senior paid staff member. There is some evidence (not least the findings reported by Shirley Otto in Chapter 7 in this book) that governance in voluntary organisations tends to be less pro-active than in their counterparts in other sectors. The extent to which the boards studied tended to depend on the leadership of their senior paid staff was nonetheless remarkable.

Some boards had played a significant role in *securing resources* for the agency. In one case, members included senior professionals in local authority or health service agencies and were able to advise on, support and generally smooth the path of funding applications to those bodies. In another, it was members of the board who had developed and carried out a successful programme of fundraising from charitable trusts. In other cases board members had been able to help secure premises and equipment. The first two cases, however, were drawn from agencies which had been established comparatively recently and were unusual. In the majority of cases, boards effectively delegated resource acquisition to the senior member of staff.

The ability of the boards of small agencies to act as '*boundary spanners*' (Saidel and Harlan, 1998), as depicted in the resource dependency perspective on boards (see the Introduction), was generally also limited. Some organisations found it useful to have board members who were employees of other voluntary agencies but this was far from universal. There was one outstanding exception, however. One agency had made substantial changes to the composition of the board. The original group of people with access to statutory funding, having carried out their task, had been replaced by people who could help the agency reach out to and deliver its services to members of the various minority ethnic communities in the city. And another board had explicitly reshaped its role to become more distant from the day-to-day work and less 'hands-on'; this enabled board members to act as a conduit between the agency and other organisations with which they were involved.

Board–staff relations

In a number of the agencies studied, the 'rubber stamp' model discussed in the Introduction could be seen in action; the senior member of staff ran the organisation without much – or any – direction from the board. Some staff were content with this arrangement: 'they're very sweet – they do what I tell them' or 'they let the staff get on with the work and that's how it should be'. Others, however, saw a passive or acquiescent board as a problem: 'I have to tell them how to manage' and 'unfortunately the management committee agrees with everything I say'. Most of the people we interviewed felt that the senior member of staff – and to a lesser extent his or her colleagues – had the major responsibility for ensuring the organisation had an effective board. The key role of the chief executive in ensuring that the voluntary agency board functions effectively – or not – has been highlighted by Herman (1989). But for those who ran the small agencies studied it was one task among many: 'It's a full-time job just servicing a management committee. Sometimes you feel it could be done better but time is a constraint.' It also involved a difficult challenge – that of making board members aware of their responsibilities 'without frightening them'. In addition, some staff were uncomfortable with one possible aspect of the task; was it appropriate for the staff to recruit (and therefore select) the people who should be holding them to account? This unease reflected the tension between models of the board role based on ideas of control and, sometimes, democratic accountability (which informants felt were important) and those based on partnership and performance (which tended to guide their actions).

The development of an effective governing body, however, was not seen as a challenge for the staff alone – important though their contribution was – but one that needed a response from staff and board members in partnership. One interviewee included on his/her list of board functions 'to work as a team with the staff'. Many of the board members in the agencies we studied had achieved that aspiration to a greater or lesser extent. But the partnership was perceived as fragile: one agency chair felt that the effectiveness of the board and the constructive nature of board–staff relationships depended on the 'people involved and not because of a good system. If the paid staff or trustees changed, it could be a very different story.'

Overcoming the liability of smallness

Small agencies faced three sets of problems. In the first place they experienced problems with recruiting board members and retaining their commitment. Second, the ability of their governing bodies to carry out the functions commonly ascribed to the boards of voluntary agencies was limited. And, third, there were difficulties for senior staff members in finding enough time to provide their boards with the support and servicing they felt were needed. It can be argued that these problems are not peculiar to small voluntary agencies but part of the common experience of all voluntary sector organisations. On the other hand, the liability of smallness discussed earlier in the chapter suggests that they experience them in a particularly acute – and sometimes distinctive – form.

The extent to which individual agencies in the study were able to manage the impact of the liability of smallness on their governance systems varied quite markedly. Five key factors help to explain these differences. The first of these was to do with the nature of successful leadership in small voluntary organisations. Our study tended to support Elsdon's (1995: 144–145) view that effective styles of leadership in local voluntary organisations were likely to be 'nurturing and enabling' and that leadership was 'exerted modestly by example ... rather than aggressively by demands'. In many of the agencies we studied those who led them (usually but not exclusively the senior staff member) reported that they relied on diplomacy, encouragement, negotiation and persuasion to mobilise and organise the work of others. They described organisational settings where informality was the norm and relationships which were based on trust and an absence of hierarchy rather than authority and prescribed roles. Exercising leadership of this kind requires skills and qualities that are rather different to those needed by a manager in a more formal or bureaucratic organisation.

One of the strengths of small agencies is their ability to attract creative individuals and offer them the opportunity to exercise flexible and imaginative leadership. One experienced trust administrator suggested to us that small organisations flourished because of 'inspired, committed – or wacky – people'. On the other hand, it was clear that the organisations we studied had combined high levels of informality with formal measures to set some boundaries, clarify responsibility and authority and introduce systems, polices and procedures. One key to effective governance was thus to manage the ambiguity or paradox of combining formality and informality. Successful boards were those where there were systems for the recruitment and induction of new members; where meetings were planned and conducted in a business-like manner; and where there was a high level of clarity about what was being decided. But they also needed the 'personal touch' and an atmosphere of friendly informality both in terms of the conduct of meetings and of nurturing individuals through contacts between meetings.

A third factor also involved the ability to perform a balancing act, in this case between concentrating on the day-to-day work of the organisation and longer-term considerations. One of the attractions of small agencies – to board members and staff alike – was their closeness to the action. Many of those we interviewed were as interested in and motivated by the chance to play an active role in the day-to-day work of their agency such as direct care, advice giving, counselling or mediation as they were by the need to manage and lead their organisations. This 'hands-on' approach could have significant benefits in terms of a first-hand and intimate know-ledge of the work which enables staff and board members to identify prob-lems at an early stage and provide an authentic account of the organisation's activities to potential funders. On the other hand, inter-viewees were conscious of the dangers of too single-minded an application to the day-to-day work; they also needed to spend time on longer-term and more strategic activities like planning and budgeting, raising funds and recruiting volunteers and paid staff.

Fourth, effective boards were those in which the work of the board was shared among the many rather than concentrated in the hands of the few. The cycle that led to a diminishing number of people taking an increasing share of the workload could be and, in the more effective agencies, was prevented by clear and explicit strategies aimed at 'spreading the load' by delegating discrete and manageable tasks and forming task groups to tackle particular issues. One organisation, for example, brought together a team of board members and staff who shared among themselves the task of representing the agency at meetings of local forums and partnership bodies.

Finally, successful boards tended to be those which were able to access and use external sources of information, advice and support. More formal non-profit organisations like Housing Associations are encouraged to adopt a 'pick and mix' approach (Harris, 1999) to recruiting board members so that the result will be a governing body whose members between them possess all the knowledge, experience and expertise that the organisation needs (National Housing Federation, 1995). This approach is not generally open to small organisations and it is not, in any case, without its disadvantages. Technical knowledge and expertise are, however, available to them through national and regional networks and local infrastructure organisations and the extent to which they were able to make use of this was an important factor in determining how effective their boards might be. One agency was able to set up new systems for financial management with the help of a local community accountancy service and another developed its fundraising strategy as the result of sending its co-ordinator on a course run by a national specialist provider.

Conclusion: the nature of governance in small voluntary organisations

These five factors thus appear to hold the key to an effective response to the challenge of developing and maintaining an effective governing body, on the one hand, and overcoming 'the liability of smallness' on the other. They are underpinned by a number of assumptions about the nature of

small voluntary organisations which have implications for their governance.

The first of these is that small organisations represent extreme examples of the fundamentally ambiguous or hybrid voluntary agency
described by Billis (1993) which combine elements of two 'worlds' – the
very different organisational forms of association and bureaucracy. Small
voluntary agencies are not 'pure' associations dependent entirely on the
voluntary work of their members; by employing staff they have entered
bureaucratic territory. On the other hand, they are at best incomplete
bureaucracies because the time and energies of the paid staff – however
dedicated the individuals concerned – are insufficient to carry out all of
the activities needed to enable the organisation to meet its objectives and
to maintain its existence. The overall work of the agency is thus shared
between paid staff, board members and volunteers. That being the case,
the 'rules' of bureaucracy are an inadequate guide to running its affairs
and a different kind of 'organisational grammar' is required (Rochester,
1998).

If we return to the idea of the spectrum discussed in the introduction
to this chapter in the light of the Billis theory, we can construct a continuum ranging from 'pure' association to unambiguous bureaucracy.
Along the way we can find different kinds of hybrids. We may also be able
to identify a point where the predominant rules and customs of the associational world give way to those where what Milofsky (1988) has called the
seductive power of the bureaucratic form is in the ascendant. The organisations in our study can be placed on or very near that critical point but,
generally, on the side of the line where associational features predominate. The small agencies studied had very important associational features
and thus needed to introduce formal measures drawn from bureaucracy
only after very careful consideration. The importance of these associational features had implications for their approach to governance.

The first of these was the nature of authority and power within the
organisation. While, on a formal level, authority was invested in elected
officers or in staff employed to 'co-ordinate', 'manage' or 'direct' the
agency's work, in practice authority was exercised on an individual or personal basis. Those who demonstrated the ability to tackle complex or difficult issues found themselves with the responsibility of undertaking this
work regardless of their formal position in the organisation. Decisions
were made and work organised on the basis of leadership – an essentially
'political' process of persuasion, example and consensus-building rather
than the use of formal decision-making procedures or managerial techniques. Understanding these processes is more likely to be gained from
the study of associations (Harris, 1998) than of management theory.

The second implication is that it is extremely difficult to differentiate
between the role of the board and the role of the staff in small agencies.
There are two very different views of the nature of the governance puzzle

found in the literature. One view is that problems of governance stem from a basic failure of agencies to draw clear boundaries between the role of boards – 'governance' – and the functions of staff – 'management' (see, for example, Carver, 1997). This view is in harmony with the distinction made by Osborne and Gaebler (1992) in their approach to governance in the governmental sector between 'steering' – the work of boards – and 'rowing' – the work of staff. On the other hand, there is a body of research findings from both sides of the Atlantic that suggests that this distinction does not reflect the reality in many organisations of a complex, blurred and shifting boundary line between board and staff roles. From this perspective Harris (1996: 106) suggests that 'there are few, if any, functions which in practice belong unequivocally or on a long-time basis to either board or staff'. In a small voluntary agency the distinction between 'steering' and 'rowing' cannot be made with any confidence and attempts to distinguish between board and staff roles in this way are unhelpful.

The third implication for small voluntary organisations is that governance is not simply a question of what boards do or what, in some ideal world, they should do. Much of the literature tends to equate governance with the expected or actual work of boards. There is, however, an emerging view that governance and the work of governing bodies are not coterminous. This is implicit in the literature, which challenges the view that we can draw a clear and meaningful boundary between board and staff roles. It has also been explored more explicitly in a recent paper from Saidel (1999). This discusses governance as a function or responsibility of the organisation as a whole. It is undertaken by a variety of actors of which the board is just one, even if it is a very important player. This approach to governance describes, very clearly, the processes at work in many of the small voluntary agencies we studied. While charity law and contractual terms might have identified the board as the body with the legal responsibility for all aspects of the agency's work, the reality was that many of these responsibilities were shouldered by groups in which the contributions and obligations of board members and staff were not differentiated. The corollary of this perception is that the conventional distinction made between the governance system and the operational system is unhelpful and may be misleading for the analysis of small agencies.

This chapter began from the premise that the nature of the board role and the ways in which it can be successfully implemented will vary according to the specific characteristics of different kinds of voluntary organisations. It argued that the generic approach adopted by the bulk of the literature did not take account of the heterogeneity of the third sector. It has concentrated its attention on small, local voluntary agencies with few staff. The ways in which these organisations have responded to the general problem of the 'liability' of smallness and the specific challenges of establishing and maintaining an effective board suggest that they do have a distinctive approach to governance. This is characterised by authority based on personal or individual leadership and an 'associational' rather than a bureaucratic approach to decision-making and the organisation of work. A third distinctive feature is that the roles of staff and board are so entwined as to suggest that the functions of governance are carried out by the active elements in the agency rather than reserved to the board. This suggests that the distinction commonly made between the operating and the governance systems of an organisation is, in this instance, inappropriate.

In this chapter I have attempted to demonstrate that 'size does matter' by arguing that 'micro' agencies experience the issues and problems of governance in ways that are different in degree and kind from those encountered by their larger counterparts. If the case has been made, there are important lessons for academics and practitioners alike. Scholars would be advised to reflect on the heterogeneity of the voluntary or non-profit sector rather than developing models, concepts and theories of governance which assume that 'one size fits all'. And size is only one of the organisational variables that might be taken into account. For their part managers and leaders of small agencies and those that work with them need to develop effective practice that is rooted in the reality of these distinctive organisational forms rather than uncritically adopting nostrums that have been successful in very different organisational contexts.

References

Billis, D. (1993) *Organising Public and Voluntary Agencies*, London: Routledge.

Carver, J. (1997) *Boards that Make a Difference: A New Design for Leadership in Non-profit and Public Organisations*, San Francisco: Jossey-Bass.

Cornforth, C. (2001) *Recent Trends in Charity Governance and Trusteeship: The Results of a Survey of Governing Bodies of Charities*, London: National Council of Voluntary Organisations.

Elsdon, K. (1995) *Voluntary Organisations: Citizenship, Learning and Change*, Leicester: National Institute for Adult and Continuing Education.

Harris, M. (1989) 'The Governing Body Role: Problems and Perceptions in Implementation', *Nonprofit and Voluntary Sector Quarterly*, 18, 4, 317–323.

Harris, M. (1993) 'Exploring the Role of Boards using Total Activities Analysis', *Nonprofit Management and Leadership*, 3, 3, 269–282.

Harris, M. (1996) 'Do We Need Governing Bodies?', in D. Billis and M. Harris (eds) *Voluntary Agencies: Challenges of Organisation and Management*, London: Macmillan.

Harris, M. (1998) *Organising God's Work*, London: Routledge.

Harris, M. (1999) 'Voluntary Sector Governance – Problems in Practice and Theory in the United Kingdom and North America', in D. Lewis (ed.) *International Perspectives on Voluntary Action: Reshaping the Voluntary Sector*, London: Earthscan.

Harris, M. (2001) 'Boards: Just Subsidiaries of the State?', in M. Harris and C. Rochester (eds) *Voluntary Organisations and Social Policy: Perspectives on Change and Choice*, London: Palgrave.

Herman, R. (1989) 'Board Functions and Board-Staff Relations in Nonprofit Organisations: An Introduction', in R. Herman and J. Van Tyl (eds) *Nonprofit Boards of Directors*, New Brunswick, NJ: Transaction.

Klausen, K. (1995) 'On the Malfunction of the Generic Approach in Small Voluntary Associations', *Nonprofit Management and Leadership*, 5, 3, 275–290.

Kramer, R. (1965) 'Ideology, Status and Power in Board-Executive Relationships', *Social Work*, 10, 107–114.

Kramer, R. (1985) 'Towards a Contingency Model of Board–Executive Relations', *Administration in Social Work*, 9, 2, 15–33.

Mason, D. (1995) *Leading and Managing the Expressive Dimension: Harnessing the Hidden Power Source of the Nonprofit Sector*, San Francisco: Jossey-Bass.

Middleton, M. (1987) 'Nonprofit Boards of Directors; Beyond the Governance Function', in W. W. Powell (ed.) *The Nonprofit Sector: A Research Manual*, New Haven, CT: Yale University Press.

Milofsky, C. (1988) 'Structure and Process in Community Self-Help Organisations', in C. Milofsky (ed.) *Community Organisations: Studies in Resource Mobilization and Exchange*, Oxford: Oxford University Press.

National Housing Federation (1995) *Competence and Accountability: Code of Governance for Members of the National Housing Federation*, London: National Housing Federation.

Osborne, D. and Gaebler, T. (1992) *Reinventing Government*, Reading, MA: Addison-Wesley.

Rochester, C. (1998) 'Neither Flesh nor Fish nor Good Red Herring: Exploring the Organisational Features of Small Nonprofit Agencies', paper presented at the annual meeting of ARNOVA, Seattle, November.

Rochester, C. (1999) *A Handbook for Small Voluntary Agencies*, London: Centre for Voluntary Organisations, London School of Economics.

Rochester, C. and Billings, C. (2000) 'Convenient Slogan or Useful Theory? In Search of the Community Sector', paper presented at the NCVO Researching the Voluntary Sector Conference, Birmingham, September.

Rochester, C., Harris, J. and Hutchison, R. (1999) *Building the Capacity of Small Voluntary Agencies: Final Report*, London: Centre for Voluntary Organisations, London School of Economics.

Saidel, J. (1999) 'Contracting and Commercialisation: An Analysis of Current Challenges to Nonprofit Governance', paper presented at the Annual Meeting of ARNOVA, Washington, DC, November.

Saidel, J. and Harlan, S. (1998) 'Contracting and Patterns of Nonprofit Governance', *Nonprofit Management and Leadership*, 8, 3, 243–260.

Salamon, L. (1998) Letter to David Horton Smith, *Nonprofit and Voluntary Sector Quarterly*, 27, 1, 88–89.

Smith, D. H. (1997a) 'The Rest of the Nonprofit Sector: Grassroots Associations as the Dark Matter Ignored in Prevailing "Flat Earth" Maps of the Sector', *Nonprofit and Voluntary Sector Quarterly*, 26, 2, 114–131.

Smith, D. H. (1997b) 'Grassroots Associations Are Important: Some Theory and a Review of the Literature', *Nonprofit and Voluntary Sector Quarterly*, 26, 3, 269–306.

Widmer, C. (1993) 'Role Conflict, Role Ambiguity and Role Overload on Boards of Directors of Nonprofit Human Service Organisations', *Nonprofit and Voluntary Sector Quarterly*, 22, 4, 339–356.

Wood, M. M. (1992) 'Is Governing Board Behaviour Cyclical?', *Nonprofit Management and Leadership*, 3, 2, 139–163.

Zald, M. (1969) 'The Power and Functions of Boards of Directors: A Theoretical Synthesis', *American Journal of Sociology*, 75, 97–11.

Part III

Roles, relationships and power

7 Not so very different

A comparison of the roles of chairs of governing bodies and managers in different sectors

Shirley Otto

Introduction

At one and the same time British voluntary organisations are increasingly pivotal in the provision of national welfare and the civic life of local communities, and under attack because of concerns about the efficiency of their management (e.g. Tumin, 1992; Deakin, 1996). Government policy in the UK has been to both devolve the provision of state social care to voluntary and commercial organisations (e.g. social housing) and to develop partnerships with voluntary organisations to deliver new initiatives. Among the changes these shifts in social policy have brought about was for local authorities to become commissioners and regulators of services rather than providers. One symptom of this transformation in the relationship between state and voluntary organisations has been demands for voluntary organisations to be more 'managerial', more 'business-like', as well as subject to greater external regulation (e.g. Penn, 1992; Batsleer, 1995). The demands that voluntary organisations be better managed have not been based on any systematic evidence of dysfunctional activity – there are few large-scale empirical studies of organisation behaviour in UK voluntary organisations – rather, it was thought to be the case because of assumptions about poor management in voluntary organisations (Landry *et al.*, 1985; Handy, 1988) and media coverage of problem organisations. The most serious charges have focused on the high levels of confusion and conflict associated with the roles of trustees and chairs and the relationship between trustees (volunteers) and managers (paid). This included volunteers being equated with 'amateurs', and therefore with unprofessional behaviour, at least by comparison with assumptions about the practice of non-executive directors of commercial companies (e.g. Carver, 1990; Kirkland, 1996; Whitlam, 1996).

Similarly influential writers of prescriptive literature in voluntary sector boards (e.g. Ford, 1992, 1993; Kirkland, 1996) were influenced by proposals made by the Cadbury Report (1992) on financial oversight and standards of behaviour in commercial organisations. To ensure financial probity the report recommended the roles of governing bodies and their managers should reflect split and separate spheres, i.e. the spheres of governance (e.g. setting standards and strategic development) and operational management. The notion that the separation of governance from management was fundamental to accountability was taken on board for voluntary organisations and not just in terms of financial probity (e.g. Deakin, 1996). Consequently, the assumption that boards governed and managers managed is a central tenet in trustee training and management development programmes.

Academic research on board behaviour is less clear-cut. Harris (1992) observed that the confusion and conflict associated with the roles of governing boards and managers might be less to do with governing bodies' comprehension of their role and more to do with the difficulties of implementing it. For example, members of governing boards, as volunteers, have other priorities that limit the amount of time and energy they can give to their organisations. Harris also argued that the roles of boards and managers were intrinsically 'interlinked and interdependent', and hence difficult to separate, and therefore a source of ambiguity and conflict (Harris, 1987; 1991). This was an observation also made by Leat who wrote, 'All those interviewed said that, in theory, management committees make policy while workers put policy into operation. In reality, however, it was difficult to distinguish clearly and easily between "making policy" and "day to day management"' (1988: 67). Cornforth (see the Introduction) describes the role of boards as paradoxical because they are expected to combine contradictory activities, for example, boards are expected to work as partners with senior staff and yet monitor and control them.

These voluntary sector centred studies are resonant with the findings of researchers in the public and commercial sectors. Stewart (1991) and Hodgson *et al.* (1965) described chairs of boards and managers as having 'mutually dependent', 'complementary' or 'closely related' jobs in which individuals negotiate the details of their roles according to circumstances, personalities and changing internal and external demands. The roles of chairs and managers were literally interdependent and the details of their remits never came to be precisely defined.

Yet it could be argued the confusion and conflict associated with these roles are not primarily located in the formal role remits themselves but in how they are realised by the role holders. Paton (1996) among others focused on the centrality of personal values, i.e. humanitarian, spiritual or political convictions, to the motivation of people working in the voluntary sector, and linked these strongly felt commitments to conflict between members of voluntary organisations. Dartington (1994) described people motivated by moral or ethical purposes as having a sense of personal authority to act autonomously so as to bring about the changes they desired. From this perspective it would not be surprising if both members of governing boards and managers preferred to have vaguely defined roles (despite the likelihood of confusing and conflictual expectations) because this gave them scope to decide priorities based on what they thought was important. Hence job satisfaction, for members of governing boards and managers, would be linked to not defining roles too precisely, nor necessarily observing the formal dictates of the Charity Commission. Investments in personal values, and taking the opportunity to realise them, could both enhance motivation and contribute to problems with roles and role relationships. In conclusion, the literature raises the following interrelated questions: are there indeed significantly higher levels of confusion and conflict associated with governing bodies and managers in voluntary organisations? And if so, is this because the role expectations of governing bodies and managers in voluntary organisations are particularly ambiguous and/or complex to understand and implement, and/or, governing bodies and managers prefer the freedom implicit in a vague job description because it allows for the expression of personal convictions, despite the confusion and conflict this can cause?

A step in clarifying these issues would be to compare members of voluntary sector governing bodies and managers' approaches to their roles with those of their counterparts in statutory and commercial organisations. This chapter is based on just such a comparative study. More specifically, it draws on a study of key members of governing bodies – the chair of the board – and the most senior manager in the organisation, whether designated chief executive, director or co-ordinator. By their 'counterparts' is meant their equivalent, in the statutory and commercial sectors, i.e. part-time/non-salaried chair working in tandem with paid, full-time managers.

Three related hypotheses were explored, namely:

- Chairs and managers of voluntary organisations have higher levels of ambiguity and conflict associated with their roles than their counterparts in other sectors.
- Chairs and managers of voluntary organisations contend with role expectations that are particularly ambiguous and/or complex to understand and implement compared to their counterparts in other sectors.
- Chairs and managers of voluntary organisations operate with higher levels of role autonomy than their counterparts in other sectors.

Study design and measures

Study design

The comparative study was designed to better understand the role behaviour of chairs and managers in voluntary organisations by contrasting them with chairs and managers in statutory and commercial organisations. As the purpose of the study was to both describe and explore role behaviour, a mix of quantitative and qualitative research methods was used. Chairs

Table 7.1 Numbers of respondents in each sector

	Numbers who filled questionnaire	Numbers who were interviewed
Voluntary sector	28 (14 chairs/14 directors)	28 (14 chairs/14 directors)
Statutory sector	30 (15 chairs and 15 heads)	12 (6 chairs and 6 heads)
Commercial sector	28 (14 chairs and 14 chief executives)	12 (6 chairs and 6 chief executives)

and managers from organisations in the voluntary, public and commercial sectors, more specifically organisations that had boards made up of part-time non-executive or volunteer members, were sent a postal question-naire (consisting of quantitative scales) and then interviewed (using open-ended and semi-structured questions) either face to face or on the phone. The interviews lasted between 60 and 90 minutes. As voluntary organisations were the primary focus of the study, more chairs and managers in these organisations were interviewed than their counterparts in the statutory or commercial organisations. The details are summarised in Table 7.1.

The three samples

Voluntary organisations

This sample was made up of twenty-eight people from charitable trusts working with homeless people in London. Fourteen were chairs of govern-ing bodies (unpaid volunteers) and fourteen managers (paid) (although not necessarily holding this job title). The choice of homelessness chari-ties was pragmatic. There existed a wide variety of organisations providing a diversity of services to homeless people, which meant it was possible to obtain a range in terms of size and type of provision. Letters were sent to all the homelessness projects (twenty) in the Greater London Area. Why fourteen chairs and managers? The original sample size was to be twelve, i.e. small enough to be manageable and yet big enough for the use of sta-tistical tests, but fourteen chairs and managers agreed to take part and it was hard to say no! All the chairs and managers filled in a questionnaire and were interviewed.

Statutory organisations

This sample was composed of thirty people, fifteen chairs and fifteen man-agers (head teachers), from Local Education Authority (LEA) primary or secondary schools in the Greater London Area. Again, the goal was to have twelve chairs and managers; however, more people agreed and were therefore included. The sample was drawn from all those who answered letters sent out to LEA schools in three London boroughs. Thirty people filled in postal questionnaires and then twelve of them were interviewed (six chairs and six heads). Why chairs and heads from local authority primary or secondary schools? At the time of the study it was state schools that provided the most established examples of statutory organisations with governing bodies made up of volunteers and paid staff. Moreover, the governing bodies of LEA schools had recently been given powers similar to those of boards of trustees of voluntary organisations.

The commercial organisations

This sample was made up of twenty-eight people from a variety of commercial organisations, all of which had chairs that were non-executive directors. Fourteen were non-executive chairs of boards (paid fees) and fourteen were paid managers. The companies were concerned with a range of activities including: brewing; electronics; software; engineering; graduate recruitment; market research; transport; manufacturing of leather, paper and electrical goods and charitable trading companies. Why these companies? These were the companies whose chairs and managers agreed to be included in the study. Letters were sent out to a wide variety of companies listed in directories and as members of institutes of directors/managers. Twenty-eight people filled in postal questionnaires, then twelve of them were interviewed (six chairs and six managers).

Background information on the people in the three samples, i.e. their time in post and number of staff in the organisations, is summarised in Table 7.2. While there were no significant differences between the samples for the length of time people had been in post, there was for the number of staff. Clearly the commercial organisations (mean 7184.79; SD 14305.58) had considerably more staff than the voluntary organisations (mean 43.36; SD 70.13) and school samples (mean 42.47; SD 27.16).

Table 7.2 Comparison between the three samples on variables: respondents' time in post and number of staff in the organisation

Samples	Time in post	Number of staff
Voluntary sector	Range: 2–156 months Mean: 54.79 SD: 37.47	Range: 2–260 Mean: 43.36 SD: 70.13
Statutory sector	Range: 3–216 months Mean: 61.20 SD: 51.93	Range: 14–117 Mean: 42.47 SD: 27.16
Commercial sector	Range: 7–180 months Mean: 56.43 SD: 51.32	Range: 26–47,000 Mean: 7184.79 SD: 14305.58

Similarities and differences across the three samples

The notion of a comparative study assumes similarities and differences across samples. The key elements are summarised in Table 7.3. As a consequence of these similarities and differences it was predicted that a comparison between the voluntary and other sectors would reveal significant differences in role issues and the amount of autonomy in roles. More specifically, these differences involved confusion and conflict associated with roles and the exercise of autonomy.

Table 7.3 Similarities and differences across the three samples

Voluntary organisations	Statutory organisations	Commercial organisations
Non-statutory	Required to exist by statute	Non-statutory
Governed by committee of unremunerated trustees	Governed by committee of unremunerated governors	Governed by boards with non-executive members who are paid a fee
Formally accountable to members and informally to range of stakeholders and interest groups	Formally accountable to Secretary of State, LEAs and to a range of local stakeholders, e.g. parents	Formally accountable to shareholders
Role and powers of chairs not prescribed	Roles and responsibilities prescribed by Secretary of State	Role and powers of chairs not prescribed
Primacy of personal values, i.e. political, spiritual or humanitarian values	Mix of personal and institutional values	Primacy of commercial values and the 'market'
Broad objects, mission and outcomes	Broad mission but specific goals, targets and outcomes	Specific goals and targets – usually financial
Rooted in loose-knit structures	Bureaucratic structures	Mixed structures
No expectation of formal inspection	Formal inspections by government-appointed inspectors	No expectation of formal inspection
Individual trustees financially liable unless an incorporated charity	Governors incur no financial liability	Individual board members financially liable unless registered as companies limited by guarantee
Support and training for trustees arranged on an *ad hoc* basis	Board of Governors serviced by Clerk from LEA Governors' Support Units; training provided by LEAs	Support and training for boards arranged on an *ad hoc* basis

Confusion and conflict associated with roles

- Voluntary vs statutory sectors – significantly higher levels of confusion and conflict associated with roles of chair and manager in voluntary organisations because the statutory organisations (i) had roles and responsibilities defined by statute; and (ii) had bureaucratic structures.
- Voluntary vs commercial organisations – significantly higher levels of confusion and conflict associated with roles of chair and manager in voluntary organisations because the commercial organisations (i) had clear goals to maximise profits; and (ii) had the notion of the chair contracted to work specific hours and be paid for them.

The exercise of autonomy

- Voluntary vs statutory sectors – there would be significantly higher levels of autonomy exercised in roles for the voluntary sector organisations because of the impact of personal values on roles and the lower levels of bureaucracy.
- Voluntary vs commercial sectors – again, the voluntary organisations would report significantly higher levels of autonomy because of the influence of the primacy of personal values on their behaviour.

Data collection

Key concepts

The key role issues under examination were defined as follows:

1   *Role ambiguity* – defined as the role holders' perception that they received unclear or non-existent messages about the requirements of their role or job.
2   *Role conflict* – defined as the perception by the role holder of differences between their views of their job, the values and/or expectations of others and resources available to do their job; also receiving different and contradictory messages.
3   *Role autonomy* – defined as the perception by the role holder of their control over, and exercise of choices in, the kind of work they do and how it is done, including shaping the role itself.

These concepts were explored drawing on both qualitative and quantitative data. The quantitative data was collected using pre-existing scales designed to measure perceptions of role behaviour which was matched with qualitative data elicited using semi-structured questions in an interview schedule. These methods are summarised in Table 7.4.

Table 7.4 Measures and methods used in the studies

Concepts/Measures	Quantitative	Qualitative
Role ambiguity	'Role ambiguity scale' 6 items on a 7-point scale (Source: Rizzo *et al.*, 1970)	Open-ended questions/ probes about respondent's experience of role confusion
Role conflict	'Role conflict scale' 8 items scored on a 7-point scale (Source: Rizzo *et al.*, 1970)	Open-ended questions/ probes about respondent's experience of role conflict
Role ambiguity	'Role autonomy scale' 5 items on a 5-point scale (Source: Nicholson and West, 1988)	Open-ended questions about respondent's exercise of discretion/ autonomy in roles

Analysis of the data

The quantitative data was first subject to non-parametric tests (Mann-Whitney U Test, Spearman's Test for correlations) as there was no reason to assume the data would be normally distributed. However, the data proved sufficiently normally distributed to carry out analysis of variance with Scheffe tests to identify role differences across the roles and sectors (Bryman and Cramer, 1990).

The qualitative analysis was carried out according to the guidelines re-commended by Ritchie and Spencer (1994). Broadly this meant identifying themes in the typescripts and then using these as a basis for coding the text. A second independent researcher then coded two-thirds of the typescripts again and a Kappa coefficient of agreement (Cohen, 1960; King, 1994; Cramer, 1998) calculated the results. A Kappa coefficient of 0.7 was adopted as a reasonable 'success' rate for the coding of this data. According to this criterion, the standard of coding (ranging between 0.55–1) was reasonably successful, and occasionally less so – it was complex separating role ambiguity from role conflict in the texts.

Findings

For the sake of clarity different terms were adopted for the paid managers in the three sectors. The terms used for the two role groups were: voluntary sector – *chair* and *director*; statutory sector – *chair* and *head*; commercial sector – *chair* and *chief executive*.

Table 7.5 summarises the key results of both the qualitative and quantitative data for the three measures adopted for the study. The details are then discussed in terms of the three hypotheses.

Table 7.5 Summary of the results of the study

Variable name	Voluntary sector	Statutory sector	Commercial sector
Role ambiguity	High levels of variance in the sample. Key issues: blurred role boundaries; chairs' role vague with unclear expectations/ responsibilities; directors uncertain about their authority	High levels of variance in the sample. Key issues: blurred role boundaries. Comparison with voluntary sector: no significant difference in scores	Lowest levels of ambiguity. Key issues: blurred role boundaries. Comparison with voluntary sector; chief executives clearer about authority than directors; commercial chairs clearer about responsibilities/expectations than voluntary chairs
Role conflict	High levels of variance in the sample. Key issues: conflict within and across roles; issues about authority and control	Very high levels for both heads and chairs. Key issues: conflict within and across roles, i.e. about authority, control and work overload. Comparison with voluntary sector: significantly higher levels of role conflict	Lowest levels of all. Key issues: conflict across roles, i.e. authority and control, impact of personalities. Comparisons: significantly lower role conflict than the statutory sample
Role autonomy	High levels of variance in the sample. Chairs lower levels than directors; chairs reactive, while director pro-active. Key issues: directors' invested in autonomy; mixed attitudes to exercise of authority and control	High levels of variance in the sample. Key issue: who is the 'boss'? Comparisons: no significant differences with voluntary sector; heads, chief executives and directors all required autonomy for performance and motivation	High levels of autonomy recorded. Key issue: importance of plans and targets. Comparison: significant differences between voluntary and commercial chairs *re* setting own agenda and deciding methods of work

Comparing levels of ambiguity in roles

First of all, there were not uniformly high scores on the role ambiguity scale for the voluntary chairs and directors. Ambiguity was an issue for some respondents but by no means all. Second, ambiguity associated with roles featured in *all three samples* with the lowest levels found for commercial organisations. The only significant difference was between the voluntary sector directors and commercial chief executives (ANOVA Test $F = 3.86$, $p = <0.05$). Scheffe Tests were used on the six individual scale items to determine the direction of any differences. In comparison with their counterparts in the commercial sector, the voluntary sector directors were:

- comparatively less clear about the nature/extent of their authority ($F = 4.43$, $p = <0.01$);
- comparatively less clear that they had given time to the right priorities, or in line with others' expectations ($F = 6.30$, $p = <0.001$).

Moreover, the Scheffe Tests also revealed interesting differences between chairs across the sectors. The chairs of the voluntary organisations, compared to their commercial counterparts, were:

- comparatively less clear about their responsibilities ($F = 8.75$, $p = <0.001$);
- comparatively less clear about exactly what was expected of them ($F = 4.43$, $p = <0.01$).

Comparing levels of conflict in roles

Again, no uniformly high level of role conflict scores was found for the voluntary sector sample. Although role conflict was recorded for all three samples, it was the statutory sample, and especially the heads, who reported considerable incongruities and significantly more so than for the other samples (chairs: $F = 3.65$, $p = <0.05$/heads $F = 17.34$, $p = <0.001$). Except that is for one item on the role conflict scale; both directors and heads had problems with receiving incompatible requests from two or more people, that is compared with the chief executives in the commercial sample ($F = 12.19$, $p = <0.001$). What sense can be made of what was common and different across the sectors and role groups?

Are roles more difficult to understand/implement in voluntary sector?

The qualitative data revealed at least a third of each sample/role group mentioned issues associated with role ambiguity and role conflict. This gave the impression that role ambiguity and role conflict were familiar features of life in all three sectors and not peculiar to any type of organisational activity, structure or size. This impression was reinforced by the quantitative data, as when the role and demographic (i.e. length of time in post and number of full-time staff) variables were correlated, no significant relationship was found.

The chairs of the voluntary organisations were concerned about the vagueness of their role. Chairs talked of 'the main problem is finding a role for yourself' and difficulties with 'judging when to push your own view and when to facilitate – it is easy for a chair to interfere'. The voluntary sector directors thought 'there is confusion over exactly where the role ends and another role begins' and as a consequence:

> It is not clear how much power the director has ... I take a lot of authority on myself and yet I am aware that I could be tripped up by someone saying 'you have not got the authority to do that' and ... everything gets unravelled.

In the statutory sample there were lots of mentions of 'grey areas', for example, a head reflected what was seen as the paradox of the chair/head relationship when he said, 'There is the greyness of the area of governors – they are there to be supporters and encouragers, but I am also aware they are my boss.' These ambiguities could tip over into difficulties about authority and control. One head mentioned, 'I myself have occasionally barked at my governors when I feel they have strayed a little too much into what I think is my area.' The unexpectedly high role conflict scores for the chairs and heads suggest these difficulties were attended, at times, by considerable tensions. It is likely these conflicts had much to do with the profound changes following the introduction of LMS (Local Management of Schools). These changes reduced the role of local education authorities, increased the authority of boards of governors and required heads to become managers as well as educators.

The commercial sample openly talked about ambiguity and conflict in roles despite having the lowest scores for both role ambiguity and role conflict. For example, a commercial chair reflected a common theme in saying: 'There isn't a clear line as to where you overstep the mark and where you don't.' Indeed, there was some suggestion that these issues were fundamental to the chair and manager relationship. A commercial chief executive described the roles of the chair and chief executive as a 'split job'; in his view, confused expectations were inevitable as separating policy-making from operations was not straightforward. The roles of chair (and governing bodies) and manager overlapped because the functions of policy formation and implementation were themselves interdependent. The roles were rooted in common management functions and processes, i.e. generating ideas, ratifying policies/standards, progress chasing and accountability. Perhaps because of this, it was not surprising people in all three samples said induction, training and regular reviews were vital. This is how one chair in the commercial sample put it:

> People often have expectations of each other that are not then ful-filled, or they expect things to happen too quickly and I think what people need to do is to learn that you need to talk about the roles more than you do, have time set aside to review and discuss . . . what I don't think you can do is legislate it all through another set of rules.

Is the exercise of autonomy in roles greater in voluntary organisations?

The hypothesis had been that chairs and directors in the voluntary organisations would operate high levels of autonomy in their work – higher than their counterparts in the other sectors – in large part because this gave them freedom to do the work they thought important according to their personal values. As ever, the data presented a more complex picture.

The quantitative data showed high levels of autonomy in roles, in voluntary organisations, but only among directors (i.e. voluntary chairs vs directors: Mann-Whitney U Test, $U = 30$, $p = <0.001$). The only difference between samples and role groups was the voluntary and commercial sector chairs ($F = 4.97$, $p = <0.01$) with the former exercising much less auto-nomy than the latter.

In the interviews the directors/heads/chief executives described them-selves as having substantial autonomy in determining the goals, methods and scheduling of their workload. They viewed having the choice to deter-mine what they did, with whom and how, as fundamental to dealing with the unpredictability of demands and constraints in their organisation. For example, the voluntary sector directors argued, 'I am the person in the organisation who knows best what's going on' and 'I couldn't do my job if I couldn't make decisions, it would be bad for the organisation . . . the important decisions I make are not operational ones but getting the framework of values and plans and reinforcing and adjudicating them.' Some of them added they had a personal preference for being in charge, and could not easily work to someone else's dictates. Although it was very common for members of the voluntary and statutory samples to describe themselves as motivated by passionately held personal values (and occa-sionally commercial respondents as well), it was the directors and heads who talked of actively creating change linked to their beliefs.

If the 'managers' were so similar, why were there differences between the voluntary and commercial chairs? Responses to the items on the role auto-nomy scale indicated the commercial chairs perceived themselves as having substantial control over their job while the voluntary sector chairs exercised initiative only over *when* they did things but not over *what* and *how* – these were decided with others, or by other people. A voluntary sector chair put it bluntly: 'I think an effective director will lead a chair by the nose.'

The qualitative data suggested this was not a simple matter of voluntary sector chairs abdicating their responsibility; there was a definite rationale for their reactive behaviour. In the words of one chair, 'There is always the potential for conflict between professional managers and lay part-time managers who are volunteers – anyway, can volunteer managers be in control?' Whatever their *modus operandi, both* chairs and directors in voluntary organisations wanted a sense of being in control – or just as important, not being out of control – and both linked being in control with effective performance of their roles. What was different was what they regarded as essential to control, and how they exercised that control. The directors required the 'freedom to get on with the job' because they 'carry the can' and 'what makes a director is the power and skill base'. For the chairs it was crucial that they could exercise choices over the use of their time so as to ensure the demands on them, especially on their time, did not go out of control. As one chair explained it, 'I stepped in because I have the chairing skills and a role in life that might help. It allowed me to control the amount of involvement I have – given I am actively involved elsewhere.' By defining their remit reactively, as a 'watching brief', the chairs retained a sense of legitimacy – and being in control – while not interfering and they could take control should circumstances require it. In the words of one chair, 'In large part you don't have very much control because there are various things that have to be done but it is important to be able to move in on an area if you want to.'

It could also be argued the chair's reactivity meant they avoided power struggles with highly pro-active directors who, by their own account, 'take a lot of authority' on themselves, and were often driven by strongly felt personal values. A chair described directors' motivation as:

> very similar to the chairs but very much stronger. It's an area where you can really control and direct the services for a particular client group. If you feel strongly for that client group, and most directors do, it's something where you can really effect some change.

Hence the chairs' desire to avoid power struggles made sense given the following applied:

- the limited time chairs were able to devote to their role (and being involved in conflict and change usually demands time and energy);
- the realities about what chairs could actually control;
- the view that the key actors were the managers (and legitimately so);
- the ambiguities about the allocation of authority and responsibilities.

Managing this 'split role' needed careful handling, as it was essential the relationship worked, whatever the formal role requirements of governing boards and their chairs. This was particularly emphasised by the chairs. In their view:

> [Chairs] form a relationship with a director, it's like a marriage ... if you don't have an understanding and a good working relationship then it must be very difficult ... you need to work out boundaries and it is this working out that makes the relationship survive.

The importance put on negotiating and reviewing relationships by respondents, in all three sectors, suggest training *per se* in the roles and responsibilities of boards would not be sufficient without active commitment by both parties to re-framing expectations with changing circumstances and personalities.

Both the chairs and the heads/chief executives in the statutory and commercial organisations described themselves as pro-active. Whereas this contributed to high levels of role conflict in the school's sample (e.g. tensions about who was boss), the commercial chairs and chief executives described more amiable relations. The chief executives described themselves as having considerable autonomy delegated to them by their chairs/boards *within* the framework of agreed strategic targets, and in light of specified constraints (e.g. policies on borrowing money). Indeed, the commercial chairs, despite scoring significantly higher on the role autonomy scale than the voluntary sector chairs, had a similar approach to them in managing the chair–manager relationship. As one commercial chair put it, once plans were 'blessed', there was no 'problem in the chief executive driving, that's if you judge them to be competent and good'. This very pragmatic, negotiated approach to autonomy and authority might account for the finding that both commercial chairs and chief executives scored highly on role autonomy yet not on role conflict.

Taking a step back and taking into account the impact on their roles of recent external policy changes, might help explain the high levels of role conflict found for the statutory chairs and heads. The 1986 Education Act gave school governors in England a much greater part to play in the running of their schools (e.g. new responsibilities for the curriculum, staffing and parts of the school budget). Moreover, as the implementation of LMS (i.e. local management of schools) further dissolved the power of the Local Education Authorities, heads were transformed from being primarily head teachers to managers (Davies and Braund, 1989). Although these 'reforms' detailed the conduct, role and duties of governing bodies and heads, they did not resolve who had ultimate authority when the territories of education and governance overlapped, for example, the expulsion of pupils. While chairs might think 'at the end of the day you're the boss', a head spoke for many of her peers when she said, 'I work on the basis that anything that happens in the school at the end of the day is my responsibility, ultimately.' Clearly, having a highly regulated environment did not remove the ambiguity and conflict inherent in the grey areas where their roles/functions overlapped.

Conclusion

Instead of discovering whether or not the roles in voluntary organisations were particularly confused and conflictual, they were found to be features of organising, albeit in different degree, in all three sectors. Not only were these issues not unique to voluntary organisations but also they were inherent in the 'split' roles of chairs and senior managers. However, although the voluntary organisations did not necessarily have more or less ambiguous or conflicting roles than other sectors, the directors and chairs did find sorting out the allocation of responsibility and authority particularly problematic (relative to the commercial organisations). These problems seem less to do with naïvety or incompetence than managing the 'closely related' and 'complementary' roles (Hodgson *et al.*, 1965; Stewart, 1991) in organisations that (i) combine part-time volunteers (with limited time available) and paid full-time managers; (ii) have no equivalent of statutory prescribed roles; and (iii) are run by people driven by deeply felt personal values.

At the outset of the study it was assumed that chairs and managers of voluntary organisations would operate with higher levels of role autonomy than their counterparts in other sectors. What was not expected was the response of the chairs in the voluntary sector sample. While they exercised autonomy in the management of their time, they differed from their counterparts in the limited use of their formal authority. The chairs' reticence could be seen as a strategy for them to retain a sense of 'perceived control' (Evans and Fischer, 1992) over their work, in light of the pressure of demands, vague choices and strict constraints on their time (Stewart, 1982). This strategy also meant they did not compete with the directors for tasks and authority on a regular basis. It is possible from the chairs' perspective that feeling in control of demands was more important than the satisfaction gained from exercising high levels of personal power. So much depended on the quality of the relationship with their director. One voluntary sector chair described the relationship as 'more like a marriage' than 'boss and subordinate'; indeed, they 'shared leadership'. Within this framework it is clearly essential that chairs and managers worked well together, trusted each other and co-operated closely. And yet herein lies a danger; Stewart questioned (1991) the impact of close mutually dependent roles on accountability. How could chairs remain sufficiently objective to monitor the work of the manager and yet maintain a complementary relationship with them? Indeed, but there may not be a choice for, in the words of a voluntary sector chair, 'they must be a line manager providing monitoring and appraisal and . . . a trusted friend and supporter for the director'. Such is the paradox of governance.

References

Batsleer, J. (1995) 'Management and Organisation', in J. Davis Smith, C. Rochester and R. Hedley (eds) *An Introduction to the Voluntary Sector*, London: Routledge.

Bryman, A. and Cramer, D. (1990) *Quantitative Data Analysis for Social Scientists*, London: Routledge.

Cadbury, Sir A. (1992) *Report of the Committee on the Financial Aspects of Corporate Governance*, London: Gee.

Carver, J. (1990) *Boards That Make a Difference*, Non-Profit Sector Series, San Francisco: Jossey-Bass.

Cohen, J. A. (1960) 'A Coefficient of Agreement for Nominal Scales', *Education and Psychological Measurement*, 20, 37–46.

Cramer, D. (1998) *Fundamental Statistics for Social Research: Step-By-Step Calculations and Computer Techniques Using SPSS for Windows*, London: Routledge.

Dartington, T. (1994) 'Conflicting Views in the Charity World', *NCVO NEWS* Management Section, 9–10 March, London: National Council for Voluntary Organisations.

Davies, B. and Braund, C. (1989) *Local Management of Schools: An Introduction for Teachers, Governors and Parents*, Plymouth: Northcote House.

Deakin, N. (1996) 'Meeting the Challenge of Change: Voluntary Action into the 21st Century', *The Report of the Commission on the Future of the Voluntary Sector*, London: National Council for Voluntary Organisations.

Evans, B. K. and Fischer, D. G. (1992) 'A Hierarchical Model of Participatory Decision-Making, Job Autonomy and Perceived Control', *Human Relations*, 45, 11, 1169–1175.

Ford, K. (1992) *Trustee Training and Support Needs*, London: National Council for Voluntary Organisations.

Ford, K. (1993) *The Effective Trustee. Part One: Roles and Responsibilities*, London: Directory of Social Change.

Handy, C. (1988) *Understanding Voluntary Organisations*, London: Penguin.

Harris, M. (1987) *Management Committees: Roles and Tasks*, Working Paper no. 4, London: Centre for Voluntary Organisation, London School of Economics.

Harris, M. (1991) *Exploring the Role of Voluntary Management Committees: A New Approach*, Working Paper no. 10, Centre for Voluntary Organisations, London School of Economics.

Harris, M. (1992) 'The Role of Voluntary Management Committees', in J. Batsleer, C. Cornforth and R. Paton (eds) *Issues in Voluntary and Non-profit Management*, Wokingham: Addison-Wesley.

Hodgson, R. C., Levinson, D. J. and Zaleznik, A. (1965) *The Executive Role Constellation*, Boston: Harvard Business School.

King, N. (1994) 'The Qualitative Research Interview', in C. Cassell and G. Symon (eds) *Qualitative Methods in Organisational Research: A Practical Guide*, London: Sage.

Kirkland, K. (1996) 'In Trust: The Changing Role of Trustees', in C. Hanvey and T. Philpot (eds) *Sweet Charity: The Role and Workings of Voluntary Organisations*, London: Routledge.

Landry, C., Morley, D., Southwood, R. and Wright, P. (1985) *What a Way to Run a Railroad: An Analysis of Radical Failure*, Organisation and Democracy Series no. 1. London: Comedia/Joseph Rowntree Foundation.

Leat, D. (1988) *Voluntary Organisations and Accountability,* London: National Council for Voluntary Organisations.

Nicholson, N. and West, M. (1988) *Managerial Job Change: Men and Women in Transition,* Cambridge: Cambridge University Press.

Paton, R. (1996) 'How are Values Handled in Voluntary Agencies?', in D, Billis and M. Harris (eds) *Voluntary Agencies: Challenges of Organisation and Management,* London: Macmillan.

Penn, A. (1992) *The Management of Voluntary Organisations in the Post War Period, with Special Reference to National–Local Relationships,* PhD thesis, University of Sussex: Falmer.

Ritchie, J. and Spencer, L. (1994) 'Qualitative Data Analysis for Applied Policy Research', in A. Bryman and R. G. Burgess (eds) *Analyzing Qualitative Data,* London: Routledge.

Rizzo, J. R., House, R. J. and Lirtzman, S. I. (1970) 'Role Conflict and Ambiguity in Complex Organisations', *Administrative Science Quarterly,* 15, 150–163.

Stewart, R. (1982) *Choices for Managers: A Guide to Managerial Work and Behaviour,* Maidenhead: McGraw-Hill.

Stewart, R. (1991) 'Chairmen and Chief Executives: An Exploration of their Relationship', *Journal of Management Studies,* 28, 5, 511–527.

Tumin, W. (1992) *On Trust Report: Increasing the Effectiveness of Charity Trustees and Management Committees,* London: National Council for Voluntary Organisations/Charity Commission.

Whitlam, M. (1996) 'At the Top: The Role of the Chief Executive', in C. Hanvey and T. Philpot (eds) *Sweet Charity: The Role and Workings of Voluntary Organisations,* London: Routledge.

8   What are chief executives' expectations and experiences of their board?

Veronica Mole

Introduction

'Can you ever get it right?' This was the rueful response of a long-standing chief executive of a voluntary organisation, discussing board–chief executive relations. It points to the often problematic relationships existing between chief executives and 'their' boards. The subject has received extensive research attention, primarily from the board perspective, and variously identifies a range of conflictual, consensual and complementary relations, in which alternative patterns of power and influence are identified. A growing prescriptive literature in the UK examines the ways in which relations between the board, the chief executive (CE) and other paid staff ought to work and sets out templates for those working relations. However, a series of paradoxes affect the chief executive role. Such post-holders, by virtue of their title, are an elite; yet for many such organisations, challenging other elites is part of their role. In many organisations, the CE will not be at the top of a massive employee pyramid, but one of a handful of staff. Chief executives are conventionally expected to lead their organisations; yet whatever chief executives do, boards remain ultimately responsible for their organisation's work, product and reputation. Implicit in discussions about the board–CE roles and relationships therefore, is the issue of how governance systems work in a context where paid staff are in the employ of volunteer board members.

This chapter examines chief executives' experiences of and expectations of their working with boards from a perspective that places the CE, rather than board members, at centre stage. It compares theorising on 'what boards do and are for' with CE expectations of boards' activities and purposes, as these relate to their roles. The work in the Introduction, identifying the paradoxical nature of the board role and weight of expectation placed on board members, and in Chapter 7, where interdependence of boards and CEs is a key theme, are also drawn on. It goes on to report the author's recent research on CEs in small and medium-sized voluntary organisations in the UK, using a narrative research approach to examine these CEs' career biographies. This research highlights the importance of boundary issues between boards and CEs, whether leading simply to overlaps of function or to more serious tensions around 'who governs'. The issues of interdependence and contradictory or multiple board roles are revisited, in terms of respondents' experiences. Conclusions are drawn that there is 'no one best way' to organise and manage board–CE relationships and a 'horses for courses' perspective is presented, whereby different approaches are appropriate to particular situations. Such an emphasis on responding to, even recognising, contingencies in voluntary organisations and their environments, however, raises problems for the development of templates for intra-organisational relations.

Board–chief executive relations, expectations and experiences: the literature

A central finding of the empirical literature on non-profit boards is that board members are uncertain both of their roles and those of their senior managers. Harris (1993) found that members of boards as well as paid staff and volunteers find it difficult to know what is expected as well as where boundaries lie, while discussions among management committees and paid staff revealed a variety of ideas about who should be doing what. In practice, the search for clear and permanent boundaries to the roles may be a chimera (Harris, 1992). Murray *et al.*'s (1992) typology of five distinct patterns of board–CE relations – CE-dominated, chair-dominated, fragmented power, power-sharing and powerless – shows how styles of governance and relationships vary between voluntary organisations. Golensky (1993) found different patterns of interaction within the leadership core not only from setting to setting but also at different times in the same organisation. Kramer (1985) puts forward a 'contingency model' in which behaviour in the leadership core may move back and forth from collaboration to difference. In sum, patterns of power change over time, possibly influenced by the life cycle of the organisation (Wood, 1992). Other variables that may impact on the relationship between boards and CEs include the age and history of the voluntary organisation, its size and purposes, the extent of professionalisation and its stage of organisation development (Zald, 1969; Fink, 1989; Murray and Bradshaw-Camball, 1990; Harlan and Saidel, 1994; Leat, 1996).

The chair–chief executive relationship appears pivotal: a dynamic one, dependent on changing personalities and environments (Harris, 1993). Herman (1989) argues that CEs have a key role in managing the board, while studies of managing the 'closely related' and 'complementary' roles of CE and chair highlight the importance of good personal relationships (Hodgson *et al.*, 1965; Stewart, 1991). A study of chair and CE relationships in health authorities found that unsatisfactory working relationships are far more likely to lead to problems in organisations than external pressures (Robinson and Exworthy, 2000; Exworthy and Robinson, 2001).

Roberts and Stiles (1999: 36), researching the relationships between 'chairmen and chief executives in major UK corporations', argue for complementarity, thus placing 'a co-operative relationship at the heart of the organisation, displacing to some degree the hierarchical model of the organisation that the duality of roles embodied'. The extent to which 'complementarity' of roles between these two players is a feature of voluntary sector life, rather than a pious hope, is, however, difficult to tease out.

Studies of 'what chief executives do' in the voluntary sector emphasise the importance of 'people relations'. Thus, for example, Dargie (2000) reports her research on chief executive activities, which used Mintzberg's ten behavioural roles that characterise managerial work. This studied eight CEs, two from local authorities, two from health service trusts, two from private firms and two from national voluntary organisations, using observation and interview methods, and year-long diary analyses. Dargie reports that for voluntary sector CEs, 'the interpersonal roles were very prominent'; and that they acted in 'a supportive role for trustees, members and volunteers' (ibid.: 41). Although for these CEs, the stability of their funding environment was a 'key concern', perhaps surprisingly, they were seen as being 'able to exercise greater control over their environment' than their counterparts in other sectors (ibid.: 43).

Studies of board and CE roles suggest considerable overlap. Harris (1996) describes the functions of the board as responsible for the employment of paid staff in the organisation; formulating policy; both safeguarding and securing resources for the organisation; acting as the link with the external environment and providing accountability for the voluntary organisation's activities. However, even if the functions of the board are understood, in practice many do not perform them as officially prescribed (Bradshaw *et al.*, 1992). Thus, explanations for the shortcomings of boards include ignorance of their role and function (Ford, 1992), aping the corporate model (Hodgkin, 1993), and not taking implementation of their official roles seriously (Harris, 1989).

The problematic nature of board roles – whether over-involvement in organisation routine or under-involvement in critical decision-making – all leave the chief executive vulnerable. Disappointment on both sides may be compounded by underlying disagreements as to 'who should be doing what'; with the issue of organisation leadership among the most complex. This is well illustrated by the response of a board in a study of governance in the Jewish voluntary sector, commenting on a CE's lack of contribution: 'the longer-term vision is left to the board. It would be easier if the chief executive were driving all this' (Harris and Rochester, 2001: 21). Yet some prescriptive texts emphasise that long-term strategy making is precisely the responsibility of the board, making this CE's limited contribution both an appropriate stance, in responsibility terms, and perhaps even a tactic to engage the board with their most critical role.

However, the much vaunted 'partnership' model between CEs, chairs and board members also makes for CE vulnerability. What happens when partnerships dissolve? How are the imbalances in most partnerships maintained? Do all parties subscribe to the perception of partnership that often one prominent partner asserts? In Chapter 7, Otto quotes a chair who describes the CE–board relationship as 'more like a marriage' – presuming good starting relationships, and continuing trust and co-operation. However, the marriage metaphor may be extended more uncomfortably, for example, to include overt pressure to stay when all the instincts are to leave. The author's pilot work for the study discussed below identified examples of CEs in such close partnership relations that they felt greatly burdened by their desire to leave organisations, with some pressurised by their boards to remain (Mole, 1999b).

Cornforth in the Introduction outlines the competing theories that have been proposed to understand the role of boards. How do chief executives see boards, in the light of these theoretical frameworks? As stewards, checking on what they do? As partners in organisational strategy making? As representative of different stakeholders; as symbolic figureheads? Do they see boards having one or all of these roles and qualities at the same time? What are the implications of these paradoxical expectations of board members for chief executives? The following section presents findings from the author's research on voluntary sector CE career accounts, which has demonstrated the inter-linking between career progress and expectations of CEs, their work content and work support mechanisms and the quality of relations between CEs and board members (Mole, 1999a; 1999b; Harrow and Mole, 2000).

The chief executives' career accounts study: insights into CE–board relations

In this study, sixty chief executives (thirty-three men and twenty-seven women) in small and medium-sized voluntary organisations participated in interviews concerning their careers, the role of the CE and aspects of governance in the sector, during 1998–2000. The organisations span an income range between £80,000 and £3 million and operate in a variety of fields including professional associations, social services and healthcare, research, education and training charities, grant-making and intermediary organisations, housing associations, community development, law/advocacy and professional associations. Lengths of time in post for the CEs range from eight months to twenty-six years, with a variety of functional backgrounds and experiences inside and outside the voluntary sector, including both the public and private sectors. Following a pilot, based on snowball sampling, the main study sample of sixty CEs was obtained from organisations listed in the *The Voluntary Agencies Directory 1997/1998*. To qualify as 'small/medium-sized', a voluntary organisation had to have an annual income of less than £5 million.

The narrative or career history method uses one-to-one semi-structured interviews to collect data from an individual's perspective covering the objective career or work history and the subjective career, their career story. The method is based on a saturation of knowledge (Bertaux, 1981). The key methodological problems involve the issue of retrospective recall of information by participants; memories are fallible and selective recall likely. Notwithstanding, Dex (1991) in her review of research work on recall suggests that it can be reliable for certain topics; and this study yielded rich ethnographic data on the careers and work experiences of chief executives in the voluntary sector.

Board–CE interdependence

The core research questions aimed to discover the extent to which 'careers' were a recognisable construct and aspiration in the sector, and the ways in which men and women CEs' background, career experiences and plans compared and contrasted; they were not about governance or organisational regulation *per se*. Nevertheless, issues and experiences of working with boards appeared within respondents' discussions, in a variety of ways. For this chapter, two questions from the interview schedule were identified as most likely to prompt such responses. They were: 'What are the key factors that enable or support you in your job?' and 'Are you able to identify any barriers that prevent you from doing your job in the way that you would like to do it'? The transcript responses for these questions were therefore re-analysed, to review where, if at all, any of the sixty CEs had cited aspects of their relations with their boards, as supportive or limiting factors in their work; and if so, which issues regarding their relations with their boards could be identified as especially significant.

Thirty-four of the sixty CEs discussed board–CE relations in the contexts of supporting or limiting their work. Given the size of organisations being studied, it is not surprising that a key theme arising from the findings was that of the 'interdependence' of chief executives and their boards – Otto's 'marriage' thesis (see Chapter 7). Within this overarching theme, three further sub-themes were identifiable: those of boundaries, levels of involvement in decision-making and the expertise and commitment of board members. In addition, some respondents also reflected on what may be described as the contradictory aspects of working with boards. Table 8.1 provides a picture of the breakdown of CE responses, by their primary issue in the three sub-themes, and by gender of chief executive. The primary issue for half of the thirty-four CEs was 'boundaries between roles and responsibilities'. The remaining half were virtually equally divided in their primary issue between 'levels of involvement' and 'expertise and commitment of the board'.

Table 8.1 Chief executives' identification of primary issue in board–CE relations: by category and CE gender

Category of primary issue	Numbers of CEs identifying this issue	Women CEs	Men CEs
'Boundaries between board and CE'			
Good support from chair	6	4	2
Mentoring relation with chair	1	0	1
Line management from chair	1	1	0
Strikes right balance	4	2	2
Uncertainty over roles	1	1	0
Does not give support where needed	1	1	0
Unsupported by chair	4	2	2
Sub-total	18	11	7
'Levels of involvement between board and CE'			
Very involved/lots of contact	1	0	1
Need right level of involvement/more consultation	2	1	1
Interfering (by board)	2	1	1
CE takes lead managing involvement	3	1	2
Sub-total	8	3	5
'Expertise and commitment of board'			
Good expertise from board	1	0	1
Conflicts of interest	1	0	1
Lack of commitment from board	4	2	2
Lack of expertise from board	1	0	1
Sub-total	8	2	6
Total	34	16	18

Boundaries

For those CEs citing 'boundary' issues regarding relationships with their boards, key aspects of their work were 'leadership' and 'defining the vision'. One CE encapsulated the wide-ranging aspects of the job: 'Running the whole show – fundraising, strategic planning, staffing, liaising with government departments, you name it.' Chief executives reporting positive management of boundaries, 'striking a balance', emphasised that these arrangements worked for them; and were right for their organisations also.

Where differing interpretations of the locations of boundaries between boards and CEs were reported, these were closely connected to the working relationship between the CE and the chair. One CE explained: 'Uncertainty over the respective roles of the management committee and me and my team creates a lack of understanding of issues with the chair.' For another, chair support was intermittent at best and had to be coaxed: 'The chair I will seek out sporadically, but he is not hugely supportive.'

Where CEs felt unsupported by the board, conflict was possible though not inevitable, and the organisation as a whole was the loser. For example, uncertainty over roles could result in an absence of leadership which affected the organisation moving forward: 'I go into meetings not knowing if the chair is with me and that is an impediment to progress.'

For some CEs, their board offered very little support, whether deliberately or through a chronic lack of interest. Thus for one CE: 'There are management difficulties and the lack of trustee and board understanding of that can make things more difficult'; while for another, 'Support from trustees is variable, some are very good and others just turn up to meetings.' One CE identified, enigmatically, the 'wrong kind of support': 'My board are behind me but do not give support in the way I need.'

Lack of support turning into open conflict was rare and appeared a function in part of past arguments and battles. The one CE citing this development noted:

> The relationship between the management committee and the chair has a long and difficult political history in this organisation. Now I have the chair being openly critical and I have thought about taking the case to constructive dismissal. He has resisted attempts to sort out the problems. There is conflict of interest resulting in tension that finds its way back to the organisation.

Difficulties and tensions in identifying working boundaries were also exacerbated by organisational change, such as rapid growth; which seem to have been largely unrecognised (or unacknowledged by board members). A CE of a social service organisation, where staff numbers had risen from three to twenty-five within three years, and where the board was seen to be too involved in matters that were staff's responsibility, complained 'they [the management committee] need to understand we are doing the work and we need to fulfil our own roles, they do not need to fulfil our roles'. Where the CEs described positive working relationships, there is support for Otto's finding in Chapter 7 that CEs and board evolve complementary behaviours. At the same time, the CE perspective was focused on 'what works for them', that is to say, for the CEs themselves, with the board expected to provide leadership and support on their terms.

Levels of involvement

Less than a quarter of the CEs cited this as a primary concern regarding their work with their boards. However, those who did were in the main describing a considerable mismatch between their expectations of the board, and the board's own interpretation of their role; in particular, this often concerned CEs' attempts to gain the right level of involvement from their chairs. A spectrum of involvement in decision-making from 'joint decision-making' and 'partnership' to 'rubber-stamping' with the CE taking the lead in the decision-making process was described. Some CEs wanted more involvement from the chair, and a partnership with the board on decision-making: one CE saw this as a mutual gain situation: 'I need/want to get more consultation on decisions. It is for mutual protection. I will not go ahead on key issues without making sure the chair is satisfied.'

Others described their preference for an increased monitoring role from the board, partly to safeguard themselves and make sure they were doing what was required.

> I have a very nice group of trustees but I would like them to be more decisive. I pose questions or make other suggestions but seldom get any answers. I would like to be appraised, to know if I'm doing things right, to be reassured that I'm going in the right direction but do not get that.

Where CEs have taken the lead, they recognised their responsibilities for managing the board: 'I made it clear to the board I wanted collaborative working, I keep them fully informed but they must involve themselves in decision-making.' At times, the relationship suggested managerial domination with the board following the CE's direction, for example: 'The relationship with the management committee had to change, I adopted a more confrontational approach and said this is the way we are going to do things.' Where CEs were not able to manage the 'right' (for them) level of involvement with the board, they described the board as 'meddling' and 'overly interfering'; with the worst case scenario that of getting in the way of decision-making. For one CE there were: 'too many decision-makers who need to be consulted and informed, it is a complicated way of trying to get things done'. Complicated ways of working slowed down decision-making, 'the slowness of the board to make decisions when rapid decision-making is necessary'. In one case, the board, though multi-skilled, was seen as reluctant to make any decisions at all: 'The board has a good range of talent but is reluctant to deal with key issues. There is a problem of personalities. Negative things are not allowed to surface but need to be said.'

A key issue for the relationship between the CE and the board from this study is at what stage the CE involves the board in decision-making, rather than the other way around. An early involvement gives the board more opportunity to help shape key issues; albeit on the CE's terms. Late involvement may mean the board feels it is being presented with a *fait accompli*. A CE explains:

> Trustees have ultimate responsibility and therefore you have to remember you cannot say this is the way to develop, without their

formal approval. That stems partly from misreading how they are going to react. The first time this occurred I realised I should have sounded one or two out beforehand but I did not see it as an issue that they would latch onto but they did and that can hinder progress. Ultimately, you will get there in the end but you have to remember their role.

Expertise and commitment

While only a quarter of the CEs cited the expertise and commitment of board members as their primary concern in facilitating their work, only one emphasised satisfaction and the remainder referred to difficulties. One CE had a more skilled (and presumed thereby contributing) board in mind: 'I would like to change the committee structure ... to involve more specialised people like solicitors, accountants and people with contacts they are willing to share.' Growing competition within the sector for funding also led CEs to look for increasing commitment to their organisation from the board. One noted that, 'Many [of the board] are also involved with other charities and it is hard to wear two hats.' This increased commitment extended especially to the chair where their role as 'champion' for the organisation was seen as working on developing external relationships and making 'warm contacts' with funders. One CE lamented: 'The chair is equivocal, has his mind on other things and is not a champion for us.' Decision-making on strategy was also linked to board commitment and their general approach to their responsibilities. Thus one CE noted, 'the philosophical conservatism of the trustees ... They are traditional followers of charity fashion and change is difficult to implement'; another remarked the 'lack of nerve of the trustees. We have a five-year plan but it took time for them to trust that we can expand and stay in control.'

Multiple models of board working: some contradictions

In addition to the three themes above, some respondents also highlighted some of the contradictions involved in close working with boards. One respondent was a 'founding chief executive' (a seemingly much less significant figure of voluntary sector folklore than the 'founding chair'). Here, the CE, rather than the chair, had taken on the task of putting together a board that was going to be good for the organisation; pointing to problems associated with bringing in people who may bring little other than their friendship and support to the organisation: 'You need a good chair who will really back you up and be a champion, you need a committed person. It is a big responsibility getting a good committee together, there are problems with having friends as bosses.' It was acknowledged that the daily organisational routine could swamp both the CE and the board together: 'There is the danger that administration displaces fundraising and strategy, [in particular] the amount of administration involved in the board and sub-committees.'

While the notion of 'partnership' with the board was widely cited, some responses made plain that this was being run on their (that is, the CEs') terms. One respondent seemed to include their chair almost as an after-thought: 'We function well together as a team, including the chair of the organisation.' Another CE recognised the steward-like approach of the board, as a function of the organisation's history: 'It is an organisation that believes strongly in the active governance role of the committee and [in] implementing what they decide and overseeing that it is done.' The board as representative of different stakeholders appeared, however, to leave a vacuum in terms of management support. One chief executive expressed the isolation that a stakeholder model of board–CE relations could produce:

> The committee are stakeholders/share-holders and contributors to the fund so it has become clear to me that I don't have any senior ref-erence points of support or advice that you would hope to get from your governing body in order to help guide you. The committee are customers too. There is no management support, you cannot talk to the committee about how to manage the committee.

Reflections on research

These findings provide an emerging picture of different CEs requiring dif-ferent things from their boards. Aligning different expectations and achiev-ing the right balance of activities often appears problematical. Where some boards may offer partnership, for example, CEs may prefer a stronger moni-toring role. Where CEs may look for the board to play mainly an external role maintaining good relations with key external stakeholders, boards may be seen as too internally focused and meddlesome. Much depends upon the CEs' perception of the appropriate level at which to involve the board in decision-making. Nor is it clear that even where CEs felt unsupported by their chairs, this necessarily hampered the organisation's progress; on the contrary it seems possible that these CEs were being spurred on to even more efforts on their organisation's behalf; an uncomfortable situation for all concerned. Another possible model of board–CE relations may be identi-fied as a 'desertion' model, in which boards took a lofty view of the appro-priateness of their standing back, thus leaving the CE to their own devices. Some support for this model may come from the fact that CEs were more concerned about the lack of commitment which their board displayed, than the board's expertise. However, it is also possible to interpret CEs' non-interest in boards' expertise as a function of their preferring boards where they (the CEs) were clearly the provider of the 'expert' opinions.

It may be more important from a governance perspective to note those two respondents who experienced problems associated with the *variable* commitment shown by board members. This is a characteristic which does not fit well with current board–CE typologies, which provide a continuum of relations, between dominance by either party and a series of collaborative arrangements in between. It suggests that board behaviour may be more difficult to track and predict. This may reflect board members leading pressured lives beyond their governance responsibilities, which constrains what they can do. Ironically, it may be a particular consequence of drives to recruit board members with professional standing who, in a turbulent work climate, may experience periods when their work life, rather than voluntary life, must come first.

It seems a possibility that here the smaller size of organisation involved could be a factor. In smaller organisations, boards may become very engaged with the 'one big project', or bond together to ensure organisational survival but face a loss of commitment when the major expectation (usually concerning funding) does not materialise. Existing theory and prescriptive advice on board–CE relations also tend to assume a fairly stable relationship. They are less helpful and relevant when that commitment can be described as variable, and intermittent, leaving CEs with continuing uncertainty as to where boards will support, intervene or acquiesce. (That CEs will also demonstrate 'variable commitment' to their organisations must of course also be recognised.)

The depth of material on board–CE relations provided by these respondents confirmed the complexity of those relations, and did not point to any issues being the concern of a particular type of organisation, although the small numbers preclude generalisations on this latter point. Taking an overview of the thirty-four chief executives, fourteen could be grouped together as welcoming or at least being satisfied with the nature of their relations with boards. Of all the categories of 'issues' affecting performance of their work, the experience of 'good support from the chair' was the most prominently identified, with six CEs (twice as many women as men) citing this. Twenty CEs raised issues which were problematic, with slightly more men than women in this category, twelve men and eight women. (This, however, assumes that the issue of 'CE taking a lead in managing board involvement' is included as a 'problem'.) At the same time, among these twenty, only one chief executive regarded these problems as a push to leave the sector altogether. In the main study, there is a strong commitment to sustain careers profiles in the voluntary sector particularly among women; the 'death of the career' notion was not at all in evidence (Harrow and Mole, 2000).

From a regulatory and governance perspective, however, there remains one puzzle and concern from these findings – 'the dog that did *not* bark'. Twenty-six of the sixty chief executives interviewed, in response to the questions concerning the support gained and barriers to achieving work, made no mention whatsoever about their relationships with boards! Career narrative research requires the researcher to maintain only an outline framework of questions, seeking the respondents' 'career stories', so that there was no prompting here regarding the absence of mention of the boards. It is interesting to speculate why this was. On the one hand, it might indicate that relations with the board worked so well that they do not require mention. On the other, it may reflect a situation where the board has become sufficiently sidelined or ineffective, that the chief executive can ignore it.

Even if it is accepted that these scenarios paint unlikely pictures, the possibility is again raised that CEs may be working to very different models of 'ideal' board–CE relations than the boards themselves. It must be recognised that those which suit CEs, and which they enjoy, will not always be those which suit or are attractive to board members and chairs, making the prescriptive literature's case for achieving 'balance' (if not harmony) in this field difficult and not always feasible.

This research provides mixed messages concerning the state of board–CE relations and insights into what boards and chief executives do. This suggests a 'horses for courses' approach, whereby the forms and nature of board–CE working are carried out on a contingency basis, with some effort to satisfy both parties, but with the CEs more likely to be accommodated. Tensions exist over boundary definitions between CEs and their boards, the level of involvement of boards in decision-making and issues of expertise and commitment, but these seem best handled on an organisational 'case' basis, rather than by a 'one size fits all' approach. However, taking a contingent approach has its drawbacks. A contingency theory of organisations focuses on the way in which organisational variables are in a complex inter-relationship with one another and with conditions in the environment (Lawrence and Lorsch, 1967). Too great a 'buying in' to a contingency framework for board–CE relations has the potential for limiting the application of any organisational structure or working 'good practice' template on the grounds of local lack of fit. Operating against this background may, however, encourage a string of managerial and governance alibis for inappropriate decision-making, ineffective control mechanisms or simply lost opportunities.

At the same time, its attraction as a theoretical framework is its reflection of working realities in many voluntary organisations, where both boards and chief executives work with what they have to hand, not with what they would like to have; and where a continual and mutual series of accommodatory relationships will develop. Thus, 'who leads the organisation and why?' may turn out be a perennial and constantly negotiable question between CEs and their boards, affected variably by the external environmental challenges they both face.

References

Bertaux, D. (1981) 'From the Life-History Approach to the Transformation of Sociological Practice', in D. Bertaux (ed.) *Biography and Society: The Life History Approach in the Social Sciences*, London: Sage.

Bradshaw, P., Murray, V. and Wolpin, J. (1992) 'Do Nonprofit Boards Make a Difference? An Exploration of the Relationships Among Board Structure, Process and Effectiveness', *Nonprofit and Voluntary Sector Quarterly*, 21 3, 227–249.

Dargie, C. (2000) 'Observing Chief Executives: Analysing Behavior to Explore Cross-Sectoral Difference', *Public Money and Management*, 20, 3, 39–44.

Dex, S. (1991) 'Life and Work History Analyses', in S. Dex (ed.) *Life and Work History Analyses: Qualitative and Quantitative Developments*, London: Routledge.

Exworthy, M. and Robinson, R. (2001) 'Two At The Top: Relations Between Chairs and Chief Executives in the NHS', *Health Services Management Research*, 14, 2, 82–91.

Fink, J. (1989) 'Community Agency Boards of Directors: Viability and Vestigiality, Substance and Symbol', in R. Herman and J. Van Til (eds) *Nonprofit Boards of Directors*, New Brunswick, NJ: Transaction.

Ford, K. (1992) *Trustee Training and Support Needs*, London: National Council for Voluntary Organisations.

Golensky, M. (1993) 'The Board–Executive Relationship in Nonprofit Organisations: Partnership or Power Struggle', *Nonprofit Management and Leadership*, 4, 2, 177–191.

Harlan, S. L. and Saidel, J. R. (1994) 'Board Members' Influence on the Government–Nonprofit Relationship', *Nonprofit Management and Leadership*, 5, 2, 173–198.

Harris, M. (1989) 'The Governing Body Role: Problems and Perceptions in Implementation', *Nonprofit and Voluntary Sector Quarterly*, 18, 4, 317–323.

Harris, M. (1992) 'The Role of Voluntary Management Committees', in J. Batsleer, C. Cornforth and R. Paton (eds) *Issues in Voluntary and Non-profit Management*, London: Open University/Addison-Wesley.

Harris, M. (1993) 'Exploring the Role of Boards using Total Activities Analysis', *Nonprofit Management and Leadership*, 3, 3, 269–282.

Harris, M. (1996) 'Do We Need Governing Bodies?', in D. Billis and M. Harris (eds) *Voluntary Agencies: Challenges of Organisation and Management*, Basingstoke: Macmillan.

Harris, M. and Rochester, C. (2001) *Governance in the Jewish Voluntary Sector*, Planning for Jewish Communities Report no. 1, London: Institute for Jewish Policy Research.

Harrow, J. and Mole, V. (2000) '"I Want to Move Once I have Got Things Straight...": Voluntary Sector Chief Executives' Career Accounts', paper presented at International Society for Third Sector Research, Fourth International Conference, Dublin, 5–8 July, online at: www.jhu.edu.edu/-istr/conferences/dublin/abstracts/harrow-mole.html.

Herman, R. (1989) 'Board Functions and Board-Staff Relations in Nonprofit Organisations: An Introduction', in R. Herman and J. Van Til (eds) *Nonprofits Boards of Directors*, New Brunswick, NJ: Transaction.

Hodgkin, C. (1993) 'Policy and Paper Clips: Rejecting the Lure of the Corporate Model', *Nonprofit Management and Leadership*, 3, 4, 415–428.

Hodgson, R. C., Levinson, D. J. and Zaleznik, A. (1965) *The Executive Role Constellation*, Boston: Harvard Business School.

Kramer, R. (1985) 'Towards a Contingency Model of Board–Executive Relations', *Administration in Social Work*, 9, 3, 15–33.

Lawrence, P. R and Lorsch, J. W. (1967) *Organisation and Environment: Managing Differentiation and Integration*, Boston: Harvard Business School.

Leat, D. (1996) 'Are Voluntary Organisations Accountable?', in D. Billis and M. Harris (eds) *Voluntary Agencies: Challenges of Organisation and Management*, Basingstoke: Macmillan.

Mole, V. (1999a) 'Non-profits and Women CEOs' Careers', in P. Kuchinke (ed.) *Proceedings of the American Academy of Human Resources 1999 Research Conference*, Arlington, Virginia, 3–7 March, pp. 951–959.

Mole, V. (1999b) 'Voluntary Sector Chief Executives: Careers, Gender and Organisation', paper presented at the British Academy of Management 1999 Annual Conference, 'Managing Diversity', 1–3 September, Manchester.

Murray, V. and Bradshaw-Camball, P. (1990) 'Voluntary Sector Boards: Patterns of Governance', in *Towards the 21st Century: Challenges for the Voluntary Sector*, Proceedings of the 1990 Conference of the Association of Voluntary Action Scholars. London: London School of Economics.

Murray, V., Bradshaw, P. and Wolpin, J. (1992) 'Power In and Around Nonprofit Boards: A Neglected Dimension of Governance', *Nonprofit Management and Leadership*, 3, 2, 165–182.

Roberts, J. and Stiles, P. (1999) 'The Relationship Between Chairmen and Chief Executives: Competitive or Complementary Roles?', *Long Range Planning*, 32, 1, 36–48.

Robinson, R. and Exworthy, M. (2000) *Two at the Top: A Study of Working Relations Between Chairs and Chief Executives at Health Authorities, Boards and Trusts in the NHS*, Birmingham: NHS Confederation.

Stewart, R. (1991) 'Chairmen and Chief Executives: An Exploration of their Relationship', *Journal of Management Studies*, 28, 5, 511–527.

Wood, M. M. (1992) 'Is Governing Board Behaviour Cyclical?', *Nonprofit Management and Leadership*, 3, 2, 139–163.

Zald, M. (1969) 'The Power and Functions of Boards of Directors: A Theoretical Synthesis', *American Journal of Sociology*, 75, 97–111.

9 Governing independent museums

How trustees and directors exercise their powers

Mike Bieber

It appears that identifying and examining the many characteristics of agency board, staff, executive, and so on, as well as focusing on the nature of power and organisational variables in our society, generally would bring to light more sharply what the executive–board relationship is, what the consequences of various types of relationships are, and what the respective parties need to be aware of to approach the preferred relationship. In view of this, further studies of characteristics and their effects would seem in order.

(Senor, 1965: 427)

Introduction

This research examined the governance of independent museums in England, exploring the relationship between boards of trustees and directors (the museums' senior executive member of staff, sometimes called chief executive) and concentrating on how roles are divided and carried out, and on where power lies and how it is used.

The governance of museums is a dynamic process, depending on several factors. Two in particular were considered:

- the nature of professions and the status of professionals, and how this may impinge on the realities of governance;
- the effect in practice that relationships between the trustees, and between them and the director, including congruence of aims and objectives, may have on governance in practice.

The chapter describes the research approach and the methodology used. It then considers aspects of the research findings, considering the board, the director-as-professional and the board, and board meetings. Several factors influencing how power is located in the governance of independent museums are identified and discussed, and then used to construct a tentative model. First, the independent museum sector is introduced. Following this, there is a brief account of some current issues and research relating to the two specific factors mentioned above; namely professional-isation within museums and power relations between boards and managers.

Independent museums

The Museums Association (MA) estimates that there are approximately 2,500 museums throughout the UK (MA, 1997a). Frequently they are characterised in terms of how they are controlled and financed (Kavanagh, 1994: 9). The national museums are grant-aided directly by central government, and their constitutions are set out by statute. Local government museums are part of the local council structures. University museums are run by their universities' controlling bodies. The remainder, some 1,100 museums, are referred to as independent (MA, 1997a).

Independent museums have been called 'the primordial slime from which all museums start' (MGC, 1988: 12). For Cossons, however, the sector 'fit[s] into the spaces in-between the long-established and creaking structure of publicly funded museums' (1990). Although the sector goes back a long time, most independent museums today are much younger: one estimate suggests that 70 per cent have opened since 1970 (Middleton, 1990: 17).

Independent museums are characterised by their diversity, reaching parts that other museums have tended not to, in terms both of location and collection. Income generated by visitors forms the major funding source. Approximately 16 to 18 million people visit independent museums annually (Middleton, 1990: 15). Although around forty independent museums attract annual attendances of over 100,000, the overwhelming majority get far fewer visitors: many are tiny, their visitors numbered in hundreds or thousands (Middleton, 1990: 15; Association of Independent Museums, 1995: 2). All this is achieved on a staffing shoestring. In 1986, when staffing figures were last researched, there were fewer than two full-time paid staff per museum. Although a few independent museums can be counted among the largest museums, many smaller independents are likely to have no full-time, or perhaps even part-time, paid staff (Prince and Higgins-McLoughlin, 1987: 78–80).

Many independent museums are registered charities, and often also are companies limited by guarantee. Their trustees are non-executive directors, responsible for their museum's governance in the same way as trustees of other charities. Although the MA's *Code of Practice for Museum Governing Bodies* (1995) has been distributed to all independent museums, detailed prescriptions for governance structures are not set out. Nor is information about museum governance collected: the patterns of governance, how the trustees of independent museums are recruited and how they carry out their duties, still are largely unknown. This research hoped to shed some light on these factors

Current debates

This section briefly describes some of the issues pertinent to the research, from critical reading of British and North American literature about the non-profit and private sectors and the field of museums. However, the literature on museums is still sparse: only two major surveys within the last fifteen years have considered museums as organisations (Prince and Higgins-McLoughlin, 1987; Scott *et al.*, 1993).

Professions and professionalism

When society appeared more rigidly stratified, professions could be identified comparatively easily. The 'trait' or 'criterion' approach, measuring aspirants against the characteristics of the established professions such as law and medicine, was central despite its inherent flaws, perpetuating a restricted definition of the concept of professions, and imposing a unilinear view of the movement of selected occupations to professional status (e.g. Carr-Saunders and Wilson, 1964; Johnson, 1972). The more recent 'functionalist' approach, whereby occupations become professions insofar as they perform crucial social functions relevant to the maintenance of society's well-being, appears equally self-perpetuating (Parsons, 1954).

However, as access to knowledge has increased and professional detachment has been challenged, the concept of profession now appears less significant, and the study of professions has shifted to a consideration of professionals and their roles within society. Occupational groups increasingly seek recognition as professionals: the list of aspirant occupations keeps growing (Watkins *et al.*, 1992). The concept of professional now may mean little more than full-time, paid, highly skilled, competent, reliable, accountable, or able to achieve goals (Hudson, 1989; Office of Arts and Libraries, 1991).

Further, the homogeneous professional community is being displaced by hierarchical forms of occupational practice and organisation (Johnson, 1972; Weil, 1988). Management has become the main instrument to control work, thereby lessening professional autonomy and threatening professions' individualistic values. The balance of power has shifted from the professions to the purchasers of their services. Professions are perceived now as within the continuum of occupations, rather than in a privileged place outside, thus, the possibility of acceptance as profession becomes more relative.

Within museums, however, the issues of professions and professionals delineate the battleground for issues of status, power and authority. Neither the International Council of Museums (ICOM) or the MA doubt the existence of a museum profession (ICOM, 1994; Museum Training Institute and Museums Association, 1993). However, the central tension of museum workers' drive to professionalism, as for other occupations, derives from their location within a management hierarchy. Their ethical codes and knowledge bases do not protect them from the painful truths of management control and the reality of museums' need to fight for survival. Professional autonomy exists at best only in a diluted format within an organisational framework.

The MA has found 'museum professionals' a 'troublesome term' excluding many museum occupations; its revised *Code of Conduct for Museum Professionals* is addressed to 'people who work in museums' (Davies, 1996; MA, 1996). For some museum staff, though, curatorial scholarship in particular has become linked synecdochically to professionalism. To acquire this has been described as needing 'virtually a lifetime of being exposed to art and developing taste and a sense of quality', whereas management is seen as a narrow activity which one can learn quickly (Shestack, 1978: 89; Cossons, 1990). Professionals are described as motivated by outcomes, whereas managers make best use of resources to achieve a set task; professionals' relationships are based on trust and loyalty; whereas managers' are only transactional (Hebditch, 1995). Professional input is seen as necessary for decisions on all aspects of the museum's work (Lewis, 1986).

Linked to this is the issue of allegiance. ICOM (1994: 286) believes that professional staff owe 'primary professional and academic allegiance' to their museum, but that 'ultimate loyalty must be to fundamental principles and to the profession as a whole'. The MA (1996) accepts that its *Code of Conduct for People Who Work in Museums* cannot override legal and contractual obligations, but staff should not be required to act contrary to it. In general, professional staff should not be expected to change or suppress their professional judgement to conform to management decisions (Weil, 1988; Malaro, 1994). It is this tension that infuses the governance of independent museums.

The museum director-as-professional

Broadly, although funding and other realities are challenging such values, museum directors still tend to be recruited mainly for being well versed in the subject matter of their museum, rather than for any management expertise: 'the museum community prefers that [museums] should be managed by museum professionals' (Weil, 1985: 103; Dickenson, 1988: 36; MGC, 1991: 15; Fopp, 1997).

Management continues to be viewed suspiciously by some, as narrow and inimical to museums' values: directors are said to believe 'that museums are so different to other organisations that the usual rules of good management do not apply' (Zeuner, 1986). Linked to this is the museum world's adherence to the director as heroic leader: motivating and achieving by personal example, and setting the organisational culture. This flows from a status dependent on scholarship, and can be contrasted with the emergence of the post-heroic leader, the director-as-developer, elsewhere in the non-profit sector (see, for instance, Schwartz, 1983: 19; Moore, 1994: 11; Bradford and Cohen, 1997). Thus, it is directors' names that tend to be known, not those of their chairs or trustees; significantly, the MA's *Yearbook* ceased listing the governing bodies of independent museums in 1997 (1997b).

The reality of the director's work priorities can be more complex, however: many independent museums are very small, so that directors must become generalists, combining direct museum work with functional management responsibilities, and perhaps also fundraising, public relations, marketing, administration and maintenance work. Thus, for instance, an advertisement for an independent museum's director stipulated that the post-holder get 'involved with all aspects' of the museum, and show 'a readiness to do personally, any job that needs doing' (*Museums Journal*, 1997: 2).

Trustees and the locus of power

The legal position and the prescriptive literature on boards are both unequivocal: authority for the governance of non-profit organisations must lie with the board, whose main roles are to provide leadership, state the mission and values, identify objectives, decide policies, and measure achievement. Boards should delegate to management, and define the boundaries of management authority. They should care for their organisations' assets, and ensure financial stability (for instance, Hind, 1995: xvi, 15–20; Hudson, 1995: 40–42, 50–51). The literature about museums echoes this approach, sometimes simplistically: that boards should decide policy and directors implement it (Malaro, 1994: 47, 50; Sukel, 1994: 263; Babbidge, 1995: vii, B8).

The prescriptive literature finds the board–director relationship in charities difficult. Seen as central to the organisation's success, it is based on the paradox that the board, supreme governors yet unpaid and part-time, must rely on its staff, particularly the director, who may be paid and full-time. As a result, the literature emphasises the need for mutual respect and trust, with chair and director dividing roles and duties flexibly (Vladeck, 1988: 74; Hind, 1995: 15–16; Hudson, 1995: 82; Ford, 1996: 15; Leat, 1996: 64). Once again, this is repeated in the museum world (Thompson, 1992: 138; Haldane Smith, 1995: 7).

The reality of governance is less precise, more blurred. As the chair of a non-profit organisation observes, 'if trustees deal with "ends" and [the] chief executive deals with "means", who decides when an issue is one or the other?' (Blackmore, n.d.: unpaginated). Cornforth and Edwards (1998: 11) describe the prescriptive accounts as idealised or heroic views of what boards should do. Chait *et al.* (1991: 8) refer to 'hand-me-down shibboleths', untested methodically, as forming much of the conventional wisdom about trusteeship. Boards are complex organisms, and may be involved in objectives, policies and strategies to a greater or lesser extent, and perhaps also with managerial responsibilities (Peck, 1995: 138–143); involvement may well change over time (Murray *et al.*, 1992: 180; Wood, 1992; Cornforth, 1995: 6; Blackmore, n.d.). The ways boards perceive and implement their roles vary, and new trustees and directors bring their own assumptions and approaches (Cornforth, 1995: 4–7; Peck, 1995: 138–143; Hudson, 1995: 40–41, 51). Boards are not necessarily monolithic, too; there may be different sub-groups, with leaders and followers, insiders and outsiders (Middleton, 1987: 149; Holland *et al.*, 1993: 146).

Studies of museum governance in practice are sparse. As throughout the non-profit sector, the relationship between board and director is seen as based on trust and effective communication: with the board having final authority, while relying on the director for information and policy development (Griffin, 1987: 393; Dickenson, 1991: 298).

Alongside this, there have been various considerations of different patterns of the distribution of power in governance. Thus, for instance, Kramer's (1985) contingency model dismisses the view of a partnership between board members and director as failing to reflect the potential range of relationships, and as obscuring their shifting nature. Instead, he describes a three-stage continuum, consisting of consensus, difference and dissent. The parties are interest groups with distinctive resources to influence decision-making. Whether there is collaboration or conflict depends on the nature of the issue and the extent to which agreement is possible. Nevertheless, each party needs the other to carry out their respective responsibilities.

Other typologies consider the effect of power distribution within a board, as well as in relation to the director, and also move away from a simple continuum. Thus, Murray *et al.* (1992), while recognising that boards dominated by either the chair or director tend just to ratify decisions, describe three other possible patterns. First, if power is dispersed among sub-groups and individuals within the board, and there are strong disagreements around important issues, power is fragmented and the board becomes characterised by conflict; this is more prevalent in larger organisations. Second, if power is dispersed but there is a high consensus on important issues and a strongly shared ideology, this tends to lead to power sharing between board and director, with consensus decision-making, and perhaps too with board involvement in the management function. Third, a powerless board, without strong leadership or clarity about its role and responsibilities, is characterised by aimlessness and uncertainty; action relies on the repetition of past practices or the unsupported enthusiasm of individuals.

For Pettigrew and McNulty (1995), power and influence in private sector boards are shaped by the simultaneous and interactive effects of various structural and contextual factors, and on board members' 'will and skill' in mobilising and then converting a range of power sources into actual influence. Cornforth (1999) uses this model and Murray *et al.*'s typology (1992) to consider power relations within public and non-profit organisations. He shows how regulations and social norms defining a board's role and operation affect its composition, and consequently the power sources available to its members and its expectations of its future performance. The board's own processes and procedures, often shaped by the history of its relationship with the director, then act either to enable the use of these power sources (for instance, through informal policy and strategy forums for board members and staff), or to hinder or even negate their effect (for instance, through board members given no opportunities to meet informally, or through long, unstructured agendas). The exercise of power helps shape power relations in the future, through affecting expectations and establishing new processes.

Cornforth (1999) discerns two new patterns of power distribution, extending those described by Murray *et al.* (1992): a coalition between the director and a long-standing and dominant trustee, and a move from a director-dominated board to a more equal partnership between board and director. Additionally, he notes that a strong director's power is simultaneously enhanced by and conditional upon the board's support (Cornforth, 1999: 24).

Other researchers have identified an additional dynamic, that the pattern of governance varies according to the stage that the board has reached in its life cycle (e.g. Greiner, 1972; Mathiasen, 1990; Wood, 1992; Hudson, 1995). While this approach suggests that power relations between board and director change during crises, the fieldwork here considered the governance of museums which, as far as could be seen, were in more 'normal' times.

Methodology

The research was based on the belief that relationships are socially determined: there are no absolute truths to be measured objectively. The fieldwork explored the views of trustees and directors on the dynamics of governance and their respective roles, and also ascertained their backgrounds and motivations. The governance of three case study independent museums was studied and was compared with a postal survey of twenty-two independent museums.

The three case study museums

The requirements for the case study museums were that there was a full-time, paid director; that the museum was a charity; that the board was responsible only for the museum; and that the museum was registered by the then Museums and Galleries Commission (MGC). In practice, these conditions excluded many museums. One further practical requirement was that they were in London. As there were only three case study museums, it was clear that this could not be a representative selection. The postal survey checked whether the views of those involved in their governance were paralleled by colleagues outside London.

Fifteen museums meeting these criteria were invited to take part, three of which agreed to become the case study museums. Table 9.1 summarises the main characteristics of the case study museums: their focus, history and size, including staffing, and some initial information about their board meetings. This shows some similarities, but also some important differences.

The fieldwork was carried out between 1996 and 1997, and was based on a triangulated approach (Peck, 1993, 1995), using three sources of data:

- the actors' own accounts;
- minute of meetings;
- observation of board meetings.

The actors' own accounts

As Peck points out, these rely on the actors' insight and objectivity; he could have added honesty (1995: 139–140). Nevertheless, this source provides glimpses beneath the surface of the board meetings being observed. At each museum there were five semi-structured interviews with the chair, director and three other trustees: one seen as close to the centre of board power, a relatively new trustee, and a trustee perceived more as an outsider, even a maverick. The chair and director were asked to identify individuals to fit these categories. Those trustees not interviewed were asked

Table 9.1 Characteristics of the three case study museums

	Museum A	Museum B	Museum C
Nature of collection	Social history	Social history	Social history
Opened	1990	1914 (became an independent in 1990)	1990
Annual visitor numbers	15,000 approx.	50,000 approx.	9,000 approx.
Full and part-time staff	4	28	4
Use of volunteers	Extensive	Few	Extensive
Board size (including chair)	15	11	11
Frequency of meeting	Monthly	Quarterly	Quarterly
Average length of meeting	139 minutes	87 minutes	82 minutes
Average attendance (trustees)	8	7	6
Average attendance (staff)	3	3	1
Minute taker	Staff member	Staff member	Director

to complete a questionnaire, a shorter version of the interview; seventeen of the twenty-four forms (71 per cent) were completed.

Following the conclusion of the observations of board meetings (see below), a questionnaire was sent to those interviewed: revisiting earlier questions, and covering matters occurring during the period of observation. Two trustees had resigned. In all, eleven of the thirteen questionnaires (85 per cent) were completed.

Minutes of meetings

These are a limited source, since, as Peck (1995: 140) notes, they tend to be restricted to recording decisions, sometimes accompanied by background information and a summary of the discussion; they represent the establishment view of the board's activities. In practice, too, minutes are often written or approved by the director and chair: it is a brave or stubborn trustee who challenges the overall approach and tone, rather than just specific details. Nevertheless, the minutes provided useful background reading for each museum.

Observation of board meetings

A form was devised to record the contributions of everyone at the meetings to each agenda item, based on Peck's approach (1993, 1995), adjusted in the light of the specific needs. For each of the seventeen board meetings observed over a nine-month period, every member's contribution was recorded, attributing it to one of the eleven types of activity listed, and also marking the time that each contribution took.

The categories used were: 'agreeing', 'disagreeing', 'giving an opinion', 'challenging', 'criticising', 'suggesting action', 'procedural', 'giving information', 'questioning', 'summarising', and the catch-all of 'other' (which turned out to consist largely of making jokes). They seemed to stand up well in practice to the realities of busy meetings. The first six categories together were taken to describe trustees 'engaging actively with the issues', arguably the main purpose of such meetings.

The postal survey

A survey of trustees and directors provided a broader look at the governance of independent museums, and also a comparison with the case studies' findings. Thirty museums were approached, half in London, and half outside, using the same selection criteria as for the case studies. The questionnaire was limited to two sides of an A4 page, in order to encourage a high response rate. Responses came from twenty-two museums, with 135 completed questionnaires: sixteen chairs (73 per cent), one hundred of the 278 other trustees (36 per cent), and nineteen of the directors (86 per cent) – 42 per cent overall. It had not been possible to send out reminders, so this reply level was high.

The research findings

The board

The research reveals that museum boards appeared to be homogeneous demographically, in terms of gender, age and ethnic origin. Men constituted 75 per cent of board members in the survey and case study museums. Table 9.2 shows that few board members were young: approaching half were aged over 60, almost 80 per cent over 50, and only 5 per cent were under 41.

Some 3 per cent of the trustees in the survey and the case studies classified themselves as Irish, while 2 per cent defined themselves in terms of an 'other' ethnic grouping. The remaining 95 per cent who replied described themselves as white. Altogether, two-thirds of the trustees in the survey, and three-quarters of chairs, were white, male and aged over 50. A further 13 per cent of the trustees and chairs were white, male and aged 50 or under. Only one in five of the 107 trustees and chairs whose gender, ethnic origin and age group were known, were outside the 'white male' grouping.

Although the research showed this homogeneity of backgrounds, however, it also indicated that the board members did not seem agreed on major principles of governance. The survey asked board members for their opinions on a number of governance issues. Responses from nine museums where replies had been received from at least half the board were examined, to note the level of agreement among those board members at each museum. A simple marking scheme was used: this is a complex area, and so the results can be only indicative.

Thus, for instance, the survey asked how strongly board members agreed or disagreed with a series of statements about governance issues (such as 'management expertise is more important than scholarship for a museum director'), using a five-point scale. The nine museum boards' responses showed that only between a quarter and a half of their members

Table 9.2 Age of board members (survey and case studies)

Age	No. (n = 143)	(%)
Under 30	3	2
30–40	5	3
41–50	23	16
51–60	47	33
61–70	46	32
Over 70	19	13

shared the same opinion. The survey also asked to whom should the board be responsible; respondents' replies were then collated and categorised. Although such an open-ended approach is likely to produce less agreement than for multi-choice questions, the level of agreement was very low within all nine boards. For example, while respondents in all the boards mentioned 'the public', in only two did over half the respondents make this choice. Likewise, respondents in eight museums referred to 'funders and key stakeholders', but in only three did over a quarter of the respondents there choose them. Taking the replies to all the questions asking for respondents' opinions about governance in general and within their own museums, on average less than half of board members agreed with each other.

This level of agreement was so low that it raised the question as to whether these issues had ever been discussed by the boards. Observation of the case study museums' board meetings shed further light on this. Few of the discussions touched on governance principles or practices. Instead, the time was spent largely in seeking and obtaining factual information, and in procedural matters. Perhaps such a lack of agreed governance principles may lead in practice to a greater reliance on *ad hoc* approaches to problematic issues, in turn emphasising personal relationships within the board. As will be seen, the observations indicated that this might well place relations between the chair and director at the centre of the museums' governance processes, and of the realities of decision-making.

The research showed that those involved as museum trustees in the survey and case studies tended not to have had substantial governance experience elsewhere over the previous five years, to offer different perspectives on governance issues. Thus, only 17 per cent of trustees had been a trustee of another museum in that time, most of whom had been a trustee of one or two other museums. Only a quarter of trustees of the case study museums had been a trustee of another arts organisation over the previous five years (the question was not asked in the survey), most of whom had had experience of only one such organisation. Approximately half the trustees of the survey and case study museums had been a trustee of another charity during the previous five years, although here again two-thirds of these indicated that they had been involved with only one or two others.

One possible consequence of this lack of governance experience elsewhere, and of the apparent absence of thorough discussions regarding fundamental governance issues, may be that the only views of governance that trustees brought to their boards and shared with their fellow trustees were likely to have derived from their similar demographic backgrounds.

The director-as-professional and the board

As the brief consideration above of the literature on professions and professionalism describes, professional autonomy now tends to exist in a
diluted format: professional decisions are taken within managerial imperatives. The question at issue within museums was whether directors have
professional autonomy. If so, how can boards decide policy, run the
museum, and tell staff what to do?

In practice, within the case study museums the board seldom discussed
issues concerning the museum's *raison d'être*, its collections and the uses to
which these were put. It appeared content to agree most of the items presented by the staff on these matters, without the scrutiny it applied to
other areas. The director reinforced this at times by mentioning their professional status and referring to 'my professional advice', for instance,
when talking about objects which the museum owned or which they
wanted it to acquire, as though to demarcate their area of authority. On
each occasion, the board complied with their request or recommendation
without further ado. One chair described this as the board 'relying on
[the director's] judgement; it was our judgement of [X's] judgement'.
The directors' perspective was slightly different; one wrote 'in ... more
complicated decisions we advise [the board] as professionals so they can
make informed decisions'.

Even when discussing medium- and long-term plans, board members
did not touch on these issues. Only three times were there discussions
about a museum's collection, twice initiated by a trustee; they tended to
fizzle out, and any decisions taken appeared in the minutes as only advisory. One trustee noted that in museums there were inevitable tensions
between those in charge, the non-professionals, and those doing the day-
to-day work, the professionals, leading at times to differences of view and
difficulties. The observation showed that these tensions appeared to have
been resolved by board members backing off at a director's use of the
word 'professional'.

This was all the more remarkable as the research showed it to have
been interest in these very matters that had first drawn most trustees to
join their board. Three-quarters of board members in the survey and case
studies mentioned interest in the museum or its subject matter as a motivating factor for joining, and 70 per cent of board members considered
that they brought skills and knowledge in this area with them. Given this,
one might have expected board members to have become more involved
with their museums' collections at governance level.

Board meetings

Board meetings in practice are the formal location for much of an organisation's governance; for some trustees, it may be the only contact they

have (although two of the three case study museums involved some of their trustees through sub-committees). It might have been useful to explore whether board members at the case study museums had contact with each other outside meetings; unfortunately, however, this was not asked. The observations in all three museums emphasised the director's centrality. It was the director who tended to compile the agenda, sometimes in consultation with the chair, deciding at what stage in the decision-making process each item should reach the board, and thereby setting the tone for the meeting; the trustees appeared to display little interest in how and when items reached the meetings. The director, sometimes with other staff, wrote the background papers, framed the recommendations for action, and presented these at the meeting, often indicating their preferred outcome.

Furthermore, the minutes, the formal record of decisions taken, were taken by staff members at all three museums. The chair was the only person able to amend the draft soon afterwards. Although trustees could suggest amendments at the next meeting (held up to three months later), this did not occur frequently. At the case study board meetings, then, the director, as leading staff member, acted as gatekeeper, information-provider, and decision-shaper.

The observation of the case study museums' board meetings included timing all contributions, and analysing them into categories. Table 9.3 shows that in all three museums, 'engaging actively with the issues' (as defined above) made up less than half of the contributions, both by number and by time. In particular, it took up less of the average meeting than requesting and giving information. The proportion of the third category, procedural issues, ranged from 12 per cent to 15 per cent, both by number and time.

Although Peck (1995) describes only the methodology of his observation of NHS Trust board members' contributions, not the results, he also analyses the overall mode of the board's behaviour during each agenda item observed, and reports the results. Thus, overall, the board spent 63 per cent of its time receiving information, seen by Peck as a passive mode of activity, and 21 per cent approving items, as against 13 per cent of its time challenging and amending. When considering policies and plans, this rose to 90 per cent of the time spent receiving information and approving items, as against 10 per cent challenging and amending; and when considering financial issues, to 84 per cent of the time receiving information, with the remainder spent approving items. Thus, Peck's (1995: 143–153) observations show board members appearing to engage even less actively with the issues than in the case study museums.

The contributions made at the meetings were analysed also in terms of who made them. Table 9.4 shows who contributed, separating speakers into several groupings. Thus, during the average meeting, the chair made considerably more contributions than other trustees. The chair and the

Table 9.3 Main groupings of activities at average board meetings, as percentages of the total contributions and time

	Museum A		Museum B		Museum C	
	(%) Contributions	(%) Time	(%) Contributions	(%) Time	(%) Contributions	(%) Time
Active engagement	43	36	31	27	37	36
Procedural	15	12	14	12	15	13
Questioning/giving information	39	49	52	60	44	45
Other	4	3	5	4	4	4

Table 9.4 Contributions to board meetings of different actors

	Museum A		Museum B		Museum C	
	(%) Contributions	(%) Time	(%) Contributions	(%) Time	(%) Contributions	(%) Time
Chair	23	19	32	26	27	26
Acting Chair	34	26	–	–	–	–
Average per trustee – three trustees who contributed most	12	12	9	10	16	15
Average per trustee – others	2	2	4	4	5	5
Director	17	20	21	29	25	26
All staff (including Director)	36	41	36	45	29	32
Chair (or Acting Chair) and Director	51	46	53	55	52	52
Chair (or Acting Chair) and all staff	70	67	68	71	56	58

Note: These figures are averages based on several meetings; because not all participants were present at every meeting, percentages may exceed 100 per cent.

director between them talked for half the time; adding on the contributions of other staff, this came to almost two-thirds of the time. Little time was left for the other trustees; at each museum there were trustees who spoke only two or three times in a meeting, or in several instances not at all.

Analysing the activities at these meetings, it became clear that the chairs were involved in more than just chairing the meeting neutrally and enabling other board members to contribute. They spent up to a third of their time actively engaging with the issues facing the board, and made up to a third of all such contributions during the meeting.

Looking at the contributions of the directors, between almost an eighth and a half of these were engaging with the issues; in all, between one in three and one in five of all such contributions came from the director and staff. Directors are not board members, of course, and their role tends to be seen formally as limited to providing information necessary for trustees to decide the issues.

Nearly all items at the meetings observed were agreed or accepted; very few were deferred, amended or rejected, and there was little debate. Meetings appeared to function mainly to progress plans, and thereby to form part of the management process, controlled by the director, more than to function as the central stage for governance, controlled by the board. The chair and the director of all three case study museums tended to use much of the meeting's time, and played an active part in the decision-making, and, together with the other staff, seemed to be crowding out the trustees.

People within organisations may often feel that, whether or not they have authority, power seems to be located elsewhere. Within the case study museums, board members and directors were asked who of the chair, the other trustees and the director had made certain recent governance decisions. The chairs saw decisions as mostly made jointly by the chair, the other trustees and the director, and by the trustees. The trustees saw decisions as mostly made jointly and by the director, narrowly ahead of being made by themselves. Chairs were seen as the group with the least input into decisions. In general, then, few saw themselves as having had power; as so often, people felt that it was others who exercised it. Only the directors saw decisions as made mostly by themselves: aware of their power and willing to acknowledge that they had used it.

Were these references to decisions being jointly made an idealistic view, or an accurate reflection of what had happened? If it was the latter, it might have been that the director played a larger part in governance matters in practice than generally acknowledged. It is interesting to note also that in the survey, too, under a quarter of board members felt that the board took all governance decisions. In such circumstances, it then becomes a matter to be implicitly or explicitly negotiated as to who does decide these issues.

However, one key function that most board members and directors of the case study museums did consider to have been a joint decision, was that of selecting new trustees; only one-fifth saw the chair as having contributed directly. Nevertheless, though, from observation of the board meetings it was the chair, occasionally the director, who suggested a possible new trustee; and usually the chair who then vetted the prospective trustee, before announcing their recommendation at a subsequent meeting: invariably this was ratified by the other trustees.

Factors influencing governance: a tentative model

Based on his observations, Peck (1995: 153) suggests that the NHS Trust board he studied did not play a role in setting and reviewing overall strategy, but merely approved managers' strategic directions. From the observation of power relations within the independent museums' boards discussed above, where a similar apparent lack of involvement by boards in policy issues was noted, another interpretation may be possible. Several inter-related factors that influenced the governance of these museums can be identified, which come together to form a tentative theoretical model, helping to understand how power within the governance of these museums was located.

The first factor concerns the composition of the board. The research revealed a demographic homogeneity among board members. Although one can over-estimate the effects, nevertheless one might expect some sharing of those cultural values characteristic of their common background, including assumptions and beliefs concerning non-profit organisations and museums, the status and independence of professionals, and perhaps even the roles of trustees. In the absence of discussion of the board's role, and of previous experience of governance for many board members to draw upon, this homogeneity may have been a significant element of cohesion to encourage mutual trust among trustees.

Another factor is that the director generally embodies within the museum the professional values of subject-matter expertise and fulfils the expectations of board and staff as heroic leader. When dealing with the board, the director strives to maintain this heroic stance and professional distance. In turn, the director's emphasis on professional status and values may link into board members' shared cultural regard for the status and independence of professionals.

The summary of current debates referred to the continuing emphasis on the importance of curatorial knowledge among some within the museum community. In the museums studied, trustees appeared, at least implicitly, to recognise the director's right to use professional status to secure control of the museum's collections; this may even have served to win the respect of those trustees who were enthusiasts for the museum's subject matter. They seem to have believed that perhaps their role was rather to concentrate on ensuring that conditions were right for the director and staff to exercise their professional expertise. In this way, they seemed to have found a way of functioning within one of the central paradoxes of governance, that trustees, who have overall legal responsibility, have to rely on their staff to support them in carrying out their governance role.

Another factor was the enhanced role of the chair. The main functions of the chairs were seen by their fellow trustees as chairing meetings, leadership, and working closely with the director. It seemed that, having entrusted so much of the museum's decision-making to the director's professional expertise, the board felt it important to monitor the director's general approach. From the case study research, the other trustees seemed to have entrusted their chair with establishing a relationship with the director which formed a crucial link between staff and board, and to have then looked to the chair to use this position to oversee the director's performance. In return, the trustees allowed their chair to exercise leadership over the board at its meetings. Thus, trustees' apparent lack of involvement in the collections may have been a delegation of authority, rather than an abdication of power.

It may be, therefore, that what appears initially to relate to Cornforth's (1999) account of a coalition between director and dominant trustee, in this case the chair, may instead represent a working relationship between the chair, acting on the board's behalf, and the director, linking in rather with his account of a more equal partnership between board and director. It would also confirm the view that a director's power may simultaneously be enhanced by, and conditional upon, the board's support. The partnership may serve to validate the director's position, clothing the reality of their power with authority delegated by the board through its chair and it may suit the director to have one board member with whom to relate. There may even be some give-and-take with their respective responsibilities: the chair gaining closer involvement in non-professional decisions such as finance, in return for safeguarding control over staff's professional areas of responsibility.

The final factor is a congruence of beliefs between chair, trustees and director, which can translate into the mutual trust and respect seen earlier to be considered necessary for effective governance. This can form the basis for the success of the trustee–staff relationship, enabling the constituent parts to operate smoothly; in its absence the relationship would grate and eventually break down. The boards and directors involved in this research probably would not have agreed to participate had there been any serious problems. It is not surprising, therefore, that almost 90 per cent of the survey's respondents agreed that there was a shared vision in their museums, with almost 40 per cent agreeing strongly; only 3 per cent disagreed. It is likely that the level of consensus decision-making apparent in the research would have followed from this shared set of beliefs.

This account of some of the factors coming from the research provides one explanation of the reality of power relationships in small independent museums which appeared to be running relatively smoothly. The composition of the museum boards, and the ways in which the exercise of their governance function was structured, affected trustees' ability to use their nominal power. To be effective, they seem to have concentrated their power in the chair–director relationship: a coalition between the representative of the board as the body legally charged with ultimate responsibility, and the leading possessor of professional expertise.

The typographies considered earlier of how power may be distributed in the exercise of governance suggest various patterns that may occur in different settings. As circumstances vary, for instance during an organisational crisis, the resulting patterns of power are likely to alter. The underlying theme of this research can be seen as emphasising that the reality of governance occurs in a variety of ways, despite the certainties of prescriptive writers; to understand what is happening, one must study how boards function within the broader theoretical and practical contexts.

References

Association of Independent Museums (1995) 'Wild Swings in Independents: 1994 Figures', *Association of Independent Museums Bulletin*, 18, 4, 2.

Babbidge, A. (1995) *The Effective Museum Trustee: A Working Manual*, Edinburgh: HMSO.

Blackmore, B. (n.d.) *Summary: Research into the Governance/Management Interface*, Middlesex: Association of Chief Executives of National Voluntary Organisations.

Bradford, D. and Cohen, A. (1997) *Managing for Excellence*, New York: Wiley.

Carr-Saunders, A. M. and Wilson, P. A. (1964) *The Professions*, London: Frank Cass.

Chait, R., Holland, T. and Taylor, B. (1991) *The Effective Board of Trustees*, Phoenix, AZ: Oryx Press.

Cornforth, C. (1995) *Governing Nonprofit Organisations: Heroic Myths and Human Tales*, paper presented at National Council of Voluntary Organisation's Conference on 'Researching the UK Voluntary Sector', September, London.

Cornforth, C. (1999) 'Power Relations Between Boards and Senior Managers in the Governance of Public and Non-profit Organisations', paper presented to Second International Conference on Corporate Governance and Direction, Henley Management College.

Cornforth, C. and Edwards, C. (1998) *Good Governance: Developing Effective Board–Management Relations in Public and Voluntary Organisations*, London: Chartered Institute of Management Accountants.

Cossons, N. (1990) 'Scholarship or Self-indulgence?', *Museum Management and Curatorship*, 9, 4, 359–360.

Davies, M. (1996) 'A View from Clerkenwell', *Museums Journal*, 96, 5, 54.

Dickenson, V. (1988) *Management Development for Canadian Museums*, Background Paper for Museum Policy Working Group, Ottawa: Department of Communications.

Dickenson, V. (1991) 'An Inquiry into the Relationship Between Museum Boards and Management', *Curator*, 34, 4, 291–303.

Fopp, M. (1997) *Managing Museums and Galleries*, London: Routledge.

Ford, K. (1996) 'Chain Ganged', *Charity World*, 5, 24.

Greiner, L. (1972) 'Evolution and Revolution as Organisations Grow', *Harvard Business Review*, 50, 4, 37–46.

Griffin, D. (1987) 'Managing in the Museum Organisation: (1) Leadership and Communication', *International Journal of Museum Management and Curatorship*, 6, 387–398.

Haldane Smith, R. (1995) 'Roles and Responsibilities of Trustees', paper presented to Museums Association Seminar on 'Safe in Our Hands?', January, London.

Hebditch, M. (1995) 'Contemporary Issues in Museums Governance', paper presented to the Museums Association Seminar on 'Safe in Our Hands?', January, London.

Hind, A. (1995) *The Governance and Management of Charities*, High Barnet, Herts: Voluntary Sector Press.

Holland, T., Leslie, D. and Holzhalb, C. (1993) 'Culture and Change in Nonprofit Boards', *Nonprofit Management and Leadership*, 4, 2, 141–155.

Hudson, K. (1989) 'The Flipside of Professionalism', *Museums Journal*, 88, 4, 188–190.

Hudson, M. (1995) *Managing Without Profit*, London: Penguin.

ICOM (1994) 'Code of Professional Ethics', in G. Kavanagh (ed.) *Museum Provision and Professionalism*, London: Routledge.

Johnson, T. J. (1972) *Professions and Power*, London: Macmillan.

Kavanagh, G. (1994) 'Introduction', in G. Kavanagh (ed.) *Museum Provision and Professionalism*, London: Routledge.

Kramer, R. (1985) 'Toward a Contingency Model of Board–Executive Relations' *Administration in Social Work*, 9, 3, 15–33.

Leat, D. (1996) 'Are Voluntary Organisations Accountable?' in D. Billis and M. Harris (eds) *Voluntary Agencies: Challenges of Organisation and Management*, Basingstoke: Macmillan.

Lewis, G. (1986) 'Managing Museums', in British Council (ed.) *Museum Management and Administration*, London: British Council.

Malaro, M. C. (1994) *Museum Governance: Mission, Ethics, Policy*, Washington, DC: Smithsonian Institution Press.

Mathiasen, K. (1990) *Board Passages: Three Key Stages in a Nonprofit Board's Life Cycle*, National Center for Nonprofit Boards, Washington, DC.

MGC (1988) *Report 1987–88*, London: Museums and Galleries Commission.

MGC (1991) *Report 1990–91*, London: Museums and Galleries Commission.

Middleton, M. (1987) 'Beyond the Governance Function', in W. Powell (ed.) *The Nonprofit Sector: A Research Handbook*, New Haven, CT: Yale University Press.

Middleton, V. (1990) *New Visions for Independent Museums*, Chichester: Association of Independent Museums.

Moore, K. (1994) 'Introduction: Museum Management', in K. Moore (ed.) *Museum Management*, London: Routledge.

Murray, V., Bradshaw, P. and Wolpin, J. (1992) 'Power In and Around Nonprofit Boards: A Neglected Dimension of Governance', *Nonprofit Management and Leadership*, 3, 2, 165–182.

Museum Training Institute and Museums Association (1993) *Careers in Museums,* London: Museum Training Institute and Museums Association.

Museums Association (MA) (1995) *Code of Practice for Museum Governing Bodies,* London: Museums Association.

Museums Association (MA) (1996) *Code of Conduct for People Who Work in Museums,* London: Museums Association.

Museums Association (MA) (1997a) *Facts About Museums,* Museums Briefing 15, London: Museums Association.

Museums Association (MA) (1997b) *Museums Yearbook 1997/98,* London: Museums Association.

Museums Journal (1997) Supplement, 97, 9.

Office of Arts and Libraries (1991) *Volunteers in Museums and Heritage Organisations: Policy, Planning and Management,* London: HMSO.

Parsons, T. (1954) *Essays in Sociological Theory,* Illinois: Free Press of Glencoe.

Peck, E. (1993) 'The Roles of an NHS Trust Board: Aspirations, Observations and Perceptions', in E. Peck and P. Spurgeon (eds) *NHS Trusts in Practice,* Harlow: Longman.

Peck, E. (1995) 'The Performance of an NHS Trust Board: Actors' Accounts, Minutes and Observation', *British Journal of Management,* 6, 2, 133–156.

Pettigrew, A. and McNulty, T. (1995) 'Power and Influence In and Around the Boardroom', *Human Relations,* 48, 8, 845–873.

Prince, D. and Higgins-McLoughlin B. (1987), *Museums UK: The Findings of the Museums Data-Base Project,* London: Museums Association.

Schwartz, B. (1983) 'George Washington and the Whig Conception of Heroic Leadership', *American Sociological Review,* 48, 18–33.

Scott, M., Klemm, M. and Wilson, N. (1993) *Museum Sector Workforce Survey,* Bradford: MTI.

Senor, J. (1965) 'Another Look at the Executive–Board Relationship', in M. Zald (ed.) *Social Welfare Institutions,* New York: Wiley.

Shestack, A. (1978) 'The Director: Scholar and Businessman, Educator and Lobbyist', *Museum News,* 57, 2, 27–31.

Sukel, W. (1994) 'Museums as Organisations', in K. Moore (ed.) *Museum Management,* London: Routledge.

Thompson, J. (1992) 'The Role of the Director', in J. Thompson (ed.) *Manual of Curatorship,* Oxford: Butterworth-Heinemann.

Vladeck, B. (1988) 'The Practical Differences in Managing Nonprofits: A Practitioner's Perspective', in M. O'Neill and D. Young (eds) *Educating Managers of Nonprofit Organisations,* New York: Praeger.

Watkins, J., Drury, L. and Preddy, D. (1992) *From Evolution to Revolution: Pressures on Professional Life in the 1990s,* Bristol: University of Bristol.

Weil, S. (1985) *Rethinking the Museum and Other Meditations,* Washington, DC: Smithsonian Institution Press.

Weil, S. (1988) 'The Ongoing Pursuit of Professional Status', *Museum News,* 67, 2, 30–34.

Wood, M. (1992) 'Is Governing Board Behaviour Cyclical?', *Nonprofit Management and Leadership,* 3, 2, 139–163.

Zeuner, C. (1986) 'The Alternative to Crisis Management', *AIM Bulletin,* 9, 2, 3.

Part IV

Continuity and change

10 The changing face of charity governance

The impact of organisational size[1]

Chris Cornforth and Claire Simpson

Introduction

The challenging and often problematic nature of governance in non-profit organisations has long been recognised. As Middleton (1987) and more recently Harris (1999) note, staff in non-profit organisations seldom seem to be satisfied with the performance of their boards. Boards are either accused of meddling in the affairs of management or conversely that they are not involved enough and serve a largely symbolic function. There has also been wider public concern at various governance failures (Gibelman and Gelman, 2000). A survey by the National Council for Voluntary Organisations (NCVO) and the Charity Commission in the UK rather alarmingly revealed that many trustees of charities were not even aware they were trustees (NCVO, 1992).

In response to the perceived problematic nature of governance, there have been a raft of different initiatives across the UK voluntary sector to improve governance, which were outlined in the Introduction. Recapping briefly, there has been a rapid growth in training and practical advice for new board members. For example, the NCVO established a Trustee Services Unit in 1993 to provide advice and information on governance, which subsequently evolved to provide board training and development. In addition, there have been a number of attempts to codify good practice and various handbooks, guides and codes of practice have been drawn up for board members and boards. However, it is unclear how widespread or deep an impact these changes have had upon the sector.

This chapter presents some results from a national survey of the boards of charities in England and Wales carried out in 1999. A major aim of the research was to examine how boards are changing and whether the various external initiatives outlined above have had an impact on what boards do. The survey looked at changes over the past three years in the following areas: board size, structure, frequency of meetings, recruitment practices, training and support and the use of external advisers and consultants. Data was gathered on both the nature of the changes and the reasons for them. In addition, the survey was designed to gather some basic demographic data about boards and to allow some comparisons with an earlier baseline survey of charity boards carried out in 1994 (Kirkland and Sargant, 1995).

An important hypothesis underlying the research was that 'size matters'. We hypothesised that many board characteristics would vary with the size of charity. The research also revealed that many board changes vary with organisational size.

Sample and methodology

The population chosen for study was charities in England and Wales. All such charities have to register with the Charity Commission for England and Wales and submit annual returns. Basic data about each charity, including its income, is kept on the Charity Commission's register of charities. Because the distribution of charities is very skewed and we were interested in the impact of size, we decided to construct a stratified random sample using this register. We divided the charities into six main income bands: less than £10k, £10k–£100k, £100k–£250k, £250–£1 m, £1 m–£10 m and greater than £10 m. This particular choice of bands was made for two main reasons:

*   for convenience – it followed the banding used by the Charity Commission itself;
*   to allow comparison with an earlier survey of charity trustees (Kirkland and Sargant, 1995) by combining some of the bands.

A random sample of 500 charities was selected from each of the income bands apart from the £10 m plus band where all organisations were selected (approximately 270 charities).

Table 10.1 shows the distribution of charities across the different income bands at the end of 1998. It shows that the vast majority of charities are very small: 70 per cent have an income of less than £10,000, and 90 per cent have an income of less than £100,000. Conversely, less than 2

Table 10.1 Breakdown of charities by income bands

Annual income bracket (£)	Number of charities	% of all registered charities
£0–10,000	113,697	70.51
£10,001–100,000	33,575	20.82
£100,001–250,000	6,382	3.95
£250,001–1 million	4,772	2.96
£1 m–10 m	2,545	1.58
£10 m and over	271	0.17
Total	161,243	100

Source: Charity Commission's register of charities, 1998.

per cent of charities have an income of over £1m. In the analysis presented later we have had to apply weightings when generalising findings to the population as a whole in order to reflect this very skewed distribution of charities. (The weights were calculated by dividing the percentage of charities in each population stratum by the percentage of sample replies in the stratum.)

The Charity Commission's register includes a named respondent for each charity and a contact address. Unfortunately the register does not include the position of the respondent in the organisation. The questionnaire was sent to the respondent with a covering letter asking that the questionnaire be passed on to the person who was responsible for providing clerical and/or administrative services to the board for completion. It was felt that this person was likely to have a good knowledge of the board and be more dispassionate than other role holders would be, such as the chair or chief executive. Equally, many small charities without paid staff would not have a chief executive. However, as we could not be sure who would fill in the questionnaire, or what other roles they might hold, the questionnaire included a question about what roles the respondent undertook. This meant we could compare the responses of different types of respondent

The questionnaire was designed to gather data about the size and type of organisation; the size, structure and composition of the board; changes concerning the board over the past three years; the functions the board performed and how effectively it was perceived to perform them; and various board processes. In this chapter we focus on presenting the results concerning the characteristics of boards and board continuity and change. For a discussion of the other findings from the survey, see Cornforth (2001a) and Cornforth (2001b).

Postal questionnaires were sent to a total of 2,797 charities. Returns were received from 737, an overall response rate of nearly 27 per cent. The response rate for charities in each income band is shown in Table 10.2. The response rate was lowest for the largest charities (income

Table 10.2 Response rate of charities by income bands

Annual income bracket (£)	Number of charities surveyed	Number of responses	% response rate
£0–10,000	500	103	20.6
£10,001–100,000	500	154	30.8
£100,001–250,000	500	136	27.2
£250,001–1 million	500	155	31.0
£1m–10m	500	136	27.2
£10m and over	271	43	15.9
Missing	–	10	–
Total	2771	737	26.6

>£10 m) at 16 per cent and for the smallest charities (income <£10,000) at 21 per cent. For the other income bands it was very similar, varying between 27 per cent and 31 per cent.

Research questions

A number of exploratory propositions were developed to guide the data gathering and the subsequent analysis. The first set of these concerned general board characteristics and the impact of organisational size.

As Handy (1993: 192) observes, organisational size has often proved to be the single most important factor influencing choices of organisational structure; see, for example, the Aston programme of studies (Pugh and Hickson, 1976; Pugh and Hinings, 1976; Pugh, 1997). Yet relatively little attention has been paid to the influence of organisational size in studies of non-profit organisations, and in particular their governance. In his review of the literature on voluntary participation in non-profit organisations, Horton Smith (1994: 246) notes that the study of contextual variables, such as organisational characteristics, is much less well developed than other areas of research. In a later paper he is critical of non-profit researchers for having focused their research on non-profit organisations with paid staff, largely ignoring the many small grassroots associations (Horton Smith, 1997). Earlier, Milofsky (1988) also noted the relative lack of attention paid by researchers to smaller community self-help organisations and suggests various differences between them and larger more bureaucratic non-profit organisations. Similarly, as Rochester notes in Chapter 6, a weakness of much of the prevailing non-profit governance literature is that it treats issues of governance as generic and ignores differences that may stem from size or other organisational variables. Yet a few empirical studies suggest that there are likely to be some important differences. For example, an earlier survey of charities in the UK suggested that board size and composition vary directly with organisational size (Kirkland and Sargant, 1995: 11). Stone and Wood (1997), based on research in small, religiously affiliated social service providers, propose that small size will lead to relatively simple governance structures and informal, but centralised control systems. Rochester in Chapter 6 also suggests a number of distinctive features of boards of small voluntary agencies. For these reasons we were keen to examine the impact of organisational size on boards. Broadly speaking, we hypothesised that boards were likely to become larger, more structured and formalised with organisational size. The four propositions relating to organisational size examined in this chapter are:

S1   Larger organisations are more likely to have larger boards.
S2   The boards of larger organisations are more likely to have sub-committees.

S3 Larger organisations are more likely to have written documents describing the job of board members.

S4 Larger organisations are more likely to provide induction and training for new board members.

The second set of propositions (listed below) concerned recent changes to boards. We expected that the various contextual changes would be having an impact on charity governance (see the Introduction). There was considerable speculation and anecdotal evidence (e.g. Kirkland and Sargant, 1995: 38; Maggs, 2000) that the increasing competition for and demands on trustees were making it more difficult to recruit board members (proposition C4). Partly as a result of this pressure and the desire to improve the effectiveness of boards, there was some evidence (e.g. Ward, 2000) that charities were becoming more professional in their recruitment of new board members, moving away from informal recruitment methods to more formal ones (proposition C5). Because of the difficulties of board recruitment and the move to more professional boards we expected boards to have reduced in size (proposition C1). At the same time we expected the increased demands on boards to have led to an increase in the frequency of board meetings (proposition C2). We also expected to find that boards were making more use of external advisers (proposition C6) and that the training and support available to board members had increased (proposition C7). Finally, we felt that the drive to professionalise boards was likely to mean that they were becoming more structured, making more use of sub-committees (proposition C3). These propositions are summarised below:

C1 Boards are more likely to have decreased rather than increased in size.

C2 Boards are more likely to have increased rather than decreased the frequency of meetings.

C3 Boards are more likely to have increased rather than decreased the number of sub-committees.

C4 The difficulty of recruiting new members is more likely to have increased rather than decreased.

C5 Board recruitment methods are changing and becoming more formal.

C6 Boards are more likely to make use of external advisers and consultants.

C7 The training and support available for board members are more likely to have increased rather than decreased.

Results concerning board characteristics

Board size

The results concerning the average size of boards are given in Table 10.3. The average ranges from 8.7 for the smallest organisations to 21.0 for the largest. The overall average size of boards for the population as a whole is 9.5. Table 10.3 suggests that the average size of boards increases with the size of the organisation. The bigger organisations ($>£1$ m) also have much greater variation in board size. The difference in board size for the different groups was compared using Analysis of Variance (ANOVA) and is significant at the $p<0.01$ level. Hence proposition (S1) that larger charities have larger boards is supported.

The results concerning size make an interesting comparison with an earlier survey carried out in 1994 (Kirkland and Sargant, 1995: 11). Table 10.4 compares the finding of the two surveys. Both surveys suggest that the average board size increases with the size of the organisation. However, our survey suggests that the average size of boards is larger in each income category by between two to four members. Overall, our survey shows an average board size of 9.5 compared with 7 in the 1994 survey.

Table 10.3 Average size of governing bodies

Income (£)	Mean	N	Std deviation	Std error of mean
£0–10,000	8.71	100	4.18	0.42
£10,001–100,000	10.02	152	5.85	0.47
£100,001–250,000	10.79	134	6.55	0.57
£250,001–1 million	13.02	153	11.26	0.91
£1–10 m	18.58	134	20.95	1.81
£10 m and over	20.95	43	22.47	3.43
Population (wt'd)	9.49	–	6.42	–

Table 10.4 Comparison of the average size of boards in 1994 and 1999

Income (£)	1994 survey		1999 survey	
	Mean	N	Mean	N
£0–10,000	7	57	8.7	100
£10,001–100,000	8	85	10.0	152
£100,001–1 million	9	106	11.0	287
£1 m and over	15	62	19.2	177
Population	7	–	9.5	–

Structure and frequency of meetings

The survey examined how boards are structured. It asked whether or not boards had sub-committees. The results are presented in Table 10.5. The percentage having sub-committees varies from 25 per cent in organisations with an income <£10,000 to 93 per cent in organisations in the >£10 m income band.

Using the chi-squared test showed significant differences between organisations in the different income bands at the $p<0.01$ level. Table 10.5 suggests that the likelihood of boards having sub-committees increases with the size of the organisation. This provides some support for proposition (S2) that the boards of larger organisations are more likely to have sub-committees.

The average frequency of board meetings is shown in Table 10.6. The average varies from between 5 and 6.8 meetings a year for the different income bands. Using the ANOVA F-test suggests these differences between the income bands are not significant at the $p<0.05$ level.

Support for board members

The survey gathered data on two aspects of support for board members: the availability of written documents detailing the job of board members and what is expected of them ('job descriptions'), and the availability of

Table 10.5 Boards with formal sub-committees (%)

Sub-committees	Income (£)						Pop. total weighted
	£0–10,000	£10,001–100,000	£100,001–250,000	£250,001–1 million	£1 m–10 m	£10 m and over	
Yes	25.0	44.1	48.5	67.3	86.7	93.0	32.9
No	75.0	55.9	51.5	32.7	13.3	7.0	67.1
% of total responses	14.0	21.3	18.5	21.4	18.9	5.9	100.0

Table 10.6 Average number of board meetings per year

Income (£)	Mean	N	Std deviation	Std error of mean
£0–10,000	5.33	87	3.86	0.42
£10,001–100,000	6.79	142	6.20	0.52
£100,001–250,000	6.70	123	4.22	0.38
£250,001–1 million	5.63	144	2.96	0.25
£1 m–£10 m	5.04	131	2.80	0.25
£10 m and over	5.48	40	2.60	0.41
Population (Wt'd)	5.71	–	4.47	–

induction and training for new board members. The results are shown in
Tables 10.7 and 10.8 respectively.

The availability of 'job descriptions' for board members varies between
32 per cent and 65 per cent for organisations in the different income
bands. Table 10.7 suggests the availability of job descriptions is lowest in
small charities (<£100,000) and increases for larger organisations. Using
the chi-squared test a significant difference was found between the charities in different income bands at the $p < 0.01$ level. These findings support
proposition S3 that larger organisations are more likely to provide board
members with written 'job descriptions'.

The availability of training varies between 20 per cent and 76.7 per
cent. Table 10.8 suggests that the availability of training increases with the
size of the organisation. Again using the chi-squared test, a significant difference was found between the charities in different income bands at the
$p < 0.01$ level. This supports the proposition S4 that larger charities are
more likely to provide induction and training for new board members.
Together these findings suggest that the support available to board
members increases with the size of the organisation.

Board change

Recruitment and size

The survey asked if boards were finding it more or less difficult to recruit
suitable board members. The results are presented in Table 10.9. Overall,
about 60 per cent of boards reported no change. Of those reporting a
change, the vast majority reported it was becoming more difficult to
recruit board members – overall, 38.6 per cent reporting it was more difficult compared with 1.1 per cent saying it was less difficult. The percentage
reporting it was more difficult to recruit board members decreased with
size from 41 per cent for the smallest charities to 11.9 per cent for the
largest. The chi-squared test showed a significant difference between
the samples, although there are problems using this statistic because of
the low cell counts. These findings support proposition C4 that the difficulty of recruiting board members has increased. Table 10.9 suggests that
the difficulty is inversely related to size, with the smallest charities experiencing the most problems.

However, these problems in finding suitable board members do not
appear to have had a large effect on how boards are recruiting new
members. We asked respondents if the way they were recruiting board
members had changed. The results are shown in Table 10.10. Overall,
only 7 per cent of charities had changed their recruitment practices,
although this varied between 5 and 23 per cent in the various income
bands, with most change among larger organisations (>£1 m). The differences between samples were significant at the $p < 0.05$ level.

Table 10.7 Charities with written job descriptions for board members (%)

Board job description	Income (£)						Pop. total weighted
	£0–10,000	£10,001–100,000	£100,001–250,000	£250,001–1 million	£1m–10m	£10m and over	
Yes	35.4	31.8	44.4	41.2	54.8	65.1	35.8
No	64.6	62.3	54.9	56.9	45.2	32.6	62.9
Don't know	–	5.8	0.8	2.0	–	2.3	1.2
% of total responses	13.8	21.5	18.5	21.3	18.8	6.0	100.0

Table 10.8 Charities with induction and training programmes for new board members (%)

Induction and training	Income (£)						Pop. total weighted
	£0–10,000	£10,001–100,000	£100,001–250,000	£250,001–1 million	£1m–10m	£10m and over	
Yes	20.0	26.0	37.1	33.6	57.0	76.7	23.5
No	80.0	71.4	62.1	65.1	41.5	23.3	75.9
Don't know	–	2.6	0.8	1.3	1.5	–	0.6
% of total responses	14.0	21.5	18.4	21.2	18.9	6.0	100.0

Table 10.9 Change in the difficulty of recruiting suitable board members (%)

Difficulty of recruitment	Income (£)						Pop. total weighted
	£0–10,000	£10,001–100,000	£100,001–250,000	£250,001–1 million	£1m–10m	£10m and over	
More difficult	41.0	34.9	36.6	28.1	23.9	11.9	38.6
Less difficult	1.0	0.7	3.7	2.6	1.5	4.8	1.1
No change	57.0	60.5	58.2	68.0	72.4	81.0	58.8
Don't know	1.0	3.9	1.5	1.3	2.2	2.4	1.5
% of total responses	14.0	21.3	18.7	21.4	18.7	5.9	100.0

Table 10.10 Change in board member recruitment (%)

Change in recruitment	Income (£)						Pop. total weighted
	£0–10,000	£10,001–100,000	£100,001–250,000	£250,001–1 million	£1m–10m	£10m and over	
Yes	7.1	4.6	10.4	12.5	14.2	23.3	7.2
No	85.9	88.8	87.3	83.6	83.6	76.7	86.3
Don't know	7.1	6.6	2.2	3.9	2.2	–	6.5
% of total responses	13.9	21.3	18.8	21.3	18.8	6.0	100.0

Because of the difficulties in recruitment and the drive for greater board efficiency, we also hypothesised that the size of boards was more likely to have decreased than increased (proposition C1). Findings on changes in board size are shown in Table 10.11. Overall, the size of boards has not changed for 69 per cent of organisations. In the income bands <£1m a higher percentage of charities had increased rather than decreased board size. For the largest charities the picture was reversed. Overall, 20 per cent of charities reported an increase in size, while 10.6 per cent reported a decrease. The differences between the samples were significant at the $p < 0.05$ level. The picture is more complex than proposition C1 suggests; the boards of small and medium-sized charities are more likely to have increased rather than decreased in size, whereas the converse is true for the boards of the largest charities.

Board structure and frequency of meetings

Proposition C3 suggests that boards are becoming more structured, making greater use of sub-committees. We asked respondents whether the number of sub-committees of their board had changed. The results are shown in Table 10.12 and offer some support for our proposition. These suggest that for about 86 per cent of charities there has been no change. However, where change has taken place it has mainly been in the direction of increasing the number of sub-committees, between 4 and 27 per cent of organisations in the different income bands reporting an increase, and between 3 and 14 per cent reporting a decrease. Overall, 8.2 per cent of organisations increased the number of sub-committees, whereas 4.2 per cent decreased the number. The amount of change appears to be related to size, with the most change taking place among the largest organisations, and the least among the smallest. The chi-squared test showed a significant difference between the samples at $p < 0.01$.

Again, because of the increased expectations and pressures on boards we hypothesised that they were more likely to have increased rather than decreased the frequency of board meetings (proposition C2). We asked respondents if the frequency of meetings had changed. The results are shown in Table 10.13 and again offer some support for our proposition. These show that for more than 80 per cent of organisations there was no change. However, where change had taken place, apart from one income band, the percentage of organisations increasing the frequency of board meetings was greater than that decreasing them. Those increasing the number of meetings varied between 8 and 28 per cent, whereas those decreasing them varied between 5 and 10 per cent. Most change was taking place among the boards of the very large organisations (>£10m). Only among organisations with a turnover of £250k–£1m were a greater percentage of organisations decreasing the number of meetings. However, the differences between samples was not statistically significant at the $p < 0.05$ level.

Table 10.11 Change in board size (%)

Size	Income (£)						Pop. total weighted
	£0–10,000	£10,001–100,000	£100,001–250,000	£250,001–1 million	£1 m–10 m	£10 m and over	
Increased	19.2	23.5	20.5	20.3	13.6	18.6	20.0
Decreased	8.1	14.8	16.7	12.4	22.0	30.2	10.6
No change	71.7	61.7	61.4	66.7	64.4	51.2	68.8
Don't know	1.0	–	1.5	0.7	–	–	0.7
% of total responses	14.0	21.0	18.6	21.6	18.6	6.1	100.0

Table 10.12 Change in the number of board sub-committees (%)

No. of sub-committees	Income (£)						Pop. total weighted
	£0–10,000	£10,001–100,000	£100,001–250,000	£250,001–1 million	£1 m–10 m	£10 m and over	
Increased	4.4	13.2	18.9	25.0	26.7	25.6	8.2
Decreased	3.3	5.9	7.4	2.8	10.7	14.0	4.2
No change	91.2	79.4	72.1	71.5	62.6	60.5	86.6
Don't know	1.1	1.5	1.6	0.7	–	–	1.1
% of total responses	13.6	20.4	18.3	21.6	19.6	6.4	100.0

Table 10.13 Change in the frequency of board meetings (%)

Frequency of meetings	Income (£)						Pop. total weighted
	£0–10,000	£10,001–100,000	£100,001–250,000	£250,001–1 million	£1m–10m	£10m and over	
Increased	8.1	11.8	15.0	7.8	11.2	27.9	9.5
Decreased	7.1	7.8	6.8	8.5	9.7	4.7	7.2
No change	83.8	79.7	77.4	83.7	79.1	67.4	82.5
Don't know	1.0	0.7	0.8	–	–	–	0.8
% of total responses	13.8	21.4	18.6	21.4	18.7	6.0	100.0

Support for boards

Given the various pressures and initiatives to improve performance, we hypothesised that the training and support available to board members were more likely to have increased rather than decreased (proposition C7), and that boards would be more likely to make more rather than less use of external advisers and consultants (proposition C6). We asked respondents if the level of training and support available to board members had changed. The results are shown in Table 10.14 and tend to support proposition C7. Overall, about 86 per cent of organisations reported no change, 11 per cent reported an increase and only 1 per cent a decrease. The increase in support varied with size of organisation ranging from 7 per cent in the smallest charities to 44 per cent in the largest. The chi-squared test showed a significant difference between the samples at the $p < 0.01$ level, although there are problems using this statistic because of low cell counts.

The results with regard to the use of external consultants and advisers are shown in Table 10.15 and offer support for our proposition C6. Again, about 80 per cent of organisations report no change. However, where change is taking place, it is very much towards greater use of consultants and advisers – overall, 17.5 per cent of charities reported an increase in use, whereas only 1.9 per cent make less use of them. The greatest increase in use is among the charities in the middle income bands for £100k–£1 m charities. These differences between samples were significant at the $p < 0.01$ level, although again there are problems using the chi-squared statistic because of the low cell counts. This time there is no simple linear relationship between the increased use of external adviser and consultants and size. The greatest increase is among medium-sized charities, with similar but smaller growth in the smallest and largest charities.

Summary and discussion of findings

The results of the survey supported proposition S1 that larger organisations tend to have larger boards. A similar relationship was found in a previous survey carried out in 1994 and reported in Kirkland and Sargant (1995). However, our survey suggests the average size of boards is 9.5 members, which is substantially larger than the average they found of 7, and that in each income band boards are on average two to four members larger. It is quite difficult to know how to interpret these findings. It is possible that the size of boards has grown over the five years between the surveys. Other findings discussed in this chapter concerning changes in board size in the past three years suggest there has been some growth in board size among small and medium-sized charities but, in contradiction to the findings above, a decrease among the largest charities (see Table

Table 10.14 Change in the level of training and support available to board members (%)

Level of support	Income (£)						Pop. total weighted
	£0–10,000	£10,001–100,000	£100,001–250,000	£250,001–1 million	£1m–10m	£10m and over	
Increased	7.1	16.2	29.5	25.2	36.6	44.2	11.2
Decreased	1.0	1.4	–	0.7	0.7	–	1.0
No change	89.9	81.1	69.7	72.8	61.9	55.8	86.1
Don't know	2.0	1.4	0.8	1.3	0.7	–	1.7
% of total responses	14.0	20.9	18.7	21.4	19.0	6.1	100.0

Table 10.15 Change in the use of external consultants and advisers (%)

Use of external support	Income (£)						Pop. total weighted
	£0–10,000	£10,001–100,000	£100,001–250,000	£250,001–1 million	£1m–10m	£10m and over	
Increased	15.8	18.8	25.2	32.7	25.4	16.3	17.5
Decreased	2.1	0.7	2.3	0.7	4.5	–	1.9
No change	80.0	79.2	71.0	66.0	70.1	79.1	79.8
Don't know	2.1	1.3	1.5	0.7	–	4.7	1.7
% of total responses	13.5	21.2	18.7	21.4	19.1	6.1	100.0

10.11). It is possible this discrepancy concerning large boards may be accounted for by statistical error or by methodological differences between the two surveys. Both studies used a similar approach surveying a stratified sample of charities and asking one person to give information about the governing body of their organisation. However, although they were defined in the same way, our survey mainly used the language of 'board member', whereas the previous survey mainly used the language of 'charity trustee'. The 1994 survey asked: 'How many members/trustees does your organisation have on its governing body?' Our survey asked: 'How many members does your governing body have?', where a board member was previously defined as 'a voting member of the governing body, responsible for the general control and management of a charity or voluntary organisation'. It is possible that in answer to our question respondents may have included some staff or advisers who attend board meetings but are not board members/trustees. This is a question that deserves further investigation. If our findings are correct, it suggests that the previous estimate of the number of charity trustees in the UK by Kirkland and Sargant (1995: 11) may have been considerably under-estimated.

Another area where there were significant differences between charities of different sizes concerned the structure of boards. As one might expect, the likelihood of boards having sub-committees increased with the size of organisation supporting proposition S2. Also the support available to board members in terms of written job descriptions and induction and training increases with size of organisation, supporting propositions S3 and S4. However, the frequency of board meetings was not related to organisational size. On average, boards meet about six times a year.

Our findings concerning board change present a mixed picture. There is both a good deal of continuity, but also some important changes taking place. For each of the questions we asked, usually between 60–85 per cent of organisations said they had not changed. In many instances these changes were significantly different for different sizes of charities.

There was support for the proposition (C4) that in general boards are finding it harder to recruit new board members. Overall, 39 per cent of organisations reported increased difficulty, while only 1 per cent reported less difficulty. These difficulties appear to be inversely related to size, with the smallest organisations finding recruitment the hardest. These differences were difficult to assess statistically because of small cell counts. However, only a small proportion, 7 per cent overall, reported changing their recruitment practices.

Proposition C1, that boards were more likely to have decreased in size over the last three years, was not supported. Overall, about two-thirds of organisations reported no change in the size of their boards, while 20 per cent reported an increase and 11 per cent a decrease. There were significant differences between different size charities. In general, charities with an income >£1 m were more likely to report having decreased the size of their boards (although, as noted above, this finding was not supported by a comparison of board size with the 1994 survey), whereas organisations with an income <£1 m were more likely to report having increased the size of their boards. If the findings on changes in board size over the preceding three years are correct, then it looks as though there may be some degree of convergence occurring between large and small charities. It is possible that the normative literature, which tends to argue against very large or very small boards, may be having an effect.

There was some support for propositions C3 and C2 that both the number of board sub-committees and the frequency of meetings were increasing to meet increased demands on boards. Over 80 per cent of organisations said they were not changing. Of those that did change, a slightly higher percentage said they were making more rather than less use of sub-committees, and meeting more frequently.

Finally, there was support for propositions C6 and C7 that the amount of support available to board members is increasing. Some 80 to 86 per cent of organisations reported no change. However, of those that did change, a much higher percentage reported an increase in support and training, and in the use of external advisers and consultants. The increase in support and training appeared to increase directly with size. In contrast, the use of external advisers and consultants peaked for medium-sized organisations. This may be because small charities find it more difficult to afford external advice, whereas the largest charities may be more likely to have the necessary expertise among their staff. Alternatively, there have been suggestions that medium-sized organisations are struggling most to compete with larger charities for funding, and may feel the need for more external assistance.

Conclusion

The statistical analysis presents a revealing picture of charity boards and how they are changing, which has important theoretical and practical implications. The research clearly supports the view that organisational size matters – a number of important board characteristics vary with size, and so do many board changes. Larger charities tend to have much larger boards than small charities. In keeping with findings of the Aston programme that the structuring of organisational activities increases with organisational size (Pugh, 1997), we found that various aspects of board structure increase with organisational size. The boards of larger charities make more use of sub-committees and provide more formal support to board members. Larger charities are also more likely to provide board members with written job descriptions and provide new board members with induction and training.

There was evidence that board recruitment problems and practices were related to organisational size. There was support for the widespread concerns in the sector that many charities are finding it harder to recruit new board members, with nearly 40 per cent of organisations saying it was more difficult. This difficulty was inversely related to size, with the smallest charities nearly four times more likely to report increased difficulty than the largest charities. Interestingly only a relatively small percentage of charities had changed their recruitment practices and those that had were much more likely to be large charities. Also, on average, board size did not appear to be decreasing as a result. This raises interesting questions for policy-makers and practitioners. How can the pool of potential charity trustees be increased? How in particular can smaller charities be helped to attract trustees? Do smaller charities need to be encouraged to try new methods to attract board members?

The survey provides evidence to suggest that external initiatives to improve board performance are having some effect, but again their take-up seems to be related to organisational size, with the greatest impact among medium and large charities. Overall, about 11 per cent of charities said they had increased the level of training and support for board members against 1 per cent who said that it had decreased. However, this change was most among the largest two groups of charities where 37 per cent and 44 per cent reported increases. On average 17 per cent of charities said their boards made more use of external consultants and advisers as opposed to 2 per cent who said they used them less. This time the increase was greatest among medium-sized charities.

The findings on board recruitment and support suggest there may be a growing gap between the boards of large and small charities, with larger charities finding it easier to recruit board members and providing them with increasing support. An important question for policy-makers and voluntary sector support organisations is, does this matter? On the one hand, it can be argued that medium and large charities control the majority of financial resources in the sector and that the boards of these organisations need to be well supported. The figures also show that even here, particularly among medium-sized organisations, much more could be done to support boards. On the other hand, it can be argued that over 90 per cent of charities have an income of <£100,000, and that this is where the vast majority of charity trustees make their contribution. Yet this is where least change is taking place. This raises two important policy questions. Should more resources be devoted to supporting the boards of small charities? And, if so, how can this best be achieved, as current initiatives appear to be having a limited impact? (see Cornforth (2001a) for a more a detailed discussion of these issues).

Overall, the findings suggest that there are dangers in developing generic theories or practical prescriptions for non-profit boards. The many differences between the boards of organisations of different sizes suggest that more attention needs to be paid to developing both theory and practice that is sensitive to these contextual differences.

Note

1 This chapter is an edited version of the paper 'Change and Continuity in the Governance of Non-Profit Organisations in the UK: The Impact of Organisational Size', *Non-Profit Management and Leadership* 12, 4, 2002.

References

Cornforth, C. (2001a) *Recent Trends in Charity Governance and Trusteeship: The Results of a Survey of Governing Bodies of Charities*, London: National Council for Voluntary Organisations.

Cornforth, C. (2001b) 'What Makes Boards Effective? An Examination of the Relationships Between Board Inputs, Structures, Processes and Effectiveness in Non-Profit Organisations', *Corporate Governance: An International Review*, 9, 3, 217–227.

Gibelman, M. and Gelman, S. R. (2000) 'Very Public Scandals: An Analysis of How and Why Nongovernmental Organisations Get in Trouble', a paper presented at the International Society for Third Sector Research conference, Trinity College, Dublin, July.

Handy, C. (1993) *Understanding Organisations*, 4th edition, London: Penguin Books.

Harris, M. (1999) 'Voluntary Sector Governance – Problems in Practice and Theory in the United Kingdom and North America', in D. Lewis (ed.) *International Perspectives on Voluntary Action: Reshaping the Third Sector*, London: Earthscan.

Horton Smith, D. (1994) 'Determinants of Voluntary Association Participation and Volunteering: A Literature Review', *Nonprofit and Voluntary Sector Quarterly*, 23, 3, 243–263.

Horton Smith, D. (1997) 'The Rest of the Non-profit Sector: Grassroots Associations as the Dark Matter Ignored in Prevailing "Flat Earth" Maps of the Sector', *Nonprofit and Voluntary Sector Quarterly*, 26, 2, 109–113.

Kirkland, K. and Sargant, N. (1995) *Building on Trust: Results of a Survey of Charity Trustees*, London: National Council for Voluntary Organisations.

Maggs, L. (2000) 'Sector Crying Out for Free Trustee Recruitment Service', *Third Sector Trustee*, October, Issue 7, 5.

Middleton, M. (1987) 'Nonprofit Boards of Directors: Beyond the Governance Function', in W. Powell (ed.) *The Nonprofit Sector: A Research Handbook*, New Haven, CT: Yale University Press.

Milofsky, C. (1988) 'Structure and Process in Community Self-Help Organisations', in C. Milofsky (ed.) *Community Organisations: Studies in Resource Mobilisation and Exchange*, Oxford: Oxford University Press.

NCVO (1992) *On Trust: Increasing the Effectiveness of Charity Trustees and Management Committees*, London: National Council for Voluntary Organisations.

Pugh, D. S. (ed.) (1997) *The Aston Programme of Research, vols 1, 2 and 3*, Aldershot: Ashgate Publishing.

Pugh, D. S. and Hickson, D. J. (1976) *Organisational Structure: Extensions and Replications: The Aston Programme II*, Aldershot: Gower.

Pugh, D. S. and Hinings, C. R. (1976) *Organisational Structure in its Context: The Aston Programme I*, Aldershot: Gower.

Stone, M. M. and Wood, M. M. (1997) 'Governance and the Small, Religiously Affiliated Social Service Provider', *Nonprofit and Voluntary Sector Quarterly*, 26, Supplement, S44–S61.

Ward, P. (2000) 'Skills on Board', *ThirdSector Trustee*, October, Issue 7, 9.

11 The impact of new governance structures in the NHS

Lynn Ashburner

Introduction

In the early 1990s the NHS reforms introduced markedly new forms of governance structure into the NHS. These were criticised by the then Labour opposition and many academics as critical issues relating to public accountability were being disregarded in favour of a 'private sector' model of governance (Ashburner, 1997). How effective private sector boards are in their governance role and how appropriate this model is for the public sector raises further important issues about board role and performance. This chapter reviews the process of change that occurred in the health sector in the 1990s and discusses its significance in terms of its impact upon governance structures in the NHS. The extent to which changes have been introduced to counter critics and to strengthen the NHS board model has been limited. The subsequent election of a Labour government was potentially an opportunity for the issue of public accountability to come to the fore and to be addressed within the large new policy initiatives which focused on the 'modernisation' process for the NHS. In the White Paper *The NHS – Modern and Dependable* (DoH, 1997), one of the six key principles is to 'rebuild public confidence in the NHS as a public service accountable to patients, open to the public and shaped by their views' (ibid.: 11), while at the same time ensuring that 'financial confidence and probity are maintained' (ibid.: 39). The expansion of the 'board' model into the primary health care sector with the creation of primary care groups, which eventually became primary care trusts, offered an opportunity to develop and evaluate new forms of governance structure. Given the role of primary care boards in the choice and purchasing of care across the health sector, greater accountability here could be argued to be of particular relevance. While some small changes of emphasis are evident in the creation of primary care groups, there has been no attempt to introduce local, democratic decision-making in any formal sense. Primary care groups are only required to have 'accountability agreements and have a named Accountability Officer' (ibid.: 49). This chapter assesses the implications of this inertia and maintains that further

changes are still possible and desirable if the government is truly committed to greater levels of 'participation' and to ensuring the probity and
effectiveness of boards in the management of the NHS.

Underlying this debate there are a number of inherent tensions which
are experienced within NHS boards that are also reflected in other types
of public, private and not-for-profit boards. Of great value in this sector
has been the extent of the study of the development and operations of
NHS boards from direct observation of boards in operation which offers a
more realistic perception of what boards actually do. Research by Ferlie *et
al.* (1996) at Warwick observed public and private board meetings of
eleven different NHS boards over a period of three years. Other studies
looked at the role of a single board, for example, Peck (1995). The findings from such studies can be compared with what boards are required to
do and what they claim to do, as well as with the literature on prescriptions for board success. Compared with the latter, which forms the majority of the literature on boards, especially those in the private sector, the
advantages of direct observation cannot be emphasised too strongly. Tensions exist across different aspects of board structure, objectives and operation. The perception that boards can only be efficient and effective at the
cost of reduced levels of accountability has long been held and needs to
be questioned. That such tensions exist should not be reason to see this as
an 'either/or' situation. Similarly, with the tensions between the board's
roles of performance and conformance, it is necessary to explore how
these can best be balanced and managed within each specific context. As
Cornforth notes in the Introduction, particular tensions experienced
within the individual roles of board members need to be addressed to
avoid weakening the ability of the board to perform effectively.

Governance roles in public and private sectors

Up until 1990 there were no boards of directors within the National
Health Service. Various forms of 'authorities' performed the necessary
governance functions, and changes to these structures are central to issues
of public accountability. Governance structures define the role and composition of the board of an organisation, and relate to the issue of probity
as well as the range of types of accountability (Day and Klein, 1987). In
the private sector accountability is predominantly to shareholders and
includes the responsibility for maximising the performance of the organisation. In the public and non-profit sectors there are different and wider
accountabilities with a need to balance these, as well as ensuring probity
in the spending of public money. Ranson and Stewart (1994) argue that
because it is public money, there should therefore be *more* stringent
accountability mechanisms for the public sector. Clatsworthy *et al.* (2000)
also believe that the need for confidence in the stewardship of the organisation is stronger in the public sector. They also emphasise the key differ-

ences in financial accounting and auditing functions between the sectors, concluding that it is problematic to take a private sector model and apply it to the public sector. While there are strong parallels between the governance responsibilities across sectors, there are marked differences in structures and roles. Even between public services, governance structures vary, with resultant differences in the relative power positions of managers, professional and lay members of boards, or non-executives (Ashburner, 1997).

The term '*public* accountability' has different interpretations, and within the National Health Service has not been interpreted as direct accountability to the public, but accountability (to the public) via government. On the other hand, '*democratic* accountability' is taken to refer to *local* democratic accountability which is very weak or non-existent. The issue of probity is more fundamental to a board's role, and is the key role of independent members, whether termed non-executives or lay members. There have been several instances in the private sector where structures were insufficient to maintain probity (Guinness, Maxwell, etc.), which have raised concerns. The Cadbury Report (1992), and subsequent reports, address some but not all of the issues raised by recent corporate failures, but all are just guidelines and thus are only advisory. The recommendations of the Cadbury Report are based upon the requirements of the private sector, and although it has been used as a basis for public sector bodies, in this respect it does not go far enough, limited as it is to financial accountability issues.

In practice, probity can also be compromised with an over-emphasis on operational issues. The role of boards across sectors, in deciding and promoting the mission of the organisation, in enabling performance and helping formulate strategy, has tended to predominate (Ashburner, 1997). As a consequence, there has been a greater emphasis on managerial and operational issues. This has made the role of the non-executives who have the main responsibility for probity more problematic, as their involvement in 'management' issues draws them away from a strategic and independent perspective. Garratt (1996), similarly, has described the increasing tension for boards between 'conformance' and 'performance'. What is important here, therefore, is the level of power of the board in relation to senior management, and the board's level of independence, which focuses on the role of the lay member or non-executives. Unlike many private sector and non-profit organisations, boards in the public sector have the constraint of deciding individual organisational strategy within the limits of government policy. This can be compared to the role of a subsidiary board responsible to a holding company, where the subsidiary is responsible for the interpretation and implementation of policies which are decided upon at a higher level. In this way government policy may constrain the extent of the strategic choices open to a board, as well as imposing decisions that a board would otherwise not wish to make

(Ashburner, 1997). Also, given the public sector board's role in interpreting government policy, then the question of the relative power and independence of politically appointed chairs and non-executives in relation to managers can be critical.

NHS governance changes

Among the multitude of reforms that have beset the NHS over the last few decades, there have been various changes made to the governance structures. Whether the reforms address governance issues indirectly, or directly as with the 1990 NHS and Community Care Act, there are important consequences for the way that power, accountability and influence are distributed. Klein (1983) described the creation of the NHS as a compromise between those who wanted the governance of the health service to be in the hands of elected local government representatives, and the medical professionals who were the dominant group. Although managers as a group were not formally members of health authorities or boards before 1990, there has been a long-standing perception of a 'trade-off' between managerial efficiency and the representation of different stakeholder groups (Klein, 1983; Ashburner and Cairncross, 1993). The role of the lay member (or non-executive) and the question of whether members on the board should be representational, and thus more directly accountable to certain groups, have been central to the developments in governance within the health sector.

Early compromises meant that the principle of representation of key stakeholders on health authorities and governing bodies of hospitals was not part of the governance structures at the birth of the NHS. Members were appointed by the Secretary of State to Regional Boards and Management Committees. It was not until a Green Paper in 1970 by Richard Crossman that the principle of representative membership was introduced and thus, from their creation in 1974, health authorities were composed of a combination of people appointed by the Secretary of State, from the various groups of health professionals and local authorities. The third group comprised lay members in what came to be known as the tripartite system. Their 'selection' was never formalised and they were perceived to comprise personal contacts from within 'the great and the good' locally. Managers were not members, but reported to the board, and received the board's policy decisions. Minor changes in 1982 with the abolition of area health authorities saw fewer local authority nominees, but no significant change occurred until 1990 when governance structures underwent a total transformation.

The criticisms of health authorities prior to 1990 have been greatly over-simplified, for example, in their description as being mere 'rubber stamps' (Ashburner and Cairncross, 1993). Day and Klein (1987) identified a high degree of role ambiguity for members, with a resultant lack of corporate identity as the main cause of the authorities' limited effectiveness and reactive management style. In policy terms, their apparent lack of decision-making was blamed on the representational nature of members' roles. In addition to this, there was a wider government agenda of increasing 'managerialism', to challenge the power of professional groups, which was manifest in policy changes across the public sector. The 1990 NHS and Community Care Act marked a significant break with the past in that it removed all local authority and most professional members. Medical and nursing members were statutorily required on hospital trust boards, but not on health authorities, and they were there only in an individual capacity and not a representational one. Lay members remained as part of the board; they were still politically appointed, but were now called non-executives.

The change of terminology, not just for the newly formed 'boards' but across the health sector, was indicative of the introduction of processes, practices and concepts from the private sector. The specific advice that was sent out from the Department of Health, in the search for non-executives, was that directors of large companies were to be approached and the CBI and other local trade organisations were to be canvassed. Alongside this very direct attempt to get 'business people' onto the boards was the inclusion for the first time of managers from the organisation. The model being followed was that of some private sector boards in the UK. The General Manager, now chief executive, was to be included along with four other senior managers or directors. Thus board membership was restricted to eleven: five senior managers, and five non-executives, most of whom had a business background, but some with some experience of health charities or patient groups, two of whom were there as 'local' members (Ashburner and Cairncross, 1993). There was increased ambiguity in the role of the non-executive when the concept of 'representation' was abandoned. Even when nominated informally as 'local representatives', they were not actually appointed to represent local people but to speak for themselves *as* local people.

Clear distinctions need to be made between the different types of accountability and their relevant roles and importance in this debate. Financial accountability is central to probity issues, with the non-executives having the ultimate power to sanction or remove the chief executive, or other directors. Local democratic accountability has probably never existed to any significant degree on public bodies where there are no direct elections, but it was claimed to exist via the local authority elected members who were appointed to health boards. When significant changes were made to governance structures in 1990, there was a conflation of issues of representation, accountability and effectiveness, which obscured the intentions behind the reforms and the effects. In reality there was little in the policy to indicate any real understanding of the issues or the needs facing boards or the new organisational structures in the NHS. The broad shift of focus was to mimic the structures in the private sector, despite the fact that these, on several significant occasions, were repeatedly failing to ensure accountability and probity. However, this still represented a fundamental challenge to the representative traditions of public services. The assumption being made, which led to abandoning any pretence of representation, was that the new accountability context was aimed at increasing effectiveness and efficiency and that this was incompatible with local democratic accountability. No attempt was made to try to balance operational effectiveness with local democratic accountability, and to explore what part representation should play in this.

As the ideals of representation and democratic accountability were being abandoned in the search for effectiveness and efficiency, it becomes important to establish whether the new bodies could or were delivering improved performance. The changes introduced as part of the 1990 reforms had put the responsibility for lack of effectiveness on the nature of the membership, rather than examining the wider aspects of composition and role. The Warwick research (Ferlie *et al.*, 1996) concluded that the defined role of the board, and how it operated, were critical, in conjunction with composition and individual roles. The research showed that changing the structure and composition of boards alone would not make them more effective, and that there was a need to look at how power and influence were shared, how individuals on the boards interpreted their roles and how they operated as a group. Key in this is the risk that the increasing focus on boards as strategic decision-making bodies could compromise their role in corporate governance and ensuring probity, i.e. performance at the expense of conformance. With the more recent emphasis on openness and accountability, however non-specific and limited, it has led some such as Harrison (1998) to argue that 'encouraging these measures still reflects a rather greater concern with conformance than performance. Whilst such a balance may increase public confidence, it does little in terms of boardroom creativity and director contribution.' Again, the effectiveness of boards is being presented as being at risk, when accountability issues are recognised. What is more relevant and what needs to be examined are how boards operate and the tensions between the two main roles of the board (conformance and performance) and how those same tensions implicit in the roles of individual members are managed.

Tensions in board roles

How can a board balance its responsibilities to its roles in relation to accountability, probity and effectiveness? Having noted the increased emphasis on accountability, the notion of effectiveness, which includes overall performance and the competence of senior managers to run the organisation effectively and in the direction of policy, has not been diminished in importance. Essential in this is the need for boards to identify their main purpose and objectives and for this to be a tangible guide to roles and behaviour. After nearly ten years of experience of NHS boards in operation, the question remains as to the extent to which the performance of boards has been addressed.

At their creation there was a lack of policy about what exactly the new NHS boards were there to do and what their main purpose was. This mirrors the main weakness in earlier authorities where there was a lack of clarity overall on what their role, and that of the board, was. The 1990 Act was solely concerned with the composition of NHS boards and led initially to 'role ambiguity', among both non-executives and executives because there was no defined role (Ferlie *et al.*, 1996). The concept of being on the board, as a medical professional or as a locally appointed non-executive, but without any requirement to represent your group or the locality, but to contribute as an individual, was difficult to define. The scope and definition of executive and non-executive roles and the responsibilities of the board emerged over the next few years, via a series of guidelines from the Department of Health. If 'accountability' is interpreted as more than just to government, then there are issues still to be addressed about how boards reconcile their multiple accountabilities to different stakeholders, which might include patients, the local community, and other employees. However, such a debate has been notable by its absence. As outlined above, since 1990, NHS boards have focused on developing a more executive and strategic role with a growing emphasis on organisational performance.

The idea that boards should, in effect, take on an executive role and decide strategic direction, rather than just ratify it, is relatively new. Lorsch and MacIver's (1989) study of private sector boards was based upon extensive empirical evidence and listed the main roles of boards studied, and this suggested boards played an increasing, but limited, strategic role. Earlier research in the private sector also shows a lack of clarity over what the board's role should be, when it was involved in strategy formulation. Fama and Jensen (1983) make a useful distinction between board responsibilities and management responsibilities, which they call 'decision management' and 'decision control', the former being the role of management and the latter the role of boards. Ambiguity has appeared because of the preponderance of executives on boards, and the increasingly managerialist nature of board activities. There is no ideal distinction between what should be the responsibility of the board and what of the executive, but it is the lack of an explicit agreement upon where the distinction *should* lie that can cause problems. Exactly where the line is drawn will vary according to the type of organisation. More recent studies such as those by Pettigrew and McNulty (1998) show that boards often play an important role in at least shaping strategy.

Current theories of boards such as agency theory, stewardship theory, resource dependency theory or stakeholder theory, as outlined in the Introduction, tend to reflect specific perceptions of what the board role should be, rather than reflecting the range of roles. Research suggesting a typology of boards, their roles and appropriateness for different contexts is embryonic, but presents a useful starting point to understand how governance issues might be addressed by government and the boards themselves. Molz (1985), in looking at boards across all sectors, classified them according to the degree of control they assigned to management. He showed how boards were increasingly giving away their control and decision-making powers to managers and raised questions as to how the board might reclaim some of these, especially where there were other stakeholder interests to consider. This issue of relative power refers not to separate groups of decision-makers within an organisation but to processes *within* the board room as more boards are dominated by managers and operational issues. Given the relatively weaker powers and influence of the independent, non-executive board members, this is a difficult trend to counter. The argument for strong involvement by the board in strategy and performance issues is that this may clarify organisational objectives and priorities. However, if the role becomes one of formulation as opposed to evaluation, then the board is taking on a specifically management role. The argument against this is that strategy formulation is an executive task and that if strategic planning and control are in the hands of a single body, then there is a loss of an independent evaluation of the strategic plan.

As roles and expectations change and a strategic role for the board is seen as a 'norm' (Pettigrew and McNulty, 1998; Cornforth and Edwards, 1999), then there is a need for boards to acknowledge and define their roles more explicitly, to ensure that their responsibility *re* probity and their ability to take an independent overview are not compromised.

The Introduction identified a number of types of board organisation that can be seen across the public and non-profit sectors. The *agency* perspective originated in economics where it was recognised that managers and owners may have different interests and so the board was there to ensure the 'conformance' of managers to the interests of the organisation. If the 'owners' of public services are seen as the government and other stakeholders, then the old-style boards, where managers were not included on authorities, can be seen as similar. Here the emphasis in interpreting policy is on accountability. The second type, based on stewardship theory, reflects a *managerial* perspective where it is assumed that managers and owners share a common interest; boards and managers are partners with the aim of improving performance. This correlates with the model of governance that has emerged since 1990 in the health service. With the change of emphasis to performance, there are concerns that issues of accountability are marginalised. The question raised earlier about whether there can be a structure where efficiency and accountability are not seen as mutually exclusive has never been seriously addressed with regard to NHS governance structures. A new model, based more on a *democratic* or *stakeholder* perspective, might be a way of ensuring that the range of stakeholder interests is taken into account while also holding the board responsible for performance.

Role of the non-executive

The role of the non-executive is critical in ensuring probity, independent evaluation and as a balance to the domination of managers. One fundamental tenet of governance is that the non-executives can hold the executives to account, but it is questionable as to how realistic this is. For this they needed to have the knowledge, skills and time to develop a corporate overview and understanding of the organisation, as well as to have some basis of power or influence. The Warwick study showed that it was problematic for non-executives to exert real power. They had limited time and were reliant upon managers for information and for them to bring important issues to the board. They were on the board as individuals, as political appointments, with no 'democratic' legitimacy as elected members or even as representatives. The study also found that the corporate nature of the non-executive role was being compromised, and with it their ability to retain complete objectivity, and feel able to challenge management should there be a need. Non-executives were being drawn into the management of the organisation, being assigned to particular functions and sitting on a range of committees. As the role develops into one which is complementary to management, then the capacity for challenge is diminished. This is a very important tension, because on the one hand it can be argued that without such involvement non-executives would not gather the necessary knowledge and information that they need in order to be able to understand what managers are really doing, but on the other it can lead to identification with certain roles or functions which can comprise objectivity. The responsibility for keeping the necessary 'balance' can be difficult for non-executives without this tension being formally acknowledged, discussed and dealt with. For example, on some boards non-executives did not become associated with only certain committees or functions but in time rotated their roles.

If those selected as non-executives are from a narrow range of backgrounds, whether this be from big business or local councils, the consequence will be a limited range of inputs and debates. This both reduces the inputs prior to actual decision-making and leaves executive power relatively untouched. There is a need to move beyond a focus on making boards more strategic, towards ensuring better corporate governance, but without losing effectiveness. This again requires a careful balance. Whereas it is a fair conclusion to say that 'better' corporate governance is more strategic (Cornforth and Edwards, 1999), this must not be at the expense of the conformance role. Although many recent reforms have concentrated on the conformance role, this reflects its past weakness in practice, rather than a strengthening that will divert attention from strategy. In this the type of non-executive appointed, and their power to influence, are critical. There are clear benefits from having a non-executive group that are supportive and advisory, but there also needs to be distance and independence. Such a role is inherently difficult and conflictual.

A later study by Harrison (1998) of three NHS boards showed that many directors were still unclear about matters of accountability and their statutory obligations and responsibilities. He describes how many boards demonstrated poor scrutiny of policy implementation and executive performance. The lack of clarity over the non-executive role clearly persists, and was described as creating tensions between them and the executive members. The non-executives perform the critical role in relation to probity, and in this the role of non-executive chair can be critical. The chair's role is invariably portrayed in terms of the relationship with the chief executive. This relationship has a significant impact on the operation of the board and the relative power of executives and non-executives. Harrison's study (1998: 147) concluded that there were 'unacceptable governance risks', when the chair/CEO axis was strong. This suggests that the power of the other non-executives becomes relatively diminished. A report by Robinson and Exworthy (1999) on the relationship between NHS chairs and CEOs, however, cites this as being the critical factor in the overall performance of the board, and suggests that a strong relationship with trust and respect needs to be established. As Ferlie *et al.* (1996) conclude, it is necessary for the chair and chief executive not to monopolise power but to create trust among all board members to allow all to perform their roles to greatest effect.

Comparing the later studies, albeit few and much smaller in scale, with the Warwick study, it is disappointing to see how little learning appears to have taken place and how few lessons from earlier research have found their way into practice. The Warwick research emphasised the importance of each board identifying its roles and objectives, recognising its corporate responsibility and defining boundaries to give clarity to individual roles and responsibilities. Harrison echoes this, saying that it is the responsibility of the *whole* board to ensure good performance and in this especially they do need to be held to account.

The current situation

Since the change of government in 1997 with its much heralded return to traditional public sector values and promotion of partnership and equity in the NHS, there have been very few changes made to governance structures. The issues remain unresolved as non-executives are still appointed and whatever their specific remit, still have no democratic basis on which to 'represent' the community. In the NHS Plan (Secretary of State for Health, 2000) the only change has been that the appointment of non-executive directors will pass to a new NHS Appointments Commission, which will report annually to Parliament. Informally there appears to be a greater willingness to acknowledge the interests of different stakeholders, but how meaningful notions such as cross-sector and inter-sector collaboration will be, in the absence of mechanisms to ensure accountability, needs to be assessed. Formal accountability remains solely to the Department of Health. The change of focus in how NHS organisations are to be evaluated by the introduction of quality issues, is one clear change, but again the definition of 'quality' remains as defined from above. There have also been new requirements that organisations must show that they have taken measures for the inclusion of local views, but how this is possible is not clear. Whose local views? How are these to be obtained? There are no democratic mechanisms in place to ensure a wide constituency. The role of CHCs (Community Health Councils) in the past has never embraced such areas, for example, they have not had any access to NHS boards or decision-making processes. It is important to recognise that their replacement by other forms of local voice does not necessarily mark a decrease in opportunities for local people to be heard. In opposition, the Labour Party was critical of quangos and the growth of the non-elected elites in the governance of the country, but there is nothing currently on their policy agenda to address such issues in the future.

There are important governance issues still facing the health sector, not just in relation to the existing bodies and boards, but for the newly emerging primary care trusts, as noted earlier. These are distinctive bodies, which bear little resemblance to existing NHS organisations, and as such will have specific requirements that will need to be reflected in the type of governance structure adopted. The new trusts will not have a clearly defined organisation to oversee, but one which consists of a network of small and disparate organisations, based on general practice. Their role in the past has been limited to the provision of primary health care, with fundholders having the power to purchase limited additional health care for their patients. Now they have many additional responsibilities, for example, the purchase of all health care for their populations, health promotion, public health and preventative care. As such, they will inherit many of the corporate tasks currently carried out within Health Authorities. This presents a very heavy agenda representing significant change to both the structures and cultures of existing systems. The precursor to primary care trusts were the primary care groups which were dominated by the members of the medical profession who took the role of chair and are in the majority among members. Accountability in the corporate governance sense is not a concept that will be very familiar to medical professionals in primary care, whose tradition has been as independent practitioners. GPs are the entrepreneurs of the health service and are likely to guard their independence fiercely. Although GPs are responsible for spending significant sums of public money, prior to the 1990 reforms there were no mechanisms of accountability, and subsequently these have been very slow in emerging. Clearly the new system will continue to change this situation, but GPs are almost certain to see this as curtailing their power and clinical autonomy.

The power exerted by the medical profession has led to compromises being made by the government, in relation to the composition of primary care groups. There was pressure from GPs with regard to their representation on, and control of, the new primary care groups, and as a consequence there can be up to eight GPs on each group. This compares with only one or two nurses, and single members from the health authority, the local authority and from related professional groups such as pharmacists and dentists, and also a lack of user or community involvement. As a transient organisational form, this may not be seen as too great a price to pay for collaboration. More importantly, such an imbalance of power will not exist on primary care trusts themselves, but there will be a much narrower range of professionals as members. As with all other NHS boards, there will be eleven members, the chair, five lay members including those from the local authority, the chief executive, finance director and three professionals (NHSE, 1999). No group has a statutory right to be represented on the board and it is not yet clear what this will mean for all the various stakeholders which includes other health professionals, those in the wide range of different nursing roles, dentists, pharmacists, the community in general and patients. As across the whole of the NHS, new policies require the involvement of users and communities. However, the GP role has always been one of acting as the patient's advocate, rather than consulting them directly. In primary care in particular, where the great majority of health care is delivered, the question about the need for some form of local democratic accountability needs to be addressed.

Conclusion

The pattern of governance structures over the lifetime of the NHS has seen a move from earlier forms which could be seen as 'conformance' models, to the 1990s where the emphasis was clearly on 'performance', and now a small move back towards recognising the importance of accountability. The 'old' health authorities with the inclusion of local authority counsellors and representatives from each of the key professional groups had some claim to local democratic accountability, however weak. With the 'new' authorities and trusts, however, there has, until now, been no pretence that they are democratically accountable. Despite current rhetoric on openness and accountability to patients and community, no real mechanisms exist to ensure that this happens. Developments over the last decade have put at risk key aspects of governance such as ensuring probity and local accountability to all stakeholder groups. Neither of these models can deliver across the range of needs of an organisation for effective governance, so there is a strong argument for exploring further models which have a stronger democratic basis. To combine the corporate membership of executives and non-executives in a process whereby the latter are elected, is only one possibility. The candidates could be selected on the basis of both their understanding of health issues and their local knowledge. Other ideas might be to have separate supervisory boards as in many European companies or the Whitehall model with separate 'scrutiny' committees. Importantly, however, there needs to be a move away from the assumption, grounded in political dogma, that efficiency is not compatible with accountability.

Such moves would serve to strengthen boards by strengthening the role of the non-executives. This is just as important for board effectiveness as there being a good relationship between the chair and the chief executive. There is a need for strong boards to ensure a balance of power between different stakeholder groups, as well as effective management and performance. The need for strong boards is particularly great in the primary care sector given the numerous new roles and responsibilities it is taking on, its domination by GPs, and its multiplicity of activities. Given the increasing role of Primary Care Trusts in the decision-making process of which services and how many are to be purchased for the community, there is a real need for them to be seen to be responsive to local needs.

As in the early 1990s, the governance structures of the new trusts may feel pressured to reflect policy objectives rather than focusing on local needs, in which case, yet again, they will have to be rapidly redeveloped during the first few years of their lives. There remains the possibility that inadequate structures and processes will present the trusts with problems that will divert attention away from their main role and will risk weakening the key group in the management and organisation of primary care. The development of the new Primary Care Trusts could be taken as an opportunity to put the rhetoric of 'partnership' and increased accountability to the test and to explore new forms of governance.

References

Ashburner, L. (1997) 'Corporate Governance in the Public Sector: The Case of the NHS', in K. Keasey, S. Thompson and M. Wright (eds) *Corporate Governance*, Oxford: Oxford University Press.

Ashburner, L. and Cairncross, L. (1993) 'Membership of the "New Style" Health Authorities: Continuity or Change?', *Public Administration*, 71, 3, 357–375.

Cadbury, Sir A. (1992) *Report of the Committee on the Financial Aspects of Corporate Governance*, London: Gee.

Clatsworthy, M. A., Mellett, H. J. and Peel, M. J. (2000) 'Corporate Governance Under New Public Management: An Exemplification', *Corporate Governance*, 8, 2, 166–176.

Cornforth, C. and Edwards, C. (1999) 'Board Roles in the Strategic Management of Non-profit Organisations: Theory and Practice', *Corporate Governance*, 7, 4, 346–362.

Day, P. and Klein, R. (1987) *Accountabilities: Five Public Services*, London: Tavistock.

DoH (1997) *The NHS – Modern and Dependable*, London: HMSO.

Fama, E. F. and Jensen, M. C. (1983) 'Separation of Ownership and Control', *Journal of Law and Economics*, 26, 327–349.

Ferlie, E., Ashburner, L., FitzGerald, L. and Pettigrew, A. (1996) *The New Public Management in Action*, Oxford: Oxford University Press.

Garratt, B. (1996) *The Fish Rots from the Head: The Crisis in our Boardrooms: Developing the Crucial Skills of the Competent Director*, London: HarperCollins.

Harrison, J. H. (1998) 'Corporate Governance in the NHS: An Assessment of Boardroom Practice', *Corporate Governance*, 6, 3, 140–150.

Klein, R. (1983) *The Politics of the National Health Service*, London: Longman.

Lorsch, J. and MacIver, J. (1989) *Pawns or Potentates: The Reality of America's Corporate Boards*, Boston: Harvard Business School Press.

Molz, R. (1985) 'The Role of the Board of Directors: Typologies of Interaction', *The Journal of Business Strategy*, 5, 4, 86–93.

NHS Executive (1999) *Primary Care Trusts: Establishing Better Services*, London: National Health Service Executive.

Peck, E. (1995) 'The Performance of an NHS Trust Board: Actors' Accounts, Minutes and Observation', *British Journal of Management*, 6, 135–156.

Pettigrew, A. and McNulty, T. (1998) 'Sources and Uses of Power in the Boardroom', *European Journal of Work and Organisational Psychology*, 7, 2, 197–214.

Ranson, S. and Stewart, J. (1994) *Management for the Public Domain: Enabling the Learning Society*, London: Macmillan.

Robinson, R. and Exworthy, M. (1999) *Two at the Top: A Study of the Working Relationships Between Chairs and Chief Executives at Health Authorities, Boards and Trusts in the NHS*, Birmingham: The NHS Confederation.

Secretary of State for Health (2000) *The NHS Plan*, Cmd 4818-I, London: HMSO.

12 The changing face of governance in women's organisations

Jane W. Grant

This chapter draws on a research study which looked at the governance of seventeen organisations which form part of the organised women's movement – eight 'traditional' organisations which came out of 'first-wave feminism' around the beginning of the twentieth century; eight which came out of 'second-wave feminism' in the 1970s and one, the Fawcett Society, which, going back as it does to 1866 but having managed to convert itself into a very modern campaigning organisation, acts as a bridge between the two categories. In this study I have interpreted the term 'governance' in quite broad terms 'to embrace all the functions performed in organisations by the members of their governing bodies' (Cornforth and Edwards, 1998: 2), including their relationships with paid staff, rather than specifically as the performance of boards, although the latter, of course, is a recurring theme. The research[1] explored three broad questions:

- What are the criteria against which to measure the successful governance of women's organisation?
- How can organisations ensure that their governance empowers rather than disempowers?
- What helps organisations cope successfully with change?

It was also partly intended as a 'scoping' exercise to encourage others to carry out much needed in-depth analyses of this important but very under-researched sector. It used both desk research and semi-structured open-ended interviews with at least two representatives from each organisation, including at least one representative of its governance. Detailed questions were adapted for type of organisation. For instance, a recurrent theme with the 'modern' women's movement organisations was the move away from collective or flatter structures. This chapter is informed by this research as a whole, but addresses itself in particular to the way in which the governance of women's organisations has changed over time.

Perhaps the first thing that strikes one about this sector is its diversity.

The traditional end of the continuum which makes up the organised women's movement has always understood the significance of boards, which form the apex of very complex hierarchical structures leading from the local, to the regional, to the national (and sometimes the international as well). In contrast, the groups which came out of the women's movement in the 1970s were usually collectively run, very loosely structured and thus with not much concept of a board as such. In fact, in the early days of groups born out of the fervour of the women's liberation movement like Rights of Women (ROW), the Women's Resource Centre, the Feminist Library, rape crisis centres or women's refuges up and down the country, it would have been very difficult to distinguish between management and governance at all since it was usually the same women who made the decisions in the collective and then carried out the work. It was only gradually, as funding was obtained and workers employed, that the distinction between management and governance began to become real (although even now they can still be blurred). Jill Radford describes how ROW, founded in 1975 as a 'feminist organisation which informs women of their rights and promotes the interests of women in relation to the law'[2] in the 1980s:

> struggled to transform itself from an autonomous and Women's Liberation group into a voluntary sector feminist organization. This involved developing new structures of accountability as ROW began to employ paid workers. We established a voluntary policy group, with a sub-group to deal with managerial matters.
>
> (Griffin, 1995: 55)

These staff were to form a workers' collective (with, by 1999, five members, all but one part-time) with the management provided by a Management Committee/Policy Group elected from the membership of ROW (currently around 500). ROW was to retain its collective structure until the end of 1999 when a combination of internal and external pressures led to the decision to re-structure and appoint a Director but, like many similar organisations established on participatory – or 'fully collectivised democratic' lines (see Rothschild-Whitt, 1979) – it had even before then become very much a modified or hybrid collective. And, as we shall see, like most organisations which have moved from their roots in the women's liberation movement into, or near, the mainstream of the women's voluntary sector, they have carried with them a commitment to participatory democracy, without the limitations of full collectivity.

The governance of traditional women's organisations

This was a far cry, however, from the highly structured, bureaucratic organisations which responded to the challenge of 'first wave feminism' in

Table 12.1 Traditional women's organisations studied

Name of organisation	Date founded
Mother's Union	1876
Co-operative Women's Guild	1883
British Federation of Graduate Women (formerly British Federation of University Women)	1907
Guide Association	1910
National Federation of Women's Institutes	1915
Soroptimist International of Great Britain and Ireland	1921
Townswomen's Guilds	1929
Standing Conference of Women's Organisations	1940

the late nineteenth and early twentieth centuries and particularly to the opportunities afforded to women by the winning of the vote, finally achieved for all women in 1928. The 'traditional' women's organisations I chose to look at in depth all, except the last, came out of this period, and are shown in Table 12.1.

I would argue that they could all be defined as feminist in that they were set up to provide support and opportunities to different groups of women, to (working my way down the list) mothers, working-class women, the small, but growing, number of women gaining access to a university education, to young women and girls, to women in rural areas, to professional women and to women in towns, and that they each in their way played a transformational role in women's lives. The Standing Conference of Women's Organisations is rather different both in that it was established later, in response to evacuation and other challenges of World War II, and because it is an umbrella organisation with a membership of women's groups in different areas around the UK rather than individual women.

However, although in *purpose* these organisations may be closer than is usually appreciated to the women's movement organisations of the 1970s – with even the WI fulfilling a radical role by providing 'a significant female controlled public space for women who had, in rural areas, previously had few such opportunities' (Andrews, 1997: 67) – in *structure* they are every bit as hierarchical and bureaucratic as many other contemporary organisations. In fact, most of them could stand in as classic examples of machine bureaucracy which is characterised by:

> highly routine operating tasks, very formalized rules and regulations, tasks that are grouped into functional departments, centralised authority, decision-making that follows the chain of command, and an elaborate administrative structure with a sharp distinction between line and staff activities.
>
> (Robbins, 1990: 283)

They might not be able, or have been able, to afford many paid staff (of the organisations I studied, the Guide Association employed far the most at 168, while several only employed 'a girl in the office' with almost all the work carried out by a network of volunteers, mainly honorary officers and members at national, regional and local level) and in fact often had a decidedly ambivalent attitude to paid staff. Mary Stott's (1978) classic study *Organization Woman* of one of these organisations, the Towns-women's Guilds (although in fact it could apply to almost any of them), is admiring but clear-eyed about the strengths and weaknesses of 'organisa-tion woman' and the organisations in which she operates. She notes how 'these self-help, mutually supportive organisations gave their members confidence and assurance in a largely male-dominated world' (Stott, 1978: 3), and highlights the importance of rules and structures in achieving this: 'Groups without rules run into difficulties because they have no machinery to resolve differences' (ibid.: 23).

But rules for their own sake can also be dangerous. She quotes a retir-ing warden of the WI's Denman College:

> Rules are a great hazard for women. When they get together the easiest thing to do is to put themselves into running a meeting and carry out all the procedures ... You think you are awfully good but you have ended up with a meeting with no content.
>
> (ibid.: 216)

She identifies a challenge which is found in almost all voluntary organisa-tions but, as my research bears out, particularly acutely in women's organ-isations, of the relationship between staff and volunteers:

> The relationship of paid and unpaid officials has always been tricky, as many a large women's organisation has found ... the old story, which seems to run through big organisations, that voluntary workers are apt to be suspicious of those who get a salary for doing very similar work.
>
> (ibid.: 116, 127)

This relationship can be particularly problematic when it is that between the chief volunteer and the chief of the paid staff – the Chairman (and even today most are still called chair*men*, when not Presidents) – 'Organisation Woman' herself – and the chief executive (although she is more likely to be called something like National, General or Organising Secretary).

> No paid chief officer of a national voluntary organisation can have an easy life. To maintain a balance between being an efficient secretary to her immediate employers, the national executive, being a good controller and trainer of the head office staff, giving leadership to the

whole movement and being available for collaboration with other organisations and able to answer questions from the media … must be of nightmare complexity.

(ibid.: 132)

One great satisfaction of top office in voluntary movements … is being able to travel all over the country, to be met, entertained, welcomed and honoured as a VIP by nice women whose admiration and gratitude shine from their eyes. It can be heady stuff, and not every woman whose talent for inspiring leadership is expressed from the platform is anxious to share the glory with her 'professional' colleague. Not every woman elected to high office in an organisation really thinks of even the top paid official as a 'colleague' … Many professional women working for voluntary associations will privately assert that … even very experienced committees tend to treat their professional staff rather as middle-class Victorian housewives treated their maids, cooks and governesses. Almost inevitably the voluntary workers tend to think of themselves as slightly superior beings because they are doing for nothing but love what the paid staff do for a salary.

(ibid.: 132–133)

As Stott explained, these bureaucratic structures – with their endless rules and regulations, with their elected positions at every level – initially served a very useful purpose: they gave women confidence, they allowed them to occupy leadership positions, they enabled mass membership organisations to be run on a shoestring. (At their height the Co-operative Women's Guild had a membership of 87,246; the WI had a membership of 462,000 in 1956 and the TG of around 250,000 in the late 1960s – and it is estimated that half the female population of the UK has been involved with the Guide Association at some time in their lives.) The problem came when these bureaucratic structures ceased to be a means to an end, a way of supporting the organisation's main purpose, and became an end in itself. Gaffin and Thoms' study (1983) of the Co-operative Women's Guild charts how this once brave and extraordinarily effective organisation, which gave so many working-class women the opportunity to grow in political and civic awareness and take these new-found talents into all aspects of public life, has dwindled to the stage where, with only 3,300 members in 108 branches it cannot even find enough people to fill the officer slots and sustain the bureaucracy. This decline owes much to loss of political purpose, particularly its unpopular 'white poppy' pacifist campaign in World War II, but also substantially to the fact that it gradually developed a structure which was taking it further away from the women it represented:

The Guild was steadily transformed into a more hierarchical and autocratic organisation whose constitution enabled the leadership to maintain firm control of policy, and suppress dissenting voices ... a two-tier structure consisting of a bureaucratic, elite leadership and a subscribing but largely impotent mass membership. Senior members of the Guild were able to 'represent their members' interests' on an array of national bodies, speaking for, yet unaccountable to, tens of thousands of women. The priority of the leadership was no longer to 'bring into active life' ordinary Co-operative women but to put the Guild at the service of the causes which they supported. Chief among these, from the late 1920s, were right-wing Labour-Co-operative politics, a malignant anti-Communism, and an unyielding commitment to absolute pacifism.

(Scott, 1998: 268–269)

By 2001 this structure has become empty, form without content, a classic example of a near total democratic deficit. Although a few local branches are able to continue to run as 'Wednesday clubs' for old ladies, paid for by the local Co-operative branch, most of those who have admired the Guild in the past now feel it has reached what Hudson (1995) would characterise as the decline stage of its life cycle, where organisational renewal is no longer possible.

The Co-operative Women's Guild is an extreme example of a bureaucracy which has outlived its usefulness but to a greater or lesser extent most of the traditional women's organisations face similar problems which they are tackling with varying degrees of courage and resolution. The British Federation of Women Graduates (BFWG) has also faced an enormous drop in membership (from around 8,000 in 1968) and with an increasingly ageing membership. This has resulted in quite a dramatic change of purpose (selling the lease of its famous Crosby Hall, with accommodation for visiting women students, and investing the money in a Charitable Foundation to help women graduates with living expenses on the basis of need) but not such a dramatic change of structure and governance. The Conference Programme for the Annual Meeting in July 1998 reveals only 1,560 paying members for 1997/8 (with a downward projection of 1,400 for 1998/9) and the Regional Executives Annual Reports, although describing lively programmes of local events, are peppered with comments about 'membership problems', 'low' or 'reduced' numbers and of the need and plans for recruitment. It also reveals a structure and governance which is extremely top-heavy and very complicated rules and regulations for such a reduced membership.

Some streamlining structural changes have been made and BFWG no longer has standing committees, since it was too expensive to provide the secretariat although they do now have open forums on international affairs or education which in many ways are more democratic. Otherwise, as with many organisations with a reduced membership, there can be a great 're-cycling' of the same people at national level, while local groups find it increasingly difficult to find women to take on officer positions and many have to fold as a result (and once there is no longer a local branch, with monthly meetings, women tend not to renew their membership).

It is not clear whether these rather minimal changes will be enough to save the BFWG from further decline. Other organisations have been much more drastic. The Mothers' Union still has a membership of 140,000 in this country (750,000 worldwide) but has made dramatic changes to its governance, reducing its Central Council or governing body from 561 to 22 and, under its last chief executive, building a new, stronger working relationship and model of leadership between the president and chief executive. The Guide Association (GA), the UK's largest women's and girls' organisation with more than 700,000 members, has made dramatic changes not just to its 'vision' and uniform but to its governance. The GA is massively dependent on volunteers and in 1998 introduced a comprehensive review of their volunteer structure. 'The aim was to provide a streamlined and efficient organisation ... the resulting volunteer committee structure is more focused so that decision-making is faster and more effective.'[3] This reduced thirty-eight committees down to nine. There are 'fewer positions for people to hold but more opportunities to participate'[4] (e.g. through forums of up to a hundred around particular issues). At the same time the staff structure has been overhauled and fully integrated with the volunteer structures and, both the current chief executive and Chief Guide have given a great deal of time to nurturing this key relationship. As a result, there is now a clear understanding that ceremonial duties and leading the work of the Trustees are the responsibility of the Chief Guide, while the chief executive manages business processes and personnel, with the relationship dependent on mutual respect and a professional approach. This is certainly not the case in all organisations where relationships between paid staff and trustees can remain every bit as difficult as those Stott described above. When I was Director of the National Alliance of Women's Organisations (NAWO), I became very aware of the whole vexed relationship between elected boards and paid staff and the way in which many boards are suspicious of evidence of leadership from women in paid positions, preferring senior staff to 'run' the organisation rather than in any way 'lead' it. This seems to be the case even when organisations are large and complex and urgently in need of skilled leadership and management. Evidence of good, high profile leadership is often met not with approbation but with remarks like: 'Who does she think she is?'

When I was at NAWO I used occasionally to attend the lunches arranged for General Secretaries of the large women's organisations. I have never met a group of professional women who felt less professional satisfaction in their work. Several gave priority to organising opportunities for training and development for the staff they were managing but were given no such opportunities themselves (some were not even officially 'allowed' to attend these lunches). Far from being given chances to develop, several were facing attempts to have their job description and their whole position eroded (in the words of one, 'whittled away under our feet'). The only one who admitted to finding her job reasonably satisfactory gave as her reason the fact that she had learnt to 'manipulate' her chair rather than be manipulated.

However, as we have seen above, and other examples show, things are changing. Perhaps the most far-reaching example of changing governance is the Young Women's Christian Association. The YWCA is even older than the main organisations I examined, established in 1855 and part of a world-wide movement in ninety countries. But although the 'Y' is almost a household name, that has not insulated it from external changes and pressures which have necessitated a radical re-assessment. An ageing housing stock which it could not easily convert to offer young women the sort of accommodation which, with changing expectations, they now require, plus changes in housing finance, made it imperative for the YWCA to confront the need to move away from its primary purpose of being direct providers of social housing for young women. The financial imperatives were so strong that this decision, however painful, was unanimous. This means that the YWCA is now seeking to dispose of its housing stock to other appropriate landlords, with more than half the total stock transferred by 31 March 2001. Parallel with this transfer is a re-focusing of its work into youth and community work and into campaigns like 'Stop Violence Against Women'.[5]

Alongside this re-focusing of its purpose, the YWCA in England and Wales has continued with a parallel and almost equally momentous revamping of its governance structures which has led to a completely different composition of the board. Instead of the main criterion for being on the board being to have worked your way up the YWCA membership hierarchy, it was proposed that recruitment 'should primarily be on the strength of appropriate skills ... [and] ... a skills audit ... in a focused way, for example by advertisements, scanning CVs and interviewing candidates ... [and with] a standing recruitment committee'.[6] The optimum size of the board should be not less than fifteen; recruitment should be from individuals both inside and outside the YWCA (with one-third reserved for YWCA members) and, to increase understanding, suitable candidates should be encouraged to attend a number of board meetings prior to appointment. This was approved in April 1999. By August 1999 they had been able to put together a board 'team which balanced continuity with new blood and gave us a broad range of skills in the areas we wanted'.[7] All this is moving immeasurably further and faster than any other of the multi-layered traditional organisations among the case studies. The move away from social housing may also allow further simplification of the parallel governance structure of both an incorporated company and an unincorporated Association.[8] This is a major move towards a partnership model of governance (see the Introduction).

Of the remaining case studies, the Townswomen's Guilds has made some attempts to update its governance, and allow its senior manager the title of chief executive, at least externally, and the Standing Conference of Women's Organisations, having struggled for years to sustain a complex hierarchy with virtually no funding, is having something of a revival with a very energetic young National Secretary who has been allowed to introduce dynamic elements of 'adhocracy'[9] into a classic machine bureaucracy. The Soroptimists, a worldwide organisation of classified service clubs for women, have done very little to streamline their exceptionally complicated hierarchical structure – with local clubs, regional, federal and international structures, all with different layers of officers and committees and a parallel programme structure administered by a programme action committee, co-ordinators and advisers – and are losing members as relentlessly as almost all the other organisations. What seems very clear is that these organisations will not survive unless they are able to face up to the fact that they are operating in a very different world, where the position of women has changed dramatically, and that a very different, more streamlined governance structure is required. The only organisation which seems to be doing quite well without doing this is the National Federation of Women's Institutes and this seems to be because of external factors – the renewed concern about the countryside, the fact that in many areas the WI may be almost the only sign of civil society left once the school, post office, doctor, bank and even bus have all gone, which, at least for the moment, override the need for more appropriate forms of governance.

The Fawcett Society

Before I look at the very differently structured groups which came out of the women's movement in the 1970s I would like to examine an organisation as traditional in its origins as any we have looked at, yet thoroughly contemporary in its governance. The Fawcett Society, under a variety of different names, goes back to 1866 when a small group of women collected more than 1,500 signatures for John Stuart Mill to present to Parliament with his Women's Suffrage Amendment to the Reform Bill. It remained in the forefront of the suffragist wing of the fight for the vote and, once this battle was won, transformed itself from a substantially single-issue group to a broad-based organisation concerned with a wide range of equality issues for women. Fawcett's comparatively small but very active membership, made up mainly of high-minded, intellectual feminists, ensured the organisation was regarded with great respect for, among many other things, its renowned library (now transformed into the Women's Library), for its extremely successful campaigns on the Sex

Discrimination and Equal Pay Acts and for equal taxation, for excellent work on education and the media, for its Women's Action Day in 1980, and for the key role it played in the setting up of the European Women's Lobby. Throughout this period the organisation was overwhelmingly member-led, never employing more than one and a half paid staff and allowing these staff little or no 'agency' or responsibility. Their approach to governance most closely resembled a 'compliance' model (see the Introduction) as we have seen in so many of the other traditional organisations, where one of the main functions of the board is to monitor and, if necessary, control the behaviour of managers.

Until 1992, the Fawcett Society had a small and mainly older membership (400 and falling) and a highly respected but rather staid image. It had an executive board of twelve and specialist sub-committees in education, public affairs, health and media. However, moves for change, which had been brewing for several years, came together in the decision to appoint for the first time a director who would actually be allowed to direct. Since then Fawcett has expanded in every direction; its membership has grown five-fold and grown progressively younger and more diverse; its work on taxation, pensions, political representation and equal pay has been influential and high profile; it has built effective partnerships not just with women's organisations, but with pro-democracy organisations, with women MPs, with the Women's Unit, etc. With a young chair and a young director it had, by the end of the millennium, an image of a youthful, dynamic, campaigning organisation. It is evolving more flexible structures, with the specialist committees being replaced by expert groups who are only called on when needed. It is now working to involve more – and more diverse – members in its governance, in its local groups and in its Activist Network. Fawcett seems, thus, to have succeeded in making the very rare transition from traditional to very modern organisation and at the same time providing a bridge between the world of the organised women's movement and that of wider campaigning organisations.

The governance of women's organisations from 'second-wave' feminism

Certainly Fawcett is now much closer to those organisations which came out of second-wave feminism – the women's movement of the 1970s – and managed to make the transition into the more mainstream women's voluntary sector. The group of case study organisations or movements which came out of second-wave feminism were all founded within twelve years of each other and are shown in Table 12.2.

They shared a strong commitment to the rights and advancement of women with the organisations of the first wave of feminism. Where they differed dramatically was in their belief that the *process* of their organising was as important as the *product*, that *how* they did it was as important as *what*

Table 12.2 'Modern' women's organisations studied

Name of organisation	Date founded
Refuge Movement	1971
Rights of Women	1975
Feminist Library	1975
Rape Crisis Movement	1975
East London Black Women's Organisation	1979
300 Group	1980
Maternity Alliance	1980
Women's Resource Centre	1983

they did – 'they see their organisations as ends in themselves, not simply as means to an end' (Ferguson, 1984: 189). Whereas the earlier organisations had felt quite at home with bureaucracy and hierarchy, the women's movement tended to see hierarchy as synonymous with patriachy and thus to be avoided at all costs. Thus organisations (although that term is in itself inappropriate to many of the small consciousness-raising groups, which were hardly organised at all) which came out of second-wave feminism were not only intended to change the world and women's place in it but they were intended to do it in a particular way which mirrored the ideals they were fighting for, replacing the structures of patriarchy with ways of organising that better reflected women's ideals. These came to be known as participatory democratic or collective ways of working. An example of what this means in practice is described in a guide to running refuges published by the Women's Aid Federation England (WAFE):

> The term [collective working] is defined in the WAFE Statement of Aims and Principles as referring to a participative and non-hierarchical way of working. In practice, people interpret the term in different ways ... this way of working derives from the women's movement of the early 1970s where it meant a commitment to certain values about how we work together. These values include: valuing everyone's contribution; participative and consensus decision-making – having a right to be consulted and heard; sharing knowledge, skills and power.
>
> The most important insight from the early Women's Aid movement which has continued today is the valuing of women's personal experience, and an approach which means there is no 'them and us'.
>
> There is still a commitment to maintaining these values today in Women's Aid, but in practice this is very hard to do without effective structures.
>
> (Turner, 1996: 41–42)

The last sentence of this quotation is revealing. The commitment to collective working was part of a deeply held ideology but that did not make it easy to do in practice. Rothschild (1993: 597) identified six characteristics of the ideal 'feminine model of organisation' which can be summed up as:

1   Valuing members as individual human beings.
2   Non-opportunistic.
3   Careers defined in terms of service to others
4   Commitment to employee growth.
5   Creation of a caring community.
6   Power sharing (information generously shared).

In reality, these ideals were very hard to achieve. Riordan (1999: 33), for instance, sees this idealised model as part of the 'myth of power': 'difficult to achieve, especially when organisations grow larger and more complex. And when women find they cannot live up to the ideal, they experience strong feelings of betrayal, anger and resentment.'

The literature[10] is repetitive about what Freeman (1984) famously called the 'tyranny of structurelessness' – the endless time and repetition needed to reach consensus, the difficulty in distinguishing between critical and routine decisions, how fear of conflict can lead to its suppression rather than dealing with its causes. Even when more structure has to be built in to accommodate paid workers, this can bring further problems:

> There was resentment on both sides; the people doing the work were working without recognition and the other side thought there was power-mongering going on in secret ... women began to want recognition in the form of job permanency and a salary reflecting their skills and experience ... the women were feeling used ... they wanted leadership and people with some degree of authority over specific areas ... there was a perception of a lack of control.
>
> (Iannello, 1992: 90–94)

There is general recognition of the potentially transformational nature of collective working but also of its problems: 'levelling down ... leaving an overall deficiency in skills', the 'possible shortfall in commitment' and the dilemma that 'leadership must still be accomplished by some means if successful organisation is to be achieved' (Brown, 1992: 38).

As a result, today very few pure collectives survive intact: most have adapted themselves under overwhelming internal and external pressures (for example, the need for accountability and to meet criteria set by funders, the need for more coherent leadership in a time of growth) into 'hybrid' organisations (see Bordt, 1998) – modified collectives, participatively run hierarchies, every sort of creative alternative on the continuum between what Rothschild-Whitt (1979) identified as 'formal bureaucracy' and 'fully collectivised democracy'.

This was certainly borne out by my own research. Of the eight organisations or movements that I examined, only the Feminist Library has remained as a pure collective, run on a shoestring entirely by volunteers. All the others (with the exception of the 300 Group which is difficult to characterise since it has tended to be run much more as an 'adhocracy' by powerful, charismatic women) very much fit into this pattern of gradually moving away from collectivity and building in structure in response to the sort of internal conflicts and external pressures we have already noted. We saw above how the radical legal organisation Rights of Women has done this. The Women's Resource Centre (WRC) has gone through somewhat similar struggles to convert itself from an ailing and ineffective collective in 1997 to the vibrant and effective infrastructure body for women's groups in London that it is today. Many women's organisations are finding it very hard to find enough women to sit on their boards, and particularly to find enough ethnic minority[11] women. Part of the WRC's success lies not just in an effective Director but in the fact that she has made it a priority to 'grow' and nurture a board of very diverse women who provide the other side of a partnership model (see the Introduction) of governance.

Both the refuge and the rape crisis movement trace similar journeys from collectively run groups in the 1970s to either modified collectives or hierarchies today. As we saw above, WAFE was to remain very committed to the principles of collectivity – and to supporting its members in making it work effectively – but was also very realistic about how difficult it was to maintain this in its pure form. In practice, most of its member organisations have now moved to a modified form of collective, if not a full hierarchy, and on 15 June 1999 the chair of the Women's Aid Council, Jan Frances, was to announce that WAFE itself was to move in the same direction:

> To set up an internal management structure consisting of a Director and Team Managers ... The best aspects of collective working will be maintained in the new structure, including teamwork, equal opportunity and consultative structures within an ethos of inclusivity and participation. At the same time, the organisation will benefit from a management structure that can deliver better accountability, fast and responsive decision-making, support for staff, evaluation of performance and proper co-ordination of all national service activities.

In addition, the new structure will free up council to concentrate on the long-term strategic issues and to provide more focused leadership to the organisation.[12]

Many of the rape crisis centres still operate as modified collectives, and the Rape Crisis Federation set up in 1996 operated what they call a 'co-operative with a structure' although they have now (2001), with the acquisition of a substantial Home Office grant, moved to an openly hierarchical structure, with two staff members given director status.

The final two organisations have made successful transitions from flatter to more hierarchical structure. The East London Black Women's Organisation was set up as a collective in 1979 but in 1997 felt it was time to change and made a smooth transition to the employment of a manager to lead the team of seven permanent and at least eight sessional staff. The Maternity Alliance is perhaps the organisation to make the greatest change. Although never a pure collective, it did operate pay parity and the move away from this in 1993 was not without pain. On paper the MA is now a hierarchy with a Director but in reality the new structures and accompanying working practices have allowed far more democratic and transparent participation to develop. For example, now there is a visible planning system with progress on project management up on the wall for all to see, unlike the old days where access to knowledge depended far more on whom you knew on the management committee.

Conclusion

The research reveals a sector which, as we have seen, although it has strong historical roots, is proving very adaptive in the face of change resulting from a range of contingency factors, both internal and external. These internal and external factors both react against and reinforce each other in a highly symbiotic way. Thus an organisation's governance and development might be influenced simultaneously by internal factors like size, income, age, where the organisation is in its life cycle, the task it performs or its ideology and external factors such as pressures from funders, new legislation, the changing role of women, or the rural economy (in the case of the WI).

The research also revealed an increasingly 'hybrid' sector with traditional organisations beginning to dismantle layers of bureaucracy and hierarchy while the women's movement groups are building in more structure as they find it no longer appropriate, or even possible, to operate completely flat structures, thus suggesting a degree of 'institutional isomophism' (see DiMaggio and Powell, 1991) as they move closer together. All parts of the sector have struggled to overcome 'power illiteracy' and develop affirming models of leadership. In spite of the many challenges it faces, the organised women's movement is developing models of good governance and is transformational both in its effect on the wider community and on individual women. Many of these challenges are, of course, similar to those faced by the voluntary sector as a whole, but it is the gendered nature of these organisations which make them particularly interesting and makes their contribution to organisational theory so unique and useful.

Notes

1 See PhD thesis 'Governance, Continuity and Change in the Organised Women's Movement' for University of Kent, Centre for Women's Studies, January 2001.
2 Quoted from ROW's publicity leaflet.
3 January 1998, *Briefing Document: A New Volunteer Structure for the Future*, London: The Guide Association, p. 4.
4 Interview with Terry Ryall, Chief Executive of the Guide Association, 7 January 1999.
5 See *Women Changing Lives*, YWCA Annual Report 1999–2000.
6 See YWCA document *Implementation of the Board Review*, 25 January 1999.
7 Written communication with Gill Tishler, Chief Executive of YWCA, 18 August 1999.
8 I am indebted for details of more recent developments to telephone conversations with Dorrie Gasser on 19 March 1999 and to conversations and written communications with Gill Tishler on 30 March 1999 and 1 April 1999.
9 See Robbins (1990: 354) for a discussion of 'adhocracy'.
10 See, for instance, Mansbridge (1980); Wajcman (1983); Ferguson (1984); Landry *et al.* (1985); Brown (1992); Dobash and Dobash (1992); Iannello (1992); Riger (1994); Fried (1994).
11 This is in fact true of the voluntary sector as a whole. See Tesse Akpeki's (1997a, 1997b) work on women's involvement on boards.
12 Letter from Jan Frances, Chair of Women's Aid Council to members, 15 June 1999.

References

Akpeki, T. (1997a) *A Force for Change: Enhancing the Quality of Women's Involvement on Boards*, London, NCVO.
Akpeki, T. (1997b) *Governance in Focus: A Race and Gender Perspective*, London: NCVO.
Andrews, M. (1997) *The Acceptable Face of Feminism: The Women's Institute as a Social Movement*, London: Lawrence and Wishart.
Bordt, R. (1998) *The Structure of Women's Non-Profit Organizations*, Bloomington, IN: Indiana University Press.
Brown, H. (1992) *Women Organizing*, London: Routledge.
Cornforth, C. and Edwards, C. (1998) *Good Governance: Developing Board–Management Relations in Public and Voluntary Organizations*, London: Chartered Institute of Management Accountants.
DiMaggio, P. J. and Powell, W. W. (1991) 'The Iron Cage Revisited: Institutional Isomorphism and Collective Rationality', in W. W. Powell and P. J. DiMaggio (eds) *The New Institutionalism in Organizational Analysis*, Chicago: University of Chicago Press.
Dobash, R. E. and Dobash, R. P. (1992) *Women, Violence and Social Change*, London: Routledge.
Ferguson, K. (1984) *The Feminist Case Against Bureaucracy*, Philadelphia, PA: Temple University Press.
Freeman, J. (1984) *The Tyranny of Structurelessness*, London: Dark Star Press and Rebel Press.
Fried, A. (1994) 'It's Hard to Change What We Want to Change: Rape Crisis Centers as Organizations', *Gender and Society*, 8, 4, 562–583.

Gaffin, J. and Thoms, D. (1983) *Caring and Sharing: The Centenary History of the Co-operative Women's Guild*, revised edn, Manchester: Co-operative Union Ltd.

Griffin, G. (1995) *Feminist Activism in the 1990s*, London: Taylor and Francis.

Hudson, M. (1995) *Managing Without Profit: The Art of Managing Third-Sector Organizations*, London: Penguin.

Iannello, K. P. (1992) *Decisions Without Hierarchy: Feminist Interventions in Organization Theory and Practice*, London: Routledge, Chapman and Hall.

Landry, C., Morley, D., Southwood, R. and Wright, P. (1985) *What a Way to Run a Railroad: An Analysis of Radical Failure*, London: Comedia Publishing Group.

Mansbridge, J. (1980) *Beyond Adversary Democracy*, New York: Basic Books.

Riger, S. (1994) 'Challenges of Success: Stages of Growth in Feminist Organizations', *Feminist Studies*, 20, 2.

Riordan, S. (1999) *Women's Organisations in the UK Voluntary Sector: A Force for Change*, Centre for Institutional Studies, London: University of East London.

Robbins, S. (1990) *Organization Theory: Structure, Design and Application*, 3rd edn, New Jersey: Prentice-Hall.

Rothschild, J. (1993) 'The Feminine Model of Organization', in S. Robbins (ed.) *Organization Behaviour*, 6th edn, London: Prentice-Hall.

Rothschild-Whitt, J. (1979) 'The Collective Organization: An Alternative to Rational Bureaucratic Models', *American Sociological Review*, 44, 509–527.

Scott, G. (1998) *Feminism and the Politics of Working Women: The Women's Co-operative Guild: 1880s to the Second World War*, London: UCL Press.

Stott, M. (1978) *Organization Women: The Story of the National Union of Townswomen's Guilds*, London: Heinemann.

Turner, A. (ed.) (1996) *Building Blocks: A Women's Aid Guide to Running Refuges and Support Services*, Bristol: Women's Aid Federation.

Wajcman, J. (1983) *Dilemmas of a Workers's Co-operative*, Milton Keynes: Open University Press.

YWCA (2000) *Women Changing Lives*, YWCA Annual Report 1999–2000, London: YWCA.

13 Conclusion

Contextualising and managing the paradoxes of governance

Chris Cornforth

This concluding chapter draws out and reflects on some of the main findings and themes to emerge from the various studies and reviews presented in the book. In doing this it uses the contextually shaped and paradoxical nature of governance as set out in the Introduction as a lens through which to view and organise these findings. As well as providing interesting insights into the nature of organisational governance, these studies also throw light on the usefulness of this framework as a way of trying to understand and manage the many challenges boards face, although they were not designed to test it in any systematic way.

As noted in the Introduction and elsewhere in this book, a criticism that can be levelled at much of the theorising about boards (both prescriptive and descriptive) is its generic nature. Often little or no account is taken of contextual factors that influence or shape board characteristics or how they work. This is not something that is unique to the study of boards; similar criticisms have been levelled at much recent research in the field of organisational behaviour (Mowday and Sutton, 1993; John, 2001; Rousseau and Fried, 2001). Interestingly, an important theme that emerges from many of the studies in the book is the importance of contextual factors. This chapter draws out and examines some of these and how they both constrain and offer opportunities for boards.

The chapter then reflects again on the paradoxical nature of governance. It examines what evidence there is from the various studies for the paradoxes of governance discussed in the Introduction. It analyses the tensions and conflicts these give rise to and how these tensions are shaped by contextual factors. It goes on to discuss some of the ways in which policy-makers and boards can attempt to manage these paradoxes.

Another theme that emerges from the chapters of the book is board change. As a number of the studies show, board composition, structure and behaviour change over time. This may arise as boards react to contextual changes, such as change in regulation or as boards attempt to manage new problems and tensions they face. Finally, the chapter looks at how organisations can seek to develop *reflexive* boards that are better able to adapt to changes in their environment and maintain a dynamic balance as they steer through the contradictory tensions and pressures on them.

Contextualising the governance of public and non-profit organisations

Boards can be thought of operating across the boundary of organisations (Middleton, 1987). Boards must face two ways: outwards, relating the organisation to the external institutional and social environment – ensuring a degree of external accountability and compliance with external regulations and standards, and inwards, relating to the internal organisational environment – working with staff to provide supervision and direction. As a result, boards are influenced by a subtle combination of external and organisational factors, as the various studies in the book show. Middleton (1987), in a review of the literature on the governance of non-profit organisations, characterised it as focused on the relationship between boards and the external environment. Predominantly boards were viewed as a means of controlling environmental uncertainties and as part of power elites. Ostrower and Stone (2001) trace how the literature has developed since then. Environmental concerns are no longer to the fore and boards have become a focus of interest in their own right. In particular, there is a focus on board characteristics, roles and effectiveness, but in the process a decline in explicit attention to the impact of internal and external contingencies. In response they develop a new 'integrated' conceptual framework to guide future research, which attempts to re-establish the importance of external and internal contingencies, which is summarised in Figure 13.1. They divide external contingencies in to 'broad dimensions', such as those concerning the legal and institutional environment, and 'specific dimensions' concerning the particular type of non-profit organisation, such as its field of activity, stakeholders and funding environment. Internal contingencies include the organisation's age, size, phase of development and complexity.

Various of the studies and reviews in the book throw light on how some of these contextual factors influence board characteristics and roles. Figure 13.2 summarises some of the main contextual influences on the boards of public and non-profit organisations, which will be examined below. The summary is not meant to be exhaustive, nor does it attempt to show the often complex interaction between different factors.

In their review of studies that attempt to link individual and group behaviour in organisations to their organisational context, Mowday and Sutton (1993) suggest three different dimensions in which it is useful to think of contexts. The first dimension concerns the extent to which the context provides *opportunities for* or *constraints on* action. The second dimension concerns the proximity of contextual influences and whether they are *proximate* or *distal* influences. The third concerns the degree of

EXTERNAL CONTINGENCIES

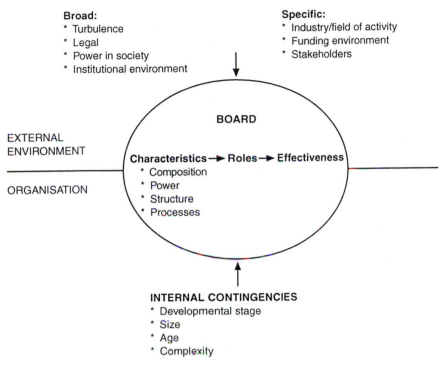

Broad:
* Turbulence
* Legal
* Power in society
* Institutional environment

Specific:
* Industry/field of activity
* Funding environment
* Stakeholders

BOARD

EXTERNAL
ENVIRONMENT

ORGANISATION

Characteristics ➡ Roles ➡ Effectiveness
* Composition
* Power
* Structure
* Processes

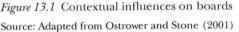

INTERNAL CONTINGENCIES
* Developmental stage
* Size
* Age
* Complexity

Figure 13.1 Contextual influences on boards

Source: Adapted from Ostrower and Stone (2001)

similarity and *difference* between different contexts. These dimensions will be used loosely to help organise the discussion here. It will start by examining some of the more distant contextual influences on governance and work towards discussing those that are closer to boards. In discussing these contextual factors, it will look in particular at how they constrain or provide opportunities for action. The section finishes by examining similarities and differences between boards operating in different sectors and fields.

Contextual influences on board opportunities and constraints

Government legislation and policy

Government legislation and policy have both direct and indirect influences on the governance of public and non-profit organisations. As might be expected, the direct impact of government legislation and policy is most apparent on the wide range of quangos that have been established in recent decades. Robinson and Shaw (Chapter 1) and Greer *et al.*

EXTERNAL CONTINGENCIES

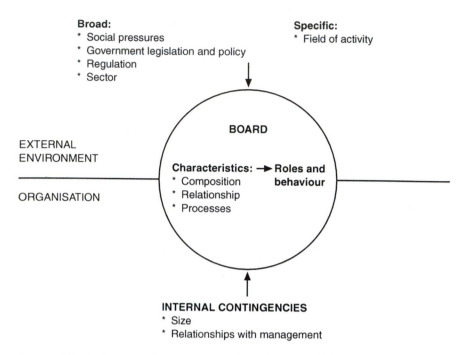

Figure 13.2 Contextual influences on public and non-profit boards emerging from studies in this book

(Chapter 2) trace many of these developments, and Ashburner (Chapter 11) looks specifically at changes in the NHS. These chapters show how since the 1970s successive governments have intervened directly to create new quangos or modify existing ones, and to shape how they are governed, through specifying board size, composition, recruitment procedures and defining their roles.

These changes have created new opportunities for boards to 'recruit' people with different expertise and experience, particularly from the commercial world, and to act more strategically, while creating concerns over their democratic accountability. At the same time government policies have also constrained the nature of the strategic choices that the boards of quangos may exercise. Greer *et al.* describe various quangos on a dependence autonomy continuum. The degree of constraint is perhaps most strong in areas such as the health service with a high degree of centrally determined priorities and targets. However, even here the picture is not black and white with the devolution of budgets and increased emphasis on local health plans.

At the opposite end of the spectrum we have voluntary organisations, which, while independent of direct government intervention, still have to operate in an environment often significantly shaped by government policy. The contracting out of public services has transformed the environment in which many service-providing voluntary organisations operate, creating important new funding opportunities, while at the same time creating new challenges and constraints. According to Harris (2001), the move to contracting, pressures for greater accountability and the growth of systems of performance measurement in the delivery of public services is creating a more complex and demanding environment for the boards of many voluntary organisations. These increasing demands may be one of the reasons behind the increased difficulty of recruiting board members in the voluntary sector observed by Cornforth and Simpson (Chapter 10). Others have suggested that growth in dependence on government funding and the imposition of performance targets that often goes with it have constrained the ability of many voluntary organisations to criticise government policies or tailor services to meet local needs. Locke *et al.* (Chapter 3) suggest that government policy towards contracting out of public services also had a somewhat contradictory impact on user involvement. On the one hand, it gave legitimacy to users as the consumers of services, on the other, the contracting process tended to favour 'safe' larger organisations with more professional staff and boards.

Regulation

The regulatory regime plays an important part in shaping the way in which boards operate. In the voluntary sector the main regulatory body is the Charity Commission. As noted in the Introduction, under pressure from the public and government, the Charity Commission has taken a more active supervisory role. For example, it has introduced new financial reporting requirements and established a small enforcement team to try to ensure charities comply with financial reporting requirements. In addition, it continues to expand the range of guidance and advice it is able to offer charity trustees (Charity Commission, 2000).

Harrow and Palmer (Chapter 5) discuss the development of new accounting regulations for charities and in particular the requirements for charities with an income greater than £250,000 to carry out risk assessment. They suggest that pressures such as these are likely to make charity boards more risk averse and reinforce a compliance model of the board's role. In a similar vein, Locke *et al.* (Chapter 3) discuss how charity law and its interpretation by the Charity Commission have constrained the development of user involvement on boards.

However, even in the face of these regulatory pressures it is important to realise boards are able to exercise some choice. Harrow and Palmer illustrate this by noting the relatively high levels of non-compliance with financial regulations among small charities. Whether this was through deliberate choice or ignorance is difficult to say. The process of influence may also be two-way. Organisations may seek to change or influence the regulatory system. As Locke *et al.* state, it was pressure by various charities and user groups that helped to influence the Charity Commission to gradually allow greater degrees of user involvement on boards.

Social and political pressures

The legal and regulatory environment in which boards operate does not exist in isolation but is shaped by wider social and political forces, which may also impact more directly on boards. It was public and political concern over declining standards in public life that led to the establishment of the Nolan Committee. Its recommendations on local public spending bodies had an important impact on setting standards and codes of practice for the governance of many quangos, and an indirect influence further afield in the voluntary sector. Subsequently, as Greer *et al.* note, it was continuing public and political concerns over politically motivated public appointments that led the New Labour government to introduce more open and accountable systems of appointment for some quangos.

It was a perceived decline in the public trust of charities, heightened by some well-publicised failures that increased pressure on government and the Charity Commission to strengthen the regulation of charities. More directly, as mentioned above, it was campaigns by groups such as the disability rights movement that led to greater acceptance of user involvement on the boards of charities.

Moving now to consider more 'proximate' influences on boards, we turn our attention to internal organisational contingencies.

Organisational size and related factors

The organisational context in which boards operate also influences how they work. In the book this is most clearly demonstrated with regard to organisational size. Cornforth and Simpson (Chapter 10) show a clear association between organisational size and various board characteristics and changes. They show that larger charities tend to have larger, more structured boards and provide more formal support for their members. The research also suggests that there is a growing gap between the boards of large and small charities, with larger organisations finding it easier to recruit board members and provide them with support. A weakness of quantitative studies like this is that they do not throw much light on how organisational size or related factors influence organisational governance. This is an issue taken up by Rochester (Chapter 6). Using case study research he examines in detail some of the constraints under which the boards of small voluntary organisations operate.

Rochester highlights the vulnerability of many small organisations, dependent on a few key people to run the organisation and on a single source of funds, which is subject to annual review and renegotiation. These constraints make certain board activities such as long-term planning and taking a strategic perspective difficult. In addition, the small size and the need to devote efforts to service provision often leave the organisations isolated. In future research it may also be useful to view small size as a source of opportunities for boards, for example, for board members to be in touch and knowledgeable about the day-to-day work of the organisation, to be flexible and able to react quickly to events.

Rochester suggests a number of factors that enable the governance systems in some of these organisations to overcome the 'liability of smallness'. He suggests that the blurring of the boundary between board and staff roles is more pronounced in small organisations, and that effective boards tend to share their work among many board and staff members rather than concentrate it in the hands of the few. These organisations are characterised by informality and successful leadership tends to be by example and involves nurturing and enabling rather than the use of formal authority. However, to be successful small voluntary organisations also need formal systems for board recruitment and to ensure board meetings are planned and conducted in an effective manner. Thus, managing the tension between formality and informality is an important skill. Given their closeness to the day-to-day work of the organisation, successful boards also need to be able to balance their involvement in operational matters with the need to periodically take a longer-term, more strategic view.

Relations with management

How boards work is crucially affected by the relationship between the board and the management or other staff they work with. In larger organisations this is most likely to be the chief executive and other senior management. As Mole (Chapter 8) notes, the interdependence of management and board roles and the difficulty of defining a clear boundary between them are key findings of the empirical literature on non-profit boards and a source of tension in many organisations. Mole's own research examined the expectations and experiences of chief executives with regard to their boards. The research reinforced the view that aligning expectations and achieving a satisfactory division of responsibilities and activities are often problematic. These findings point towards the importance of boards and managers explicitly reviewing and negotiating their relationship, trying to take account of differing expectations and circumstances.

The power of management to influence and possibly dominate what boards do is an important issue in the literature of governance, and is related to wider contextual changes. Managerial hegemony theory discussed in the Introduction highlights how the growing professionalisation of management and the rise of a managerial class have constrained the power of non-executive board members. The importance of professionalisation varies between different fields or 'industries'. This is a theme picked up by Bieber (Chapter 9) in his study of independent museums. He describes how the boards of these museums seldom discussed issues relating directly to the collections, which was surprising given that it was a particular interest in the collections that attracted people to become board members in the first place. He suggests that when issues to do with collections were raised, directors drew on their professional status in a way that limited discussion and defined these topics as lying within their area of discretion.

Edwards and Cornforth (Chapter 4) highlight how other sources of managerial power can be used to constrain the board's role. For example, they describe how the chief executive at the local voluntary organisation (LVO) encouraged the board to adopt a limited and reactive role through the careful control of information and discouraging board members from meeting outside board meetings.

Next we consider the third of Mowday and Sutton's (1993) dimensions, and examine the similarities and differences between boards and operating in different sectors and fields.

Similarities and differences between boards in different contexts

One important means of exploring the influence of contextual differences on organisational behaviour is through detailed comparative research that examines settings with 'powerful institutional and cultural differences' and looks for similarities and differences (Rousseau and Fried, 2001). The impact of sectoral and institutional differences on governing bodies has received little attention in the organisational governance literature. While there has been widespread academic criticism of the adoption of business-based models of governance in the public sector, there have been few empirical studies that systematically compared governance in different sectors or in different organisational fields. Otto's study (Chapter 7) provides an interesting exception.

Interestingly Otto's work did not confirm her initial hypotheses that chair and chief executive roles were more ambiguous and conflictual in the voluntary sector compared with the other sectors. Instead, she found that these qualities were inherent in the 'split' roles of chair and chief executive. However, there were important differences between the sectors in how this important relationship was 'managed'. The chairs of voluntary organisations were more reactive and less pro-active than their counterparts in the other sectors, which she suggests results from the voluntary nature of their role and the lack of statutorily prescribed roles. In the public sector there was a higher degree of role conflict, which Otto suggests may result from the widespread changes to governance practices in the education sector that she studied, and the resulting ambiguity over who is ultimately in control. Otto's samples were restricted to a particular field of activity in both the public and voluntary sectors, hence it is unclear whether differences may have arisen because of sectoral differences or differences between organisational fields.

Locke *et al.* (Chapter 3) suggest how differences between organisational fields in the same sector have influenced the degree of user involvement on the boards of voluntary organisations. They argue that the presence of an established disability rights movement made it easier for members of disability charities to push for and achieve greater user involvement. In contrast in the homelessness field, without such a movement and a relatively high turnover of homeless people, greater user involvement has been more difficult to achieve.

Together these studies suggest that important, and sometimes unexpected, similarities and differences exist between boards operating in different institutional and economic contexts. They also suggest that comparative studies of governance in different sectors and fields will be an important avenue for future research.

Managing the paradoxes of governance

The multi-paradigm perspective on boards set out in the Introduction suggests that all boards will face common paradoxes. Below, some of the evidence for this claim from the various studies in the book is briefly reviewed. In particular it suggests that how these paradoxes manifest themselves will be shaped by contextual factors, and considers some of the ways in which these paradoxes can be managed.

Who governs – the tension between representative and professional boards

> But there is, and will continue to be, a tension between the management driven and output related approach which is central to many recent changes, and the need for organisations providing public services to involve, respond to, and reflect the concerns of the communities which they serve.
>
> (Nolan, 1996)

In many public and non-profit organisations there has been a strong tradition that those who govern them and sit on their board should represent the communities the organisation serves. Two different mechanisms have been used to achieve this end: direct elections of board members from a defined constituency, or through giving key stakeholders the right to appoint members to the board. Over the past two decades, due in part to changes in public policy described in the Introduction, there has been a shift in emphasis towards a more business-like or managerial approach to governance with its stress on efficiency and effectiveness, and the competencies that board members need to fulfil their role effectively. This highlights an important tension: should board members be 'chosen' because of their competence and expertise, or as representatives of particular groups?

This paradox has been most apparent at a policy level with regard to the governance of quangos. Greer *et al.* (Chapter 2) chart the increasing use of non-elected bodies such as quangos, non-profits and the private sector to deliver public services, and the decline in democratic accountability. Similarly, Robinson and Shaw (Chapter 1) examine in detail these changes at a regional level and note the move from local government to more complex patterns of local governance, involving a range of elected and non-elected bodies. Implicit in the public reforms of the various Conservative governments during the 1980s and early 1990s was the assumption that democratic forms of organisational governance were inherently ineffective and inefficient. As a result there was a move to appointed boards and an explicit attempt to get more business people onto the boards of a range of quangos.

Since the late 1990s, the pendulum has swung back, at least a little way, as calls for more open and accountable governing bodies became ever more strident. Ashburner (Chapter 11) charts the impact of these changes on NHS boards. However, as Robinson and Shaw note, the move to more open and transparent board recruitment processes has been uneven and it is still quite difficult to even find out who serves on the boards of many types of quango. As all three sets of authors argue, serious doubts remain about the ability of many quango boards to adequately ensure local democratic accountability.

How, then, can the paradox between effectiveness and accountability, and between expert and representative boards better be managed? While all three sets of authors are united in calling for greater democratic accountability, it is more challenging to know how this can best be achieved. Greer *et al.* suggest one step might be to reframe the problem in terms of *board legitimacy*. They argue that board legitimacy is a product of both board effectiveness and democratic accountability. They suggest that a board that fails on either of these fronts is likely to be perceived as lacking legitimacy. They suggest that no one model of governance is likely to meet the needs of the diverse quango sector, and call for more experimentation combining different forms of three types of representation: political representation, stakeholder representation and what they call the representation of characteristics.

There is perhaps a danger that too much is expected of boards alone. As Locke *et al.* (Chapter 3) note, boards are not the only way, and may often not be the best way, of trying to achieve greater user involvement. Similarly, as Greer *et al.* discuss, boards are not the only way of achieving greater democratic accountability. Greater transparency and openness, external audit and evaluation, the development of new forums for consultation, improving the responsiveness of services to user needs can all increase local accountability.

The other side of the coin is that much can be done to try to ensure that 'elected' or 'lay' boards are effective. There has been a large increase in the availability of training, support and advice for board members in public and non-profit organisations, although there are large variations between different sectors, fields and areas. In some fields, such as education, external training is widely available to new board members. In others, such as large parts of the voluntary sector, provision is much more patchy.

Organisations themselves also have various options to help improve board effectiveness. As Grant (Chapter 12) notes, some traditional women's organisations with large, representative governance structures have streamlined and reduced the size of their boards to make them more effective. Co-options and external advisers can be used to ensure that boards have access to areas of expertise they may be missing (Cornforth and Edwards, 1998: 29–34). Chairs and chief executives can also try to ensure that their board members have opportunities to develop both individually and as a team, for example, ensuring new board members have access to relevant induction and support, and that board members and senior managers have regular opportunities to reflect on the board's role and performance.

The tension between performance and conformance

It was argued in the Introduction that boards face a paradox in having to carry out contrasting roles that required very different orientations, skills and behaviour. The 'conformance' role requires attention to detail, the exercise of care, and skills in monitoring, evaluation and reporting. In contrast, the performance role demands forward vision, strategic thinking and risk-taking, and requires boards to be more pro-active.

Various chapters in the book suggest how this paradox is likely to be shaped by contextual factors. Harrow and Palmer in Chapter 5 argue that the new financial reporting regulations on charities and the more active role played by the charity regulator, the Charity Commission, is likely to make charity boards give precedence to the conformance role and make trustees more risk averse. Interestingly, Otto's (Chapter 7) comparative study of relations between board chairs and chief executives in different sectors suggests that board chairs in the voluntary sector tend to play a more limited and reactive role than their counterparts in other sectors. However, she explains this more in terms of other sectoral differences, rather than pressures from the regulator. She suggests this is due to voluntary sector chairs trying to keep control over their work and avoid conflict with chief executives, given the voluntary nature of their role and the strict constraints on their time, the greater difficulties they experience resolving ambiguities over the allocation of responsibilities and the perception that managers are the key actors in voluntary organisations.

In the public sector the conflicting pressures arising from government policy often heighten this paradox. As Greer *et al.* note, on the one hand, public organisations are expected by government to be innovative and entrepreneurial. On the other, they are often subject to centrally imposed initiatives, performance targets and close monitoring and audit, which effectively constrain their opportunities for strategic choice. This dilemma was illustrated by the case studies of the school and FE college discussed by Cornforth and Edwards (Chapter 4), where the boards felt that the number of government initiatives and requirements imposed on them severely constrained both the time they could devote to strategic issues and their freedom of action.

In contrast, Ashburner, in her review of reforms of governance structures in the NHS, suggests that the move to a 'private sector' model means that boards are too involved with 'performance' at the expense of their 'conformance' role. She suggests that the close involvement of non-executive board members with executives in formulating strategy and other management issues may mean that the ability of non-executives to carry out their 'conformance' role will be compromised, because they lack the necessary independence to adequately scrutinise, evaluate and challenge management's proposals. The counter-argument is that if non-executives are only involved in evaluating proposals, they make lack an understanding of the thinking behind the proposals, which makes them difficult to judge. Equally, it is a big step for a board to seriously challenge or reject management's proposals and many boards may feel unwilling to take this step except in exceptional circumstances. As a result, boards may be able to exert more influence by being involved in strategy formulation at an earlier stage so they can help shape proposals. This dilemma again reflects the difficult balancing act boards have to perform.

How can boards manage this tension between their conformance and performance roles, so that issues of long-term or strategic importance do not get squeezed off the board's agenda, while at the same time the boards' capacity for independent scrutiny is not compromised? Edwards and Cornforth (Chapter 4) suggest a number of important factors that enabled some of the boards they studied to have greater involvement in strategy making, a key aspect of the performance role, without compromising their conformance role. The attitudes and experience of board members themselves were important, which in turn could be shaped by board selection processes, board training and by the attitudes of managers to their boards. Also important were board processes. It was necessary to manage board agendas so important, longer-term issues were given priority. In some organisations long, detailed agendas meant that a process of operational drift occurred, where boards became bogged down in operational detail, leaving insufficient time for longer-term strategic issues. Some of the more successful organisations regularly set aside special meetings where routine board matters were set aside to focus on strategy. This was also an important means of managing the tension that can arise from carrying out very different roles at the same time. Garratt (1996) advocates a board cycle where different aspects of the board role are to some degree separated out over time in an annual cycle of board meetings.

The tension between controlling and partnering management

A paradox perspective suggests that a simple dichotomy between boards controlling or partnering management is too simplistic. Different forms of behaviour will be appropriate at different times in the relationship. In a similar vein, Kramer (1985) suggests that the board relationship with management is constantly shifting between consent, difference and dissensus depending on the issues being faced and the circumstances. The question is more one of balance and how to manage the inevitable tensions that can arise in such complex relationships.

Again, various chapters in this book suggest that broader contextual factors shape and constrain this relationship. As discussed above, Ashburner suggests that changes in NHS boards are likely to shift the balance of the relationship too much towards a comfy partnership between senior managers and external directors. In contrast, Harrow and Palmer (Chapter 5) are concerned that the increasing regulation of the charitable sector, with its emphasis on compliance and the control of risk, may undermine trust between boards and managers and lead boards to closer control and monitoring of management.

Mole (Chapter 8) gives some insight into the relationship between chief executives (CEs) and boards from the chief executives' perspective. Interestingly, in this career history research, only just over half the sample of chief executives mentioned their boards when discussing key factors that supported or acted as barriers to achieving their work. This may suggest that boards are less important in the life of many CEs and the work of their organisation than is sometimes supposed. Of those that did mention their boards, about two-thirds raised problematic issues. The range of issues discussed and the variety of views expressed illustrate the complexity of board–CE relations. From the CEs' perspective the issue mentioned most frequently concerned the level of support they received from their boards, both as a positive factor and as a negative factor when it was absent or felt not to be of the right sort.

Bieber (Chapter 9) examines issue of power and control between boards and directors (chief executives) in independent museums. His case study research shows the central role chief executives play in shaping what boards do, through setting agendas, deciding how issues are presented to the board and controlling information. He also shows how museum directors used their professional status to keep control of issues concerned with the museums' collections. While not quite a rubber stamp, most items at board meetings were agreed and only very few were deferred, amended or rejected and there was relatively little board debate. However, Bieber notes that board chairs played a key role in mediating the relationship between the board and director. He suggests that the boards seem to have entrusted their chairs to establish a relationship with the directors and to oversee their work. Hence a board's support for its director was at least partially conditional on the chair's support. The relatively passive role of the boards may also reflect the balance of power in what Lorsch and MacIver (1989) call 'normal' times, when things are going well. They suggest it is usually in crises that the board becomes much more active.

Otto (Chapter 7) examines this important relationship between chairs and chief executives in more detail. Her comparative research suggests that the chairs of voluntary organisations may be less pro-active than their counterparts in the private sector and the relationship with chief executives may be less conflictual than those in the public sector. Otto suggests that this more limited involvement may stem from the voluntary nature of the chair role and the absence of a clear statutorily prescribed role. It was a way in which the chairs of voluntary organisations could keep control of the time they committed to the job and also avoid or minimise conflict with chief executives.

However, the relationship between chairs and chief executives may also be influenced by the type of voluntary organisation and the circumstances they face. Grant (Chapter 12) suggests not all chairs of voluntary organisations may be so reactive or careful to avoid conflict. In her analysis of the development of the women's movement organisations, she highlights the sometimes fraught relations between chairs and chief executives. The analysis suggests that in organisations which are predominantly voluntary in nature, paid staff may lack legitimacy, and there may be competition between chairs and CEs for prestige and influence.

How can the complex and paradoxical relationship between boards and senior managers and the resulting tensions best be managed? As Mole has pointed out, tension and conflict seem most likely to occur when boards and senior managers have different expectations of their respective roles. The complex and interdependent nature of the roles offers plenty of scope for different interpretations. One way of trying to establish a productive working relationship is through explicit discussion and negotiation over roles and responsibilities. Cornforth and Edwards (1998) suggest that an important determinant of effective governance was that boards regularly review their relationship with management and how they were working together. Harris (1993), drawing on action research in small voluntary organisations, goes further and suggests the value of a technique called Total Activities Analysis where boards and staff systematically review the organisation's main activities and examine who should play what part in carrying them out.

The reflexive board: maintaining a dynamic balance

A theme throughout this book has been the inadequacy of current academic theories of boards as a way of understanding boards or as a guide to action. Each of the different theories tends to give pre-eminence to one particular role of boards. They ignore the multiple and sometimes conflicting roles that boards play and the way these may shift over time in response to changing circumstances. As much of the preceding analysis suggests, contextual factors need to be explicitly built into our theories of organisational governance.

Equally, much of the prescriptive or 'how to do it' literature on boards is flawed. In the desire to improve board performance there is a tendency to portray an idealised or heroic model of the board (Herman, 1989). The board is simultaneously strategic – driving forward organisational performance; a careful steward of the organisation's resources; accountable to the organisation's stakeholders; a critical friend to management – able to offer support but also monitor and challenge poor performance; a vital source of information and contacts on external threats and opportunities, etc. The danger with this idealised view of boards is that if the gap with practice is too large, it can become demotivating and provide a poor guide to action (Herman, 1989; Cornforth, 1995).

The boards of non-profit organisations and quangos also face new challenges. There are increased pressures for improved performance and accountability. Public and non-profit organisations are increasingly subjected to scrutiny by the media, and their failings are quickly pointed out. At the same time public and political concern over the performance of many types of organisations has grown. Regulatory regimes have been tightened. Many funders are requiring organisations to specify performance targets and put in place systems to monitor and report on their performance. As the demands on boards are increasing, there are growing problems of recruitment, and many board members report lack of time as the main constraint on their involvement.

How can boards deal in a realistic way with these new challenges and the difficult and often ambiguous roles they have to carry out? Relying on how things have been done previously or simple prescriptions by themselves is unlikely to be adequate. Boards need to become more *reflexive*. This involves boards consciously trying to develop a greater understanding of their behaviour, roles and impact. As part of this process boards need to develop a capacity to regularly review their composition, the roles they play, board performance and how they work together and with management. As a result, the reflexive board will need to give a high priority to its own maintenance and development. Unfortunately, under pressure of time, this is a function that often is neglected.

This raises the question, who should be responsible for board development and relations with management? While formally it is usually regarded as the board chair's responsibility to carry out this function, they often do not have time to carry out this role. Noting this problem, Drucker (1990: 13) suggests the only answer is to assign this responsibility to the chief executive. However, this runs the danger of the board becoming the creature of the chief executive. Again it is unlikely that there is one best way to resolve this tension. What is most important is that boards and senior management find a way to ensure board review and development stay on the board's agenda.

Boards also need new conceptual tools to help them reflect on and understand the complex challenges they face. Hopefully, the paradox perspective presented in this book will provide one useful framework for enabling boards to think about their different roles and the difficult tensions and ambiguities they face. Rather than search for the right board model or approach, boards need to try to find the right balance between the different 'pulls' created by the paradoxes given the circumstances they face. Board dysfunctions or problems usually occur when boards become attracted to one 'pole' and are no longer able to maintain a 'balance', for example, when boards trust and support management so much that they forget to scrutinise their proposals and ask the hard questions, or become so involved in operational detail that they forget the big picture and neglect the organisation's strategy.

References

Charity Commission (2000) *Annual Report 1999–2000*, London: The Stationery Office.

Cornforth, C. (1995) 'Governing Non-profit Organizations: Heroic Myths and Human Tales', in *Researching the UK Voluntary Sector: Conference Proceedings*, London: National Council of Voluntary Organisations.

Cornforth, C. and Edwards, C. (1998) *Good Governance: Developing Effective Board–Management Relations in Public and Voluntary Organisations*, London: CIMA Publishing.

Drucker, P. (1990) *Managing the Non-Profit Organization*, Oxford: Butterworth-Heinemann.

Garratt, B. (1996) *The Fish Rots from the Head: the Crisis in our Boardrooms: Developing the Crucial Skills of the Competent Director*, London: HarperCollins.

Harris, M. (1993) 'Exploring the Role of Boards Using Total Activities Analysis', *Nonprofit Management and Leadership*, 3, 3, 269–281.

Harris, M. (2001) 'Boards: Just Subsidiaries of the State?', in M. Harris and C. Rochester (eds) *Voluntary Organisations and Social Policy in Britain: Perspectives on Change and Choice*, London: Palgrave.

Herman, R. D. (1989) 'Concluding Thoughts on Closing the Board Gap', in R. Herman and J. Van Til (eds) *Nonprofit Boards of Directors: Analyses and Applications*, New Brunswick, NJ: Transaction.

John, G. (2001) 'In Praise of Context', *Journal of Organizational Behavior*, 22, 31–42.

Kramer, R. (1985) 'Towards a Contingency Model of Board–Executive Relations', *Administration in Social Work*, 9, 3, 15–33.

Lorsch, J. W. and MacIver, E. (1989) *Pawns or Potentates: The Reality of America's Corporate Boards*, Boston: Harvard Business School Press.

Middleton, M. (1987) 'Nonprofit Boards of Directors: Beyond the Governance Function', in W. Powell (ed.) *The Nonprofit Sector: A Research Handbook*, New Haven, CT: Yale University Press.

Mowday, R. T. and Sutton, R. I. (1993) 'Organizational Behavior: Linking Individuals and Groups to Organizational Contexts', *Annual Review of Psychology*, 44, 195–229.

Nolan (1996) *Second Report of the Committee on Standards in Public Life: Local Spending Bodies*, 1, London: HMSO.

Ostrower, F. and Stone, M. M. (2001) 'Governance Research: Trends, Gaps and Prospects for the Future', paper presented at the Association for Research on Nonprofit Organizations and Voluntary Action (ARNOVA) Annual Conference, Miami, Florida, 27 November–1 December.

Rousseau, D. M. and Fried, Y. (2001) 'Location, Location, Location: Contextualizing Organizational Research', *Journal of Organizational Behavior*, 22, 1–13.

Index

Printed in the United States
78608LV00001B/31

9 780415 359924